Key to Main Churchhouses.

1. Garber Church.
2. Mill Creek.
3. Greenmount.
4. Fairview—Unity Cong.
5. Linville Creek.
6. Timberville.
7. Flat Rock.
8. Beaver Creek.
9. Bridgewater.
10. Harrisonburg.
11. Sangerville.
12. Staunton.
13. Mt. Vernon.
14. Elk Run.
15. Summit.
16. Lebanon.
17. Pleasant Valley.
18. Middle River.
19. Barren Ridge.
20. Buena Vista.
21. Chimney Run.
22. Valley Bethel.
23. Thorny Bottom.
24. Crummetts Run.
25. Bethel.
26. Mt. Carmel.
27. Lost River.
28. Damascus.
29. Oak Grove.
30. Cedar Grove.
31. Pleasant View.
32. Valley Pike.
33. Salem.
34. Peach Grove.
35. Rileyville.
36. Mt. Zion.
37. Oakton.
38. Cannon Branch.
39. Valley.
40. Nokesville.
41. Midland.
42. Mine Run.
43. Monta Bella.
44. Trevilian.
45. Bethel.
46. Evergreen.
47. Bethlehem.
48. Antioch.
49. Brick.
50. Snow Creek.
51. Topeco.
52. Burks Fork.
53. Pleasant Valley.
54. Beaver Creek.
55. White Rock.
56. Red Oak Grove.
57. Roanoke.
58. Peters Creek.
59. Copper Hill.
60. Cloverdale.
61. Daleville.
62. Troutville.
63. Pleasant View.
64. Mathias.
65. Chestnut Grove.
66. Crab Orchard.
67. Spring Run.
68. Pott Creek.

Other places denoted by + are where preaching and Sunday-school work is being done.

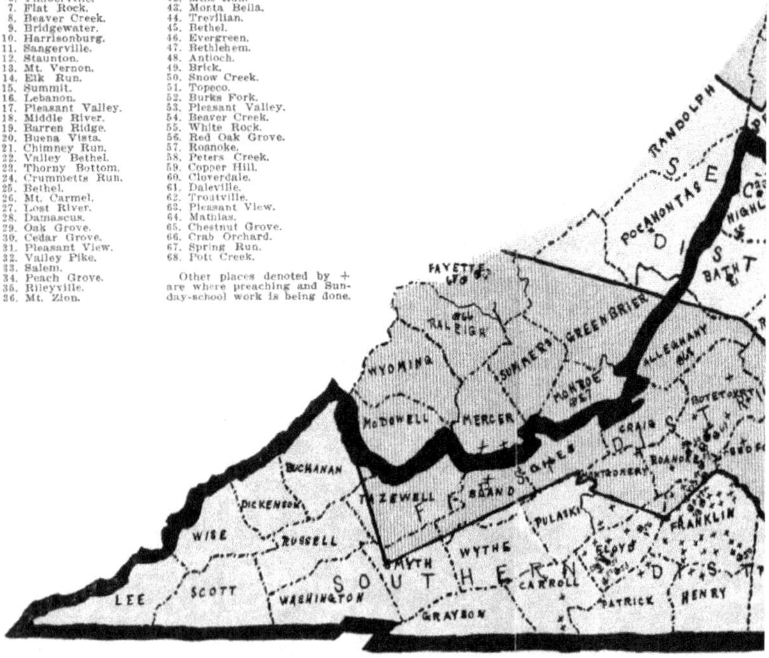

GRANT
HARDY
FREDERICK
LOUDOUN
FAIRFAX
FAUQUIER
PRINCE WILLIAM
CULPEPER
STAFFORD
MADISON
ORANGE
SPOTTSYLVANIA
AUGUSTA
ALBEMARLE
LOUISA
CAROLINE
ESSEX
WESTMORLAND
RICHMOND
NORTHUMBERLAND
LANCASTER
HANOVER
KING WILLIAM
KING AND QUEEN
MIDDLESEX
GLOUCESTER
MATHEWS
NEW KENT
CHARLES CITY
JAMES CITY
ELIZABETH CITY
NELSON
FLUVANNA
GOOCHLAND
HENRICO
AMHERST
BUCKINGHAM
CUMBERLAND
POWHATAN
CHESTERFIELD
APPOMATTOX
AMELIA
PRINCE EDWARD
NOTTOWAY
DINWIDDIE
PRINCE GEORGE
SURRY
CAMPBELL
CHARLOTTE
LUNENBURG
SUSSEX
ISLE of WIGHT
BRUNSWICK
SOUTHAMPTON
NANSEMOND
NORFOLK
HALIFAX
MECKLENBURG
GREENSVILLE
ACCOMAC
NORTHAMPTON
MISSION TERRITORY OF SECOND AND NORTHERN DISTRICTS

History of the Brethren in Virginia

by

D. H. Zigler

HERITAGE BOOKS
2011

HERITAGE BOOKS
AN IMPRINT OF HERITAGE BOOKS, INC.

Books, CDs, and more—Worldwide

For our listing of thousands of titles see our website
at
www.HeritageBooks.com

A Facsimile Reprint
Published 2011 by
HERITAGE BOOKS, INC.
Publishing Division
100 Railroad Ave. #104
Westminster, Maryland 21157

Originally published: Elgin, Illinois
Brethren Publishing House
1914

— Publisher's Notice —
In reprints such as this, it is often not possible to remove blemishes from the original. We feel the contents of this book warrant its reissue despite these blemishes and hope you will agree and read it with pleasure.

International Standard Book Numbers
Paperbound: 978-0-7884-3782-3
Clothbound: 978-0-7884-8740-8

History of the Brethren in Virginia

By

D. H. Zigler

Elgin, Illinois
Brethren Publishing House
1914

Mr and Mrs C. J. Charlton
Presented By
Bro. D. H. Zigler.

In Memory

Of the Faithful Ones of the Past and as a Token of the High Appreciation of the Consecrated Workers of the Present,

This Volume is Affectionately Dedicated

INTRODUCTION

History is always a fascinating subject. Few things appeal to us more strongly than the achievements of generations that have passed. Their trials, their difficulties, the light and the shade of their varied experiences were not very different from those that we shall have to encounter. And our prospects for acquitting ourselves in the battle of life better than they have done will depend very largely on how well we have learned the lesson of their successes and failures.

As a people, we Dunkers have been strangely careless in regard to our past. We have kept few records and many of these are imperfect and incomplete. Like true men in any great cause, our predecessors have been content to work patiently and in obscurity, trusting to Providence for results, and little suspecting the far-reaching significance with which their humble labors were fraught. They little dreamed that they were making history, and that of the truest and noblest sort. Had they done so, they might have kept a fuller and more accurate record of their doings.

The fact that, until recently, we have given no adequate account of ourselves to the world has led to endless confusion and misunderstanding. I suppose no people have been less understood and more persistently misrepresented than we. We have been accused of holding views that we never held, and have been identified with bodies with which we never had anything in common. Yet we have ourselves chiefly to blame for this state of things. We have not put ourselves to the pains of correcting the errors.

Within the last score of years, however, some highly commendable work has been done to set ourselves right before our fellow men. This period has witnessed a remarkable awakening of interest in our early history, and much valuable information has been brought to light. Every new contribution to our knowledge of these earlier times is hailed with eager interest.

There are various phases of our history as a church, however, that have not yet been exploited, and there is much interesting history of a local character that is only awaiting the chronicler. This latter is an inviting and fruitful field, and will doubtless, in the years to come, yield a rich harvest of inspiring truth, when the facts are once culled out and recorded. It is to this latter class that the present work belongs.

When persecutions and war drove many of our early Brethren away from their adopted homes in Pennsylvania, the broad and fertile valley of the Shenandoah offered them an inviting asylum. And here many of them settled. Since the first of them located here and began to build up churches one whole century and one-third of another have passed away, yet in all this time they have had no historian—no one to preserve a record of their work. Consequently many important facts of their lives, their labors, their heroism, have been irretrievably lost. But if facts have perished, the results of their labors still live.

In making a careful investigation of this field and

bringing to light its varied activities Brother Zigler has done an excellent piece of work, and has placed the church at large and the Virginia churches in particular under lasting obligations. His diligent researches have resulted in unlocking unsuspected stores of wealth. He has succeeded in giving to his narrative a degree of fulness and completeness that to the casual student would have seemed impossible.

He has done for the churches in Virginia what should be done in many other parts of the Brotherhood. It is to be hoped that his example may be an encouragement to others to do a like service for their sections.

I have read the book with a great deal of interest. It is a fascinating story, in which our own ancestors are the actors. The role that they have played in this life drama, and the noble manner in which they played it, ought to be an inspiration to us. The book will do much good and deserves to be widely circulated and read.

JNO. S. FLORY.

PREFACE

The following pages were the outgrowth of a series of lectures on the Second District of Virginia delivered at Bridgewater College during the Bible Term of 1904. For a time thereafter it was the purpose of the District Mission Board to publish the work in pamphlet form, but the lack of sufficient reliable data at that time with other causes deterred the prosecution of the plan. In the years that have intervened additional matter has been obtained to such an extent that the present volume appears much beyond its first intended proportions and now assumes the title of "A History of the Brethren in Virginia." This, however, was only accomplished by a most persistent and painstaking research.

Content with the consciousness of having done their part in the uplift of their fellow men, the Brethren in Virginia left few early records of their struggle to establish and maintain primitive Christianity in this fair Southland. If it were possible to have the story told over again by the actors themselves, or could we lift the curtain that veils the past and look upon the scenes of bygone years as they transpired, how much more complete the record would be! But the lips that then spoke are stilled forever; the hands that could have written are cold in death; and the past is obliterated by a pall as dark as midnight. Wherefore, it only remains for the writer of the present to gather the facts thread by thread and weave them in one by one until the whole record is given.

Of the works now extant none of them purport to give more than a fragmentary account of the church in Virginia. These writers have been content to circumscribe their narratives to a given period of history, or to a delineation of the lives of distinguished individuals. These have served the important purpose of giving information on the special subjects in hand. Yet little effort has been made to record the events as they transpired and the causes leading thereto. For this reason few people have been so little understood by the general public. This condition has been true throughout the different periods. Especially was this so in their opposition to slavery during that dark epoch of American history and in their refusal to participate in the unfortunate conflict between the North and the South. In no less degree is this true of the position of the church, at the present time, against hurtful and un-Christian indulgences. Wherefore, there is a growing demand for further information relative to the works of righteousness of our forefathers and more knowledge of the present activity of the church.

To meet these requirements this volume is written, and no labor has been spared to make the work authentic. But this was by no means a small undertaking on account, as previously mentioned, of a lack of direct records. In order to supply this deficiency, the facts needed to be gleaned from old letters, ancient documents, county records, and the archives of the state and the nation. Although the undertaking at first appeared by no means promising, yet the field has proven a surprisingly fruitful one and the character and amount of matter obtained has far surpassed the most sanguine expectation. This was true to such an extent that in numerous instances it became a problem which should be used to exemplify the point under consideration.

In this connection the author would acknowledge with a deep feeling of gratitude his indebtedness to the many individuals who so kindly assisted in this work and contributed of their knowledge to make this volume worthy of its present claims. To enumerate all of these would make a long list. Many of them, however, appear in connection with the articles written expressly for this work. At this place grateful acknowledgement is made of the helpful service of Eld. T. C. Denton, Daleville, Virginia, who was appointed by the District Meeting of the First District of Virginia to collate data; Dr. John S. Flory, Bridgewater College, for translation of old papers and other valuable service rendered; Eld. C. D. Hylton, Trinity, Virginia, for assistance in numerous ways; Rev. S. L. Bowman, Daphna, Virginia, for special investigation relative to early settlers in Rockingham County; Pres. W. B. Yount, Bridgewater College, for valuable suggestions; Eld. George Wine, Ottobine, Virginia, who contributed liberally of his fund of information; and David J. Wine, Forrestville, Virginia, for data relative to the settlers in Shenandoah County. In addition to these, Eld. Benjamin Miller, Eld. Samuel Driver, Eld. Daniel Hays, Eld. J. M. Kagey, and Eld. S. A. Sanger assisted in the work by helpful suggestions and personal observations. Furthermore, the author would especially make mention of old papers of exceeding value, without which a history of the church in Virginia would be very incomplete, contributed by Eld. John P. Zigler, now deceased, and Michael Zigler, Broadway, Virginia. Sisters Sadie Zigler and Rebecca Bowman furnished a number of the illustrations. To all these and to many other brethren and sisters, who contributed by helpful suggestions and words of encouragement, the author would express his sincere thanks.

The work of collating material, although arduous, was not devoid of pleasure. The discovery of an additional record; the finding of a new link in the chain of evidence and beholding a fact newly brought to light was the great power that sustained during these hours of search. The data has been carefully used as collated except the correction of grammatical errors and abridgment in some instances. If any omissions have been unjustly made, it is unknown to the author.

The title of the book has been suggested by the repeated affectionate use of the term Brethren in their correspondence. Especially was this true during the dark and trying times of the Civil War. In this instance it is used in full recognition of the name German Baptist Brethren as sanctioned by the General Conference of the church and should be so understood by the reader. The names Dunkard, Dunker, Tunker, etc., are only used as they appear in some of the old writings.

In addition to the past records of the church, a carefully prepared map is given, which shows the localities in which the Brethren live and the division of the State into the two districts. Also an account of the present activities of the church is written in the closing chapters of the book.

How successfully the work is accomplished, the reader is the best judge. May all that has been done go forth on a mission of love to the honor and glory of God.

D. H. ZIGLER

Broadway, Virginia.
February 15, 1908.

PREFACE TO REVISED EDITION

As the wheels of time move, so do advancements come to any progressive people. This is true of the Church of the Brethren in Virginia during the past six years. In this time the State Districts have been increased from two to five, the local organizations multiplied rapidly, and the membership increased in nearly every point of activity. The Sunday-school, the educational, the missionary and other lines of church work have gone forward to a creditable degree.

In all this there is a marked unity of purpose to maintain the distinctive Bible doctrine as taught by our forefathers. Younger men are taking the places of those who are called from life's activity to the home beyond. It is our duty to chronicle all these events in a way that others who follow may know of them.

To this end the former book has been carefully revised and such additional information added as to help make the work complete. In all the author is indebted to many brethren for valuable assistance. The different State Districts appointed committeemen to coöperate in the work. Their names, with those of other writers, appear in the text given.

A feature of the book is a map showing the State of Virginia from a church viewpoint. No pains have been spared to make this correct in all its details. With what success all this has been accomplished is best determined by the reader. It is sent forth in the Master's name.

D. H. ZIGLER.

Broadway, Virginia,
August 15, 1914.

TABLE OF CONTENTS

TABLE OF CONTENTS

History of the Brethren in Virginia

CHAPTER I

Organization of the Church in Germany—The Flight to America—The Sojourn in Pennsylvania.

That the reader may more fully comprehend the following chapters relative to the German Baptist Brethren in Virginia, an account chiefly from the writing of Alexander Mack, Jr., of the organization of the church in Germany and their subsequent flight from persecution in that country to America, is here given. In addition thereto, a brief notice is made of the half century of prosperity in the New World and their final dispersion caused by the hand of oppression in Pennsylvania.

From the writing of Eld. Mack, Jr., we learn that the organization of the Brethren Church was an outgrowth of the great reformatory movement that swept over Germany during the seventeenth and eighteenth centuries. The Pietists, as they are known, embraced all shades of religious opinion. They eagerly sought to restore the waning piety of the Protestant churches. As long as they kept before them this one virtue they prospered greatly. This appears to have been especially marked during the first few years of the eighteenth century. They held house-to-house meetings besides their regular services. At the meetings the young converts would present themselves for further instruction in spiritual life. Unfortunately for them, their frequent meetings and signal success awakened the jealousy of their enemies; persecution followed and many were driven from their homes. A number of them found refuge in Wittgenstein, which was governed by a friendly count. Although the country was rough and the soil barren, the leniency of this local government caused a great influx of people. Schwarzenau became a chief center of these refugees.

It soon became apparent to some of these Pietists that a closer organization was necessary in order to administer discipline among themselves, but, coming from different localities, their views were as widely different on almost all Christian duties except those of devotion and piety. It was a difficult task to collect a sufficient number of one mind to establish a congregation. Some of them rejected any form of discipline, whatever: others returned to the churches from whence they came; and still others drifted into outright infidelity. There were some, however, who, notwithstanding this state of perturbation, were sincerely desirous of finding the footprints of primitive Christianity and follow the example of the Savior. They were fully convinced of the necessity of faith and obedience in order to obtain salvation.

In the year 1708, eight persons entered into a covenant with each other, by the help of God to endeavor to attain to the answer of a good conscience by rendering obedience to all the commands of the Lord Jesus, and follow Him as their Good Shepherd and Leader through good and evil report. The names of these eight persons are George Greby and Lucas Fetter, of Hesse Cassel; Alexander Mack and Anna Margaretta Mack, of Schriesheim; Andrew Bonney and Johanna

The Valley of the Eder—near Schwarzenau.

Bonney, of Basel, Switzerland; John Kippin and Johanna Kippin, of Würtemberg. These five brethren and three sisters covenanted under the bond of the Cross of Jesus Christ, to labor together in the unity of the faith as a church. So solicitous were they of attaining unto the Truth that every evidence was prayerfully and carefully weighed. By consulting history, they found that primitive Christians in the first and second centuries were uniformly planted into the likeness of His death by baptism in water by a threefold immersion. But they were unwilling to rest their faith upon the authority of history alone. They searched the New Testament Scriptures and found abundant teaching for the same. One of their number, Alexander Mack, had labored in word and doctrine in different parts of Germany. He was chosen their minister, and, true to Scriptural precedent, their first act was to engage in Christian baptism. Early one morning, the day or month is not given, they resorted to the riverside to engage in this solemn ordinance. After a season of devotion, each of them was taken into the water and was baptized by the threefold immersion, as directed by Christ. On their return from the water and when they had changed their clothing, they were filled with much joy and the word of the Lord, "Be fruitful and multiply," came to them with great force.

The young church, thus filled with the spirit of missions, became very zealous in spreading the Gospel and during the next seven years was a period of great activity. These eight persons grew more and more in the faith of the Gospel and bore testimony of the

Truth in the public assembly. The Lord bestowed upon them His special blessing in an abundant manner. Many believers were added to them and churches were established in different places. Especially at Schwarzenau, a large congregation of believers assembled. The Lord also called a number of laborers into His vineyard. This large accession drew public attention to them and, while they received the blessings of God on the one hand, they encountered the enemies of Truth on the other. Therefore, for the sake of God's Word, they needed to bear persecution. Some were robbed of their property, which they appeared to submit to joyfully. Others were cast into prison. A minister, Christian Libe, was compelled to serve at the galleys on board one of the ships, being coupled with ungodly miscreants to work at the rudder. Yet none of these things moved them. The fact that poverty, imprisonment, and tribulations seemed but to make them more joyful, caused others to look on in astonishment. Then, they were subjected to a sort of catechism in the form of subtle questions. These were submitted to them by some of the most learned men of the land, in the hope of confusing the Brethren and thereby drawing them from the faith, or bringing them into disrepute. Forty questions were submitted to the church with a request to answer them. In this the Brethren were amazingly successful. Much wisdom and sagacity is seen in the answers given. So well pleased was the church at Schwarzenau, that it was decided to publish the forty questions with the answers for the instruction of the uninformed.

This is believed to have been the first publication

by the Brethren. Reprints have been made at different times in America both in the German and English languages. The first of these is in the German, published by Christopher Sower, Jr., in 1774. In 1854 Henry Kurtz gave them in the English through the columns of the *Gospel Visitor*. Other reprints were also made. It being the first literary work of the Brethren it is interesting to the student of history, but the scope of this volume does not admit its insertion here. This brief reference to it must suffice.

Persecution, augmented by internal troubles, put these pious people to the sorest tests. They were driven from place to place. Some went to Friesland. Others fled to Holland. In the summer of 1719, twenty families embarked on a Flemish vessel at Friesland, for America. They landed at Philadelphia in the autumn of the same year. Like Paul and Barnabas, some strong disputations arose among them on the way, but their fidelity to their religion was very marked as the following incident will show: While on their voyage, a furious storm arose. The sails were lowered and much of the merchandise was thrown overboard. The captain was about to give up all hope, but by the direction of Providence, he went to the humble apartment occupied by these brethren and sisters. In much astonishment, he beheld them engaged in singing and prayer as though the sea was calm. With renewed courage, he returned to his post with the declaration that Almighty God will never let the ship sink with such pious people on board. On landing at Philadelphia they became widely separated and began their struggles amid the wilds of the new country.

Little is known of their spiritual growth in the next few years, save that the smouldering embers of religious fervor were kept alive. At this time a plan was agreed upon to visit the isolated members and extend to them a true Christian greeting. Accordingly, Peter Becker, John Gomery, and George Bulsar Gantz were appointed. Their visit was crowned with much success and is looked upon as the first endeavor in home missions in America. From this time on. love and union prevailed. The church was aroused to greater activity. Many were added to the church by baptism and the number was augmented by arrivals from Germany.

During these years, the sorest of persecution was being experienced by the Brethren in the native land. The church at Schwarzenau was practically disbanded from this cause. From there the believers fled to West Friesland and thence went into Holland. On July 7, 1729, Alexander Mack, his three sons, and about fifty-nine families among whom were 126 members took passage on the ship *Allen,* to join their brethren in America. After a voyage of seventy-one days, they landed at Philadelphia. This large increase in membership was the occasion of much joy. The presence of Alexander Mack and other leaders of the church greatly inspired the church to more endeavor for the Lord. New organizations were formed in Pennsylvania and in New Jersey. A season of great prosperity followed, lasting nearly a half century. However, these zealous Christians were to undergo a sore trial of their fidelity to the doctrines they had been

Meetinghouse of the Brethren, Germantown, Pa.

so energetically and earnestly proclaiming to the American people.

The desire to throw off the English yoke had been smouldering in the hearts of many of the American people and it only took the adoption of such measures as the Stamp Act and the enforcement of the Writs of Assistance to fan these smouldering embers into a flame. This speedily led to the war of the Revolution. In this the Brethren could not engage, however much they may have sympathized with the Americans, for reasons that follow:

1. The Spirit of Christ and the Word of God forbade carnal warfare. As early as August 20, 1739, Christopher Sower published an article on the inconsistency of Christian nations engaging in war with each other. In this article he showed how inconsistent warfare is with the teaching of Jesus, the Prince of Peace.

2. They knew that there is a better way for nations to settle their differences, as well as individuals, than to resort to killing each other.

Yet their refusal to take up arms seemed not to be understood. They were classed among the Tories, and with the passions of men's hearts aroused by the spirit of warfare, little opportunity was given them to explain.

Again, when they were presented with an oath renouncing the king of England and swearing allegiance to the American government, the words of Jesus came to them, which says, Matt. 5: 34, " But I say unto you, Swear not at all; neither by heaven; for it is God's throne: Nor by the earth; for it is his footstool; neither by Jerusalem; for it is the city of the Great King." Also, the words of the apostle, James 5: 12, "But above all things, my brethren, swear not, neither by heaven, neither by the earth, neither by any oath: but let your yea be yea; and your nay, nay; lest ye fall into condemnation."

As a consequence of this, their property was taken from them and they suffered many indignities at the hand of the rougher individuals of the community. Eld. Christopher Sower, who was a wealthy printer, lost all of his property. Tons of Bibles ready for binding were destroyed, while he, much disfigured by maltreatment, was driven seven miles to General Washington's headquarters. However, the commander-in-chief ordered his release. Many others suffered a like deprivation of their property, and, as in the time of the apostles, "were scattered abroad" to seek protection and cheap homes for their families. Furthermore, wherever they went they preached the Gospel and churches were established. Some of them went north and west into the interior of Pennsylvania; a few made their abode in Maryland; and others migrated farther south into Virginia. It is the object of this volume to chronicle in the succeeding chapters the acts of these, mentioned last.

CHAPTER II

Migration to Virginia—The Valley of Virginia—Causes Leading to the Settlement in the Valley.

When the Brethren came south from Pennsylvania and Maryland they nearly all settled in the Valley of Virginia. This is a beautiful and fertile expanse of country between the Blue Ridge and the first ranges of the Alleghany Mountains. It extends from the Potomac River at Harper's Ferry southwest to the Tennessee line. In measurement, it averages about twenty miles in width and is three hundred miles long. It is, virtually, an extension of the well-known Cumberland Valley and is equal to it in productiveness and beauty of landscape. There were two sections in which these colonists made their homes. The first territory is now embraced by the counties of Shenandoah, Rockingham, and Augusta in the north, and Franklin, Botetourt, Floyd, and Roanoke counties include that portion farther south. This left an intervening territory of about fifty miles in width between them.

They left but few records and what is known of their lives must be gathered from diversity of sources. Yet, we are glad that enough can be secured in this way to form a correct conclusion of the noble lives they lived and the powerful influence for good in the respective communities in which they made their homes.

It cannot be claimed that these Brethren were the first to settle in the Valley of Virginia as some have presumed, but they were among the earliest immigrants to the different parts in which they located. Kerchival, in his "History of the Valley," page 50, says: "A large majority of our first immigrants were from Pennsylvania, composed of native Germans or German extraction. There were, however, a number direct from Germany, several from Maryland and New Jersey, and a few from New York. These immigrants brought with them the religion, habits and customs of their ancestors. They were composed generally of three religious sects; viz., Lutheran, Mennonites and Calvinists with a few Tunkers. They generally settled in neighborhoods pretty much together." The "Tunkers" as the author pleases to call the Brethren, were "a few." This coincides with facts that shall be presented more fully in a succeeding chapter. At this place, it is sufficient to say that it is generally accepted that John Garber from York County, Pennsylvania, was the first member of the Brethren to locate in the northern part, or the Shenandoah Valley, if not the first in Virginia. He evidently came about the year 1775 or 1776. On his first visit, he was not accompanied by his family. The purpose for which he came is not made clear. His object may have been to "spy out the land" in view of future permanent settlement. For it is known that he was joined by his family later on as the records will show. Yet, it is equally probable that his coming was prompted by a missionary spirit. He is known to have been a minister of ability, and, not unlike the Hackleton cobbler, William Carey, he made and cobbled shoes for a support, that he could preach a free Gospel to the people.

His brethren did not join him until after the oppression in Pennsylvania. This, in itself, is evidence that it was not financial gain that caused him to move to Virginia when he did.

Eld. Jacob Miller is the first minister known to have lived in the more southerly settlement of the Brethren. His home was in Franklin County and it is believed that he located there near the time that John Garber settled in Shenandoah County. Where he came from is not definitely known, but it is most likely that he migrated from Pennsylvania or Maryland, as he was a German. A few years later, he was joined by an Englishman named William Smith, who requested baptism and was subsequently elected to the ministry. His home was in Floyd County but these brethren traveled and labored together much in the ministry. The one would preach in German and the other in English.

In the introductory chapter, it has been shown how the Brethren in Pennsylvania refused to engage in warfare or take an oath. As a consequence of this, their property was confiscated. Therefore, destitute of earthly possessions they entered this new country.

Nothing but stout hearts and a firm reliance on the promises of God could have carried them through such experiences. Yet God never forsakes his people in their faithfulness to him. This is abundantly shown in this instance, for rich was the inheritance they were to possess. In their lives, we see fulfilled the words of Christ, Mark 10: 29, 30, " There is no man that hath left house, or brethren, or sisters, or father, or mother, or wife, or children, or lands, for my sake, and the gospel's, but he shall receive an hundredfold now in this time, houses, and brethren, and sisters, and mothers, and children, and lands, with persecutions; and in the world to come eternal life." A study of the Church in Virginia will convince any one of the literal fulfillment of this promise of Christ.

As a pledge to the words of the dear Master and with a spirit of paternal affection, the great Valley of Virginia lay as with outstretched arm to receive the homeless refugees and give to them cheap homes with peace and plenty. Here land could still be gotten by grant from the government, or bought at a nominal cost. In the records of Shenandoah County reference is made to a grant of four hundred acres of land on Holman's Creek to Eld. Martin Garber. Others also procured homes at a very small outlay of money. The provisional government gave them the necessary protection and the Red Man of the forest was very kindly disposed toward these settlers from the north.

A slight digression at this place is necessary to notice the unusual conditions that made it possible for the Brethren to procure such cheap homes with protection in the Valley of Virginia, while the country east of the Blue Ridge had been settled for more than a century and a half and protection not yet fully assured in that part of the colony. Notable among these was the intolerant spirit manifest throughout the older portions of the colony toward all Dissenters from the English Church. This, together with the unfavorable relationship between the English colonists and the Indians, was the main cause that brought about the conditions referred to above.

It should be remembered that the establishment of the English colony was in some degree an effort to spread Christianity among the heathen. In every charter granted the Virginia Company, religious consideration took a prominent place. One of the first acts on landing at Jamestown was to construct a place of worship. This was done by nailing an old sail to three or four trees, while the sides of the building were made of rails and the seats of unhewn trees. In this primitive church, Common Prayer was read twice a day and divine services were conducted each Sunday. The Church in Virginia was only a part of the Church of England, which, at this time, demanded strict conformity. In the instructions for the colonists in Virginia under date of November 20, 1606, it is decreed that any one who seeks to withdraw others from the established religion or from their allegiance shall be imprisoned until he reforms. If he be obstinate, he shall be sent back to England for condign punishment.

In the year 1610, prior to the departure of Lord Delaware, the new Governor for Jamestown, the Rev. William Crashaw preached a sermon before his lordship. Addressing the Governor, he said: "Remember thou art a General of Englishmen, nay a General of Christian men, therefore, looke to Religion. You go to commend it to the heathen: then practise it yourselves; make the name of Christ honorable, not hateful to them. Suffer no Papists; let them not nestle there; nay, let the name of the Pope, or Poperie, be never heard in Virginia. Take heed of Atheists, the Divel's champions; and if thou discover any, make them examplaire. And (if I may be so bold as to advise) make Atheisme, and other blasphemie capitall, and let that be the first law in Virginia. Suffer no Brownists, nor factious Separatists; let them keep

Church in King William County, built by English Government in 1734.

their conventicles elsewhere; let them go and convert some other heathen, and let us see if they can constitute such churches really, the ideas whereof they have fancied in their branes; and when they have given us such examples we may then have some cause to follow them. Till then, we will take our patterne from their betters."

In time, the Governor of Virginia became the head of the church in America and the colonists thought that they were doing God's service and fighting against the devil by suppressing all forms of Dissenters. One of the laws established by Gov. Dale in 1611, required every person, who should settle in the colony, to appear before some minister of the Established Church and explain his religious views. If he refused, he was to be publicly whipped. Upon a second refusal, he was to be twice whipped, and if he refused a third time, he was to be whipped every day until he should confess. Later on, fines were imposed for absence from divine service. The whipping-post and branding irons were measures adopted to enforce conformity. According to the new provisions of the law in 1662 to 1663, Quakers and other Dissenters were forbidden from assembling, and if more than five over sixteen years of age met together, each was fined two hundred pounds of tobacco for the first, and five hundred pounds for the second offense, and those able to pay were to be held responsible for the fines of those not having the necessary amount.

Regardless of these stringent measures, the number of Dissenters increased from year to year and a long and bitter struggle for religious liberty was being enacted throughout the colony. On the frontier, more liberty was granted at a comparatively early date. This was notably true in the year 1700, when five hundred Huguenot fugitives were permitted to take up their abode in the colony. Gov. Nicholson gives as a reason in his letter to the Lord of Trade, that it is believed that their presence will strengthen the frontier. Like privileges were given other settlers.

In this conflict for religious liberty, such men as

Thomas Jefferson, James Madison, and Patrick Henry took a prominent part in later years and did much to bring about the desired end. Finally, in 1785, the Statute of Religious Freedom was adopted by the General Assembly. By this act, Virginia was the first government in the world to establish and maintain an absolute divorce of church and state.

During the time of the enactment of these checkered scenes in east Virginia, just across the Blue Ridge Mountains lay the beautiful and fertile Valley of Virginia, practically unknown to the English colonists. Here, for centuries, the Red Man alone pitched his wigwam and with his squaw and papoose enjoyed the refreshing mountain breezes after the day's chase was over. With a feeling akin to bitter hatred, he watched the encroachment of "Long Knife," as the English were known, and from his position of vantage, he would, at times, swoop down upon his foe and many a loved one was unmercifully slain or carried away into captivity.

That this valley should not have been settled for so long after the occupation of the country east of the Blue Ridge by the English, has been a matter of conjecture by many. Beyond question, it was known to them, but it may have been considered hazardous to have ventured so far inland. Yet this alone could not be considered a sufficient reason to keep back these hardy pioneers. Therefore, we must conclude that there must have been an agreement between the English settlers and the Indians, that settlement should be made as far as the mountains and no farther. The data and full text cannot be given, but that such treaty did exist is evidenced by a letter written by Thomas Chaukley, a Quaker, to his brethren at Winchester, Virginia, under date of May 21, 1838 (Kerchival's "History of the Valley," page 39), in which reference is made to such an agreement being in force at that time. After citing a number of reasons why his brethren should respect the rights of the Indians, he continues as follows: "Consider you are in the province of Virginia, holding what right you have under that government; and the Virginians have made an agreement with the natives to go as far as the mountains and no farther; and you are over and beyond the mountains, therefore out of that agreement; by which you lie open to the insults and incursions of the Southern Indians, who have destroyed many of the inhabitants of Carolina and Virginia, and even now destroy more on the like occasion. The English going beyond the bounds of their agreement, eleven of them were killed by the Indians while we were traveling in Virginia." The above quotation makes it very clear why such English settlement was not made in the Valley of Virginia and, with equal conciseness, gives an illustration of how jealously the Indian guarded his rights. It, likewise, must be apparent to the reader how readily permission could be gotten by the Germans to make settlement there. For, as Gov. Spotswood previously said, "they became a good barrier for all that part of the country." On the other hand, the Indian welcomed his German neighbor from the north. The kind treatment the dusky man of the forest received at the hands of William Penn had reached his ears. Therefore, the settler wending his way from thence was not looked upon with suspicion as "Long Knife" from the east. They dwelt in peace for years and it is a conceded fact that never did any of our Brethren suffer an indignity in any form from the natives.

Thus we have briefly traced some of the tangible influences that brought about the conditions existing in the Valley of Virginia when it was entered by our forefathers. Furthermore, it has been seen how their footsteps have been directed thence and that homes and churches have been established in this fair Southland. Above all this was the great heart and mind of God caring for His people and directing their lives to a greater usefulness in glorifying His name.

CHAPTER III.

Additional Settlements—Character of Settlers.

In the preceding chapter a brief mention is made of the first settlements in Virginia. It has been seen that these colonies were widely separated and doubtless, for a time, they had but little or no communication with each other. Which has the just claim of priority cannot at this time be definitely settled. While it is admitted that the date of Elder Jacob Miller's early ministry in Franklin County is not so definitely fixed as that of Brother John Garber's in Shenandoah County, yet, allowing reasonable time for his successors until definite dates are known, his early ministry might be easily placed as early as the middle of the last half of the eighteenth century. In addition to this, the fact that his home was among the foothills of the eastern slope of the Blue Ridge Mountains is significant. This not only makes it probable that a nucleus of members might have located here at a very early date, but that they may have migrated here through the older settlements of Virginia instead of passing south through the Valley as usually is inferred.

In another chapter it had also been seen that Dissenters from the Established Church were permitted to settle on the frontier as early as 1700. In the lapse of time, this spirit became more tolerant. Therefore the Brethren could more readily have gotten permission at that later date. Again, as noticed, their homes were in the territory east of the Blue Ridge. If they had journeyed south through the Valley of Virginia, it would be difficult to surmise a motive for their crossing the mountains and settling where land was doubtless more expensive and the inhabitants less hospitable to them. It was here too that Eld. Miller was joined

Old-time Flax Wheel.

by William Smith, an Englishman, who doubtless came from the older settlements. These facts present a field worthy of investigation. For the present, any conclusive statement would only be conjecture.

Eld. Jonas Graybill in his research found that quite a colony of Brethren located at New Amsterdam, now Daleville, Botetourt County, in 1780. These came from

Pennsylvania and were driven thither by the same oppression in that State referred to elsewhere, but Eld. Graybill more fully tells of these in another chapter of this volume.

Because of the wide influence John Garber and his descendants have wielded in the affairs of the church in Virginia, a more extended account of his life should be made; but this is deferred in order to mention other settlers who came a few years later, and their inspiring influence on the young church. Among the first of these to come, were his two sons, Samuel and Martin, who remained in Maryland until after their marriage to the daughters of Jacob Stoner of Frederick County, of that State. In the fall of the year 1783, they with their families and those of four others settled in Shenandoah County, near the home of their father. Two years later, seven more families came, and by the end of the year 1787, thirty-two in all had moved from Pennsylvania and Maryland into the Shenandoah Valley. While some of these settled in Shenandoah County, the greater number of them located in Rockingham County. On this point, the author is favored with a letter from Eld. John M. Wine of David City, Nebraska. Bro. Wine has long since passed the meridian of life, but is highly favored with a retentive memory. He says that he distinctly remembers hearing his grandmother repeatedly relate their experiences in moving to Virginia. The letter is given below, omitting the part referring to his recollection. He says: "They (meaning his grandparents) with five other families, left Pennsylvania and Maryland in the fall of 1783. Eld. Martin Garber and his brother, Samuel (sons of John), Jonathan Miller, and a Bro. Myers settled near Flat Rock. In 1785, seven more families came and settled in Rockingham County and from that time until 1787, thirty-two families came from Pennsylvania and Maryland. The most of them settled in Rockingham, between Harrisonburg and

Preparing the Warp.

Staunton. Among them were the Florys, Myers, Millers, Bowmans, Neffs, Glicks, and others." Eld. Wine further adds that the Brethren submitted to the confiscation of their property rather than violate the teaching of Christ against going to war and against taking the oath, which was demanded of them.

Though they were destitute of earthly possessions, they were rich toward God and with a strong desire to conquer for Him, they pressed onward. However, not all of these settlers remained in the localities that they first selected. Learning of brighter prospects further on, or possibly influenced with the spirit of unrest that comes to the emigrant, some of them went as far south as Tennessee and others west to the Ohio.

Yet, the greater part of them made permanent homes in Virginia and they became quite an acquisition to the young church. Among the ministers who came at this time, were Benjamin Bowman Sr., Peter Bowman, Martin Garber, John Glick and others. From this time on, the Brethren became more active in the Master's cause. Meetings were held in the different settlements. But they were not able to erect meeting-houses. To meet this requirement, their dwellings were so constructed as to best accommodate the monthly, bi-monthly or ter-monthly service as it came to them in turn. The houses were usually one and a half story high with sides of logs, the roof of clapboards, and the floor of puncheon. The interior was divided into apartments for the accommodation of the family. This was not infrequently done by use of curtains made from homespun material. In other buildings, however, the partitions were made of boards sawed by the old whip or hand saw. In such case, the whole of it was hanging on a pivot and could be hoisted, or the lower half could be so manipulated as to throw the entire lower story into one room on meeting-day. In addition to furnishing a place for the meeting, it was the usual custom for the proprietor of the house

The Old Loom.

to provide food for as many in the assembly as desired it, and feed their horses as well. At the close of the meeting, when the appointments were announced, an invitation was given to all to remain for the meal which was then in preparation.

As time went on and the congregation increased, each member in the community in which the meeting was held was asked to contribute some provision toward feeding the people. This custom prevailed after churchhouses were erected and especially on the occasion of love-feasts when the services would usually continue from Saturday morning until Sunday evening. At night, the assembly, regardless of church affiliation, was entertained at the nearest homes of the Brethren. In this way the broad hospitality was inculcated, for which the Virginia church is noted to this day.

The Way They Did the Cooking.

Their acts of benevolence were no less marked than their hospitality. The unfortunate in life received assistance, however humble their station. Neither were their acts confined to their own number. Quite the opposite is shown to have been true. The author is in possession of some of these old subscription papers, one of which is here mentioned. It was for the relief of one Isaac Halterman. In the preamble, it recites the affliction of the beneficiary as having been that of a long sickness. While yet not recovered from his emaciated condition, an impatient creditor, through an action in court, was about to sell his property. The amount subscribed was intended to make payment of this claim, that he should not lose his home. It is evident that Isaac Halterman was not a member of the Brethren Church. This act was not great in worldly achievement, but it is a beautiful tribue to nobility of Christian character.

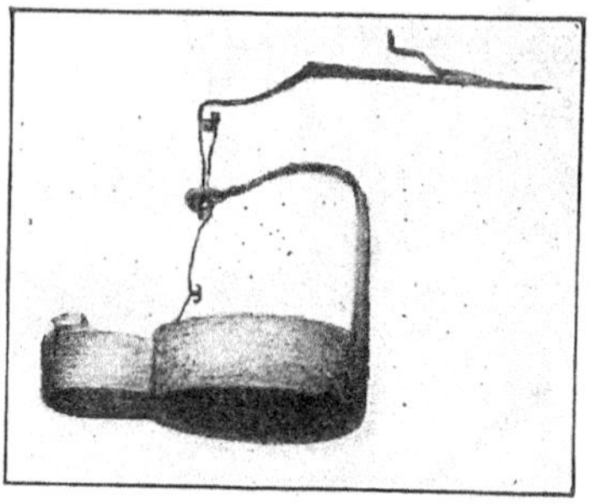

Primitive Fat Lamp of Our Forefathers.

The widow and orphan found in the Virginia church a true guardian and protector. Not only the most destitute received aid, but whenever the interest of the friendless ones was at stake, the church as a whole or as individuals did what it could for their welfare. Not through the helpfulness of an orphans' home, as in more recent years, but in their own good way they met the requirements of the times in which they lived. As an instance of such mediation, the following contract, translated from the German by Dr. John S. Flory of Bridgewater College, is here given. The agreement, somewhat abridged in minor detail, reads as follows:

AGREEMENT BETWEEN THE BAPTIST CHURCH

and

ANNA SHERFIG AND CHILDREN.

A contract: the agreement made, concluded and made binding in the following manner and form between the Baptist Church in Shenandoah and Rockingham counties, and especially with the oldest servants in the aforesaid church, namely, Benjamine Bowman, and Martin Gerber, and John Glick, and John Kagey, and Joseph Bowman, and Jacob Gerber, and as said before with the entire church already mentioned, of the one part, and with Anna Sherfig, widow, of Shenandoah County, State of Virginia, and with her oldest children who are of age, namely, John Sherfig, and Josua Sherfig, and Magdalene Sherfig, and Salome Sherfig, of the other part,

Witnesseth: Whereas the said Anna Sherfig has been complained of and has promised that she will move from the place and that the children will be put out as soon as her deceased husband, namely Abraham Sherfig, has directed in his last will and testament, so it has seemed well to be charitable and merciful with her, and it has thus been mutually agreed that she shall be allowed to give a proof (of her good intentions) in the following manner and form: that with the consent of the children who are of age, she may remain dwelling upon the place for a period of time, and farm the place according to the agreement, and bring up her children in the order and fear of God; she may thus dwell a year or two longer than her deceased husband's will says, if she can come off in peace and according to the agreement with her children. If, however, one or several of the children are not willing to follow, then shall the church have full right to put her off as her husband's will provides; but if the family comes into disorder, then the said church shall have the right to break up the household, according to their judgment; or if the children who are of age shall complain because of their inheritence or the magistrate should also be opposed, then the executive, with the advice of the church would have to break up the household and do as the will says; or if it should also fall too heavily upon her, the mother of the family, then she shall have the right with the advice of the church to break up her home if she wishes to do so; and while some of the deceased and said Sherfig's children are small and cannot earn their food and clothing and the said mother is unwilling to bring them up and provide them with food and clothes, and neither the magistrate nor the said church will assume the care or guardianship of the little children, then the church must see to it that it is just to permit her something for the place besides her third. If the third of the grain which they cut at the last harvest was not enough to maintain the children and bring them up, then the church has decided, in the hope that the magistrate would not oppose, to leave her use all the grain which she had gathered at the last harvest on the aforesaid place to maintain her family in the manner as said, and all the grain which is sowed upon the said place she shall have for her use as already mentioned. . . . . . It is further agreed that neither the mother nor the children shall sell wood from the above mentioned place without the consent of the church, and they shall keep the place well fenced and especially in good order. If they wish to clear land, they shall do it with the consent of the church. The said Josua shall keep no more stock on the place than he necessarily requires on the place to secure all the articles of this instrument. All the instruments of both parties are written, and all are signed with their own hands; and the three oldest of the children named within together with their mother named within seal it with their own seal, this day, the twenty-seventh of November, in the year of our Lord one thousand eight hundred and twelve.

In the presence of

Samuel Bowman	Yohones Kagey
David Bowman	Joseph Bowman
George Wever	John Scherfig (seal)
William Good	Joshua Scherfig (seal)
William Good	Salomy Scherfig
Michael Wine	or Miller (seal)
Benjamine Bowman	Magdalena Scherfig
Martin Gerber	(seal)
John Glick	

It is most likely that Abraham Scherfig was twice married and that Anna was his second wife. From each of these unions, children were born. At least, the older ones were of age, while the others were quite young, and became impatient to come in possession of their inheritance. Complaint had been brought against the widow, and the church here performed the very difficult duty of mediator, guardian, and trustee for all parties concerned.

As individuals, they were equally given to good works. The spirit of commercialism had not taken hold of their lives to such extent as to destroy the finer impulses of the human heart. So impressive were the acts of kindness and deeds of love, in administering to the needs of the destitute, that mention is made in the strongest terms by writers not identified with the church. A notable instance is a poem dedicated to the memory of "Kagey, the Good Man," by the eminent educator and poet, Joseph Salyards of New Market,

Virginia. Here the writer pays a most beautiful tribute to the memory of one of these benefactors of mankind. A short extract is here given from this somewhat lengthy poem. The third and fourth stanzas read as follows:

> " In yonder lane the widow lorn,—
> Naomi of our heartless years,—
> Leans o'er her orphans every morn,
> And yields to unavailing tears;
> For, he whose voice had soothed so long
> Sad memory's unobtrusive sigh,
> Whose hand secured from wreckless wrong,
> Whose bosom bled at sorrow's cry,
> He too has left our wintry shore,—
> He hears the sufferer plead no more.
>
> "Ah! never down the rocky vale
> She hastes to meet her orphans more;
> Shares the warm kiss and lifts the pail,
> White-wreathed with sweetness from his store.
> No more the fatherless from play,
> Shall run with lisping joy to tell,—
> 'The good man brings his gifts today;
> Come see his white locks in the dell.'
> Deep death hath wrapped in darkness now,
> The honors of that reverend brow."

Doubtless these lines were suggested to the writer by the many beneficent acts received in the home of his widowed mother from the bounty of Eld. John Kagey. For it is known that " Kagey, the Good Man," or Yohones Kagey, was an active minister in the Brethren Church during the first half of the nineteenth century. His name appears on the contract given on a preceding page.

In a few years the ministry had so increased that

The Old Flat Rock Church in Shenandoah County Where Brethren First Settled.

various points usually marked by churchhouses at the present day, became the centers of church activity. Chief among these are Flat Rock and Maurertown in Shenandoah County, Linville Creek, Greenmount, Garbers, and Beaver Creek in Rockingham County, and Middle River in Augusta County. Among these ministers were ordained elders, and, in order to administer discipline, a division line running east and west through Harrisonburg, Rockingham County, had been agreed upon in 1788. The members living north of this were designated Lower Rockingham and Shenandoah Brethren. Those south were known as Upper Rockingham and Augusta Brethren. This was the only division of territory for more than a quarter of a century, and seemed to meet every requirement of church regulation.

In Franklin, Floyd and Botetourt counties, like nuclei of membership were formed, which afterward developed into churches. Here, too, were an active ministry laboring for the Lord's cause. In a preceding chapter, a brief notice is made of the labors of Elders Jacob Miller and William Smith, and in the succeeding pages their work is so minutely delineated that it is unnecessary to give an extended account here. However, their methods were unique and therefore of interest. With staff in hand, they would walk ten or twelve miles to the place of preaching. Previous to the regular service, they would read a Scripture and give explanation. At the same time, permission was given to any one present to ask questions or give words of exhortion. Eld. Miller would speak in the German and Eld. Smith in the English language. Through their ministration, largely, the foundation for a number of the large and flourishing organizations in the First District of Virginia was laid. When other ministers were chosen, some were English while others were German. As a consequence of this, there were some German congregations, and other assemblies that could only speak the English. For a time these different churches were designated as the "German Arm" and the "English Arm" of the church. These differed somewhat in customs but not in Bible doctrine. In time, however, by the exercise of Christian charity and intermingling, they all learned the English tongue and were no more known by the different nationalities.

Among other ministers who labored in this part of the State at an early date, were John Bowman, Abraham Naff, Isaac Naff, Daniel Barnhart, John Eller, Christian Bowman, Austin Hylton, Samuel Crumpacker, David Rife, Henry Snider, and a number of others. The churches in the First District of Virginia stand as an evidence of their well-spent lives. Other laborers followed them of whom we shall learn more fully in succeeding chapters.

In the cemetery near the Flat Rock church stands a very modest stone with

17 J. H. G. 87

engraved upon it. Near by it is one of a somewhat more modern design, upon which is the following inscription:

Barbara Garber
ist G. W. 15 D. B. 1808
Old 75 y. 5 m.

Grave of John Garber.

Grave of Barbara Garber.

These humble slabs mark the graves of John Garber, the first minister of the Brethren Church that is known to have preached in the Shenandoah Valley, and that of his beloved wife, Barbara. Yet a far more enduring monument has been erected by their godly lives in establishing the church in northern Virginia and in giving it a most noble family of seven sons and three daughters. Of this number, six of the sons were preachers and the other a deacon. The daughters were also identified with the church, two of whom became the wives of distinguished ministers. Four of the sons permanently settled in Virginia. Two of them, Martin and Jacob, remained near their father's home. Daniel located near Harrisonburg, and Abraham near Middle River in Augusta County. Samuel went to Tennessee and John and Joseph to Ohio. Wherever they went, they were quickly recognized as leaders in the church. So closely has this family been connected with the affairs of the church in northern Virginia, that a well-written history of their descendants would give an account of the growth and development of the church in this section.

As seen on the tombstone, John Garber's death was in 1787. The correctness of this is substantiated by his will, which was written on September 4, 1787, and admitted to probate at Woodstock, December 27, 1787.

This indenture is of special interest, but of too great length to reproduce here. A few extracts must suffice. In the preamble, he states that at that time he was sick and in a low state of health bodily, but of a perfect mind and memory. He first provided for his " well beloved wife, Barbara, and five younger children to remain on the place until February 1, 1790." At that time there was to be a general division of the personal property, two-thirds of which was to be divided among his ten children; viz., John, Samuel, Martin, Anna, Abraham, Jacob, Daniel, Catherine, Joseph, and Magdalene, and one-third was to be given to his wife. This division was to be made, however, after giving his widow "her bed, her cupboard, a cow, a good spinning wheel, and the choice of two sheep so that she may have not just cause or reason to complain."

He was little past the meridian of life when he died. His widow survived him twenty-one years and was seventy-five years old at that time. This would have made her fifty-four years old at the death of her husband, which most likely corresponds closely to his age at his demise. However correct this statement, which is but reasonable, they left a posterity that have served the church faithfully and have done much to shape her destiny in this as well as other States.

CHAPTER IV.

Church Organization—Origin of District Meeting—Missionary Activity.

Until now, the simple organization mentioned in the preceding chapter existed among the churches. As already stated, they were known as the Upper Rockingham and Augusta Brethren and the Lower Rockingham and Shenandoah Brethren. Likewise, the Franklin, Floyd, Botetourt, Roanoke, etc., Brethren indicated the Brethren living in these respective counties. At this time, the membership had increased and a wider field was open for the ministry. Isolated members in various sections would call for meetings and individuals would seek to know the truth. In this way, the ministry in the different counties would go and hold meetings, and finally churches were established. The Franklin Brethren went into the surrounding territory as far as North Carolina. The Floyd and Botetourt Brethren went into adjacent counties and as far south as Tennessee. The Augusta, Rockingham, and Shenandoah Brethren went east, west, north and south. However, their uncompromising attitude against slavery stood as a barrier east of the Blue Ridge. To the west, they crossed the Ohio and preached the Gospel in the settlements beyond. They usually traveled on horseback, but for shorter distances they went on foot. In every section, a most commendable zeal was manifest. The ministers not only served the church without charge, but usually traveled the long distances at their own expense.

Yet there were some exceptions to this. Although there was no compensation asked of the laity of the church, a beautiful spirit of mutual helpfulness manifested itself among them, which may be considered one of the first missionary movements among the general membership of the church. When a minister was from home preaching, not infrequently the members would gather at his home and assist his family with his farm work. On his return, a pleasant surprise awaited him. Sometimes the crop was planted, the harvesting done, or the grain safely stored away for the support of his loved ones, while he was absent. These pretty customs prevailed to some extent to within the recollection of the author, and only gave way to a more systematic method of missionary endeavor.

Elder Austin Hylton. See Biography, Chapter X.

About this time, meetinghouses were first erected. As previously stated, the young church was not able to construct houses of worship. Their dwellings, their barns and the canopy of the heavens were dedicated to the service of the Lord. To accommodate the inincreasing congregations, it was now necessary to have more commodious buildings. Especially was this true for love-feast occasions.

The Middle River Church, Augusta County, was built in 1824.

Linville Creek, Rockingham County, 1828.
Cooks Creek, Rockingham County, 1822 (?)
Flat Rock, Shenandoah County, 1844.
Millcreek, Rockingham County, (?)
Germantown, Franklin County, 1848.
Pleasant Valley, Augusta County, 1854.
Barren Ridge, Augusta County, 1856.
Brick Church, Floyd County, 1857.
Lemontown, Botetourt County, (?)
Brush, Rockingham County, 1843.
Pine Grove, Rockingham County, 1850.
Greenmount, Rockingham County, 1859.
Beaver Creek, Rockingham County, (?)
Valley, Botetourt County, (?)
Valley Pike, Shenandoah County, (?)

This also was a period for closer church organization. For nearly a half century, the Brethren in Virginia had maintained the unity of the church successfully with little more division than geographical location. With an increased membership, and more widely distributed, this became far more difficult. Therefore, a closer organization was deemed necessary in order to maintain love and union. The wisdom of this can be plainly seen. The method of procedure at new places was usually as follows: Points for preaching were opened as opportunity afforded and as soon as the membership was sufficiently strong near the given place for a working body, they were organized into a local church or organization. In this way, discipline could be administered and the new body became a base for the extension of Gospel teaching. The definite lines between these organizations were agreed upon at a later date. The older

Old Garber Church, Two Miles Southwest of Harrisonburg. This was the First Meetinghouse Built by the Brethren in Virginia.

settlements were subdivided for the same reason. For a more detailed account of these organizations, however, the reader is referred to the respective chapters on local organization. The dates of a few of these subdivisions are given here.

In 1838, in Shenandoah County, the Woodstock congregation was formed to the north of Flat Rock with twelve members. A matter of unusual note is the fact that one-half of this membership were River Brethren. They simply formed themselves into this compact for their mutual helpfulness and the advancement of Christ's kingdom.

In 1840, the territory, in part, composing the churches of Greenmount and Linville Creek was organized into Upper Linville and Lower Linville Creek. This left Flat Rock with much the same boundary as it has today. Four years later, Upper Linville and Lower Linville were divided. The former was called Greenmount and the latter Linville Creek. In 18-(?), the territory in Rockingham County south of Harrisonburg, known as Upper Rockingham, was divided into three divisions. The central portion was known as Cooks Creek; the western portion, Beaver Creek; and the eastern portion, Millcreek. In Augusta County, like divisions were effected. The Brethren at Middle River had made preparation for such division by building houses of worship to the north in 1854, and to the south in 1856. Some years later, these points were made the centers of separate organizations. The former is known as Pleasant Valley and the latter as Barren Ridge.

In the southern district there was not much disposition to multiply the local organizations at this time. However, in 1845, the Floyd County church was divided into the East Arm, meaning that east of Floyd Courthouse, and the West Arm, meaning that portion west of the courthouse. In the other sections, they continued to be known by the name of the county in which they were organized. Yet they seemed no less active in grappling with the problems they had to meet, and some of the leading Brethren in Virginia labored in that part of the State.

The church in Virginia has always been loyal to the general Brotherhood. This is evidenced by maintaining her doctrines under the most adverse and trying conditions. The attitude on slavery gave a most difficult and perplexing problem for these churches to solve, and to uphold the principles of peace under the fearful scourge of the war in the South was an ordeal that few people could have withstood. In all these experiences, the fidelity of the church was unshaken. The Annual Meeting has frequently been held in the State and when held elsewhere, the Virginia churches have been invariably represented. This repeated contact with the membership at large tended much to instill interest in the general workings of the church and thereby maintain this marked loyalty. In turn, the frequent selection of Virginia brethren as officers of the Conference is an evidence of the high esteem in which they were held by the Brotherhood.

Elder George Shaver, First Minister of Woodstock.

Because of the increase in the number of organizations, new conditions arose and it was their great desire that love and union should continue to prevail throughout all the churches in Virginia. Devout ministers would visit the different communities; hold meetings and admonish the members to live holy lives and to labor for the peace and prosperity of the church. But their solicitation for the advancement of Christ's kingdom demanded other measures. Therefore, council meetings were held from time to time in the various localities, in which the organizations most conveniently located would unite. In time, some of these conferences were made more general in character, the work broadened, and the churches wherever located were usually represented. The name, General Council Meeting, was applied to them. However, at no time did they assume the duties of Annual Meeting, but, on the contrary, they devised measures by which her decisions could successfully be carried into effect. Such perplexing problems as divorce, fornication, slavery, etc., received repeated consideration.

These associations were productive of advanced thought, and the meetings from time to time formulated queries, far reaching in their nature, to be presented to Annual Meeting. However, to some of these measures the General Conference was not ready to give assent. To trace the entire development during this period by illustrations would cause this volume to grow far beyond its intended proportions at present. A few must suffice, although others would be of almost equal interest. In a meeting held in the old Brick church, Augusta County, on February 29 and March 1, 1856, a part of the time was devoted to mission work. Eld. John Kline in his diary, Life of John Kline, page 366, says of the proceedings: "Today we discuss the question of the propriety of making a move to more generally propagate the Gospel. Most of the brethren and sisters present seemed to be heartily in favor of the move. One brother, John Harshberger, said: 'If the Gospel is not true, let us eat and drink like other beasts, for tomorrow we die; but if the Gospel be true—and thanks be unto God, for we know it is true—it is worthy of all acceptation, for it is the power of God unto salvation to every one that believeth. But how can any one believe in him of whom he has not heard? And how can any one hear without a preacher? And how can any preach except he be sent?' I am in favor of trying to do more in every way than we have yet attempted, to spread the good news of salvation.

"'Salvation! let the echo fly
  The spacious earth around,
Till all the nations 'neath the sky
  Conspire to raise the sound.'"

As a consequence of this meeting, John Kline, Benjamin Moomaw, Peter Nininger, and John Harshberger were appointed a committee to draw a memorial asking for a plan to carry into effect the decision of Annual Meeting of 1852, which they so strongly favored. When the petition was drawn, it was carried to the Annual Meeting, near Freeport, Illinois, by Eld. John Kline. In response to this memorial, the following was enacted by the General Conference:

"Yearly Meeting. 1856. Art. 22. A letter from Virginia urging that this Yearly Meeting devise a plan, how the church could fulfill the command of the Savior, Matt. 28: 19, more effectually, so that the Article 8, on our Minutes of 1852, should not remain a dead letter. This meeting recommends the subject to the serious consideration of all the churches."

While the meeting was not yet ready to adopt a plan for more effective missionary endeavor, the letter was accorded due consideration. The zeal for the missionary cause continued unabated. In practical missionary

Elder Isaac Myers Starting to West Virginia Mission Field.

endeavor we have some of the most striking examples of devotion on the part of the Virginia ministry.

Furthermore, there was a continued strong desire that the Yearly Meeting should devise some method by which all the churches would unite in mission work. In this the general Brotherhood was not united. Therefore, as originators of the plan to divide the States into districts, they advocated a district missionary organization which they sought to have the General Conference endorse. To this end, a plan, attributed to a Virginia pen, was submitted to the Yearly Meeting of 1858, which reads as follows:

"Whereas, there is a strong desire among the Brethren in various places to have a more general exertion made on the part of the church to have the Truth more universally spread; and, whereas, the subject has been frequently talked of without any definite plan being proposed; we, therefore, have concluded by way of introduction, to offer the following outlines of a plan, subject, however, to such amendments as may from time to time be thought best. That is, let each State where there is a respectable number of Brethren, form a district; let the Brethren then hold their annual meetings; let each of these divisions (districts) have its treasury; let the churches that feel favorable have their treasury; let the churches be called upon as often as may be necessary to cast in their mite as a free-will offering. Then let these contributions be put into the district treasury and let the District Meeting appoint ministering brethren, say two or more, if necessary (such as are willing to go), to travel through the respective States for one year, their expenses being paid, and such provision made for their families as may be thought necessary."

This plan, however, met with strong opposition and the meeting withheld its approval.

In 1859, the missionary question was again before the General Conference, which evoked a very heated discussion, as a result of which a committee of six were appointed to draft a plan "by which the Brotherhood in general can take part in the good work." Of this committee, Eld. John Kline was a member and a leading spirit. The correspondence between him and a number of Brethren in different parts of Virginia shows the great interest in missions. In a letter under date of February 7, 1860, Peter Nininger, after making certain inquiries concerning their coming District Meeting, continues, "also on the missionary subject, I should like to know how the committee is getting along on that. I am hopeful that you will be well posted on that subject, and that there will be something done on that all important subject this spring." Likewise, Eld. B. F. Moomaw wrote him concerning the work of the committee. In his letter, dated January 21, 1860, he cautioned Eld. Kline not to aim at too much lest the whole of it fail. He further says, "as respects the missionary cause, I entertain fears that there will be no improvement, if it is not injured. . . . As yet, I have no plan matured, but of this I am fully convinced that it will not do to aim at too much, less the whole scheme be paralyzed."

After further discussion of the matter at some length, he adds, apparently as an afterthought, "I have lately been thinking that there is a plan by which much good might be done. It is this: If some brother gifted with the pen would write out a summary of the principles of the church in a brief, comprehensive way and have it published for free distribution, it would greatly aid in the propagation of the truth and arrest some of the errors that are in circulation. I think it would also cause many to inquire more fully after the doctrines of the Divine Record."

These old letters give us some additional glimpses of the earnestness of the spirit that ruled the lives of these brethren and no doubt permeated the churches they served. The reader can well recall that these three, with Eld. John Harshberger, constituted the committee, four years previous, that drafted a memorial on missions, that was presented to Annual Meeting of that year.

The committee of which Eld. Kline was now a member, according to appointment, met at the Limestone church, Tennessee, on May 25, the day prior to the Conference. Not all the members were present, most likely on account of the excited condition of the South at that time, due to the John Brown episode. Of the committee meeting, Eld. Kline in his characteristic manner wrote in his diary, " All the members of the committee seemed to be impressed with the importance of the matter under consideration. All agreed that it is not contrary to Gospel order for the church to help such preachers as are not able from poverty to do what their ability as ministers would enable them to do, if they could spare the time from their work at home to go more. Many fields are still white unto the harvest. The Lord may be today saying: 'I have much people in this city,' or in this place. By this he means, ready to accept salvation and become his people when the doors of the church are fairly opened up to them." Life John Kline, Page 431.

The records of the Conference show the plan that was adopted.

In the meeting held at the old Brick church in Augusta County on February 29 and March 1, previously mentioned, the Brethren became the prime

Elder S. A. Sanger, One of the Ardent Missionaries of Virginia.

movers for the division of the States into districts and that general council or district meetings be held in them. In his notes on this, Life of John Kline, p. 366 Eld. Kline enters the following items:

"Saturday, March 1. Council continues. The subject of divorce and adultery is considered today. It is decided to send it to Annual Meeting as also a query on proposition to district the churches, and have general council meetings in those Districts."

The minutes of that year's Annual Meeting, Art. 23, states that "A proposal" was submitted in favor "of forming districts of five, six or more adjoining churches for the purpose of meeting jointly at least once a year, settling difficulties, etc., and thus lessening the business of our General Yearly Meeting. We believe this plan to be a good one, if carried out in the fear of the Lord."

While this act gave the approval for holding general council meetings, they had been held in Virginia for years previous to this time. However, the minutes referred to gave to these meetings a new aspect. Prior to this, they had not the authority designated to them to settle difficulties, but were the outgrowth of a desire to more extensively spread the Gospel and to prevent differences by maintaining love and union among the churches. Furthermore, it was the constant desire of the Brethren that the influence of these meetings should be broadened and that all the churches receive the greatest benefit from them. To this end, at the District Meeting held at the Valley meeting-house, Augusta County, on March 11 and 12, 1859, a committee of twelve were appointed to set forth the purposes and intent of the District Meeting. Likewise, they were to devise a plan for holding future meetings and secure the representation from all the churches. The committee's report which reads as follows, was unanimously adopted by the meeting.

The committee appointed by the general council meeting held at the Valley meetinghouse, in Augusta County, Virginia, on March 11 and 12, 1859, report, that this meeting appoint another meeting of the same kind, to be held at some central point, between this time and the spring of 1860, in which all the churches favorable to holding general council meetings (District Meeting), shall be represented, if possible.

This meeting also recommends that B. F. Moomaw, Peter Nininger of Botetourt County, Martin Garber of Augusta, Solomon Garber of Upper Rockingham, and Jacob Miller of Lower Rockingham, be appointed a corresponding committee to invite all the churches in Virginia, Tennessee, and North Carolina to represent at said meeting at time and place of appointment, that we may determine what can be done for the great cause of the Gospel.

This meeting is further of the opinion that the many calls from the various parts with the extensive spread of the Brotherhood, demand that some systematic regulation should be made to facilitate this great cause. [Wherefore,] this meeting recommends

1. That it shall be the duty of such conferences to grant similar meetings, for the purpose named, to applicants from the various parts of the territory represented in these general council meetings as in their wisdom they may deem proper.

2. It shall be the privilege of any of the churches in the bounds above stated to make application for such meetings when desired.

3. Said meeting shall in no way supersede Annual Meeting, but they shall be assistants thereto, by discussing and settling all differences so far as possible, in order to lessen the labor of Annual Meeting. Also

they shall labor to keep love and union in all the churches. But,

4. These meetings shall not have the power to finally settle questions of general doctrine. This duty shall devolve upon Annual Meeting alone.

Signed by

Daniel Thomas	John Kline
Abraham Garber	Daniel Brower
Martin Cösner	Peter Nininger
Jacob Miller	John Harshberger
John Wine	John Wine
Solomon Garber	Martin Cosner

The above report shows how nearly the purpose for which the District Meeting was first inaugurated accords with its present usefulness. While the Brethren were not forgetful to labor for the purity, love, and union of the church, the one all-absorbing problem was the adoption of some measures by which the Gospel could best be propagated. Although the plan for district missionary organization did not receive the approval of Annual Meeting the previous year, they did not think it an act of disloyalty to adopt some measures by which the work could be made more aggressive. For this the Brethren elicited the greatest interest by their correspondence. Arrangements were made to hold the next meeting at the Valley meeting-house, Botetourt County, March 30, 1860. A number of the ministers from Rockingham and Augusta counties were in attendance, among whom were Elders John Kline and Solomon Garber.

CHAPTER V.

Slavery.

Among the great problems the Church of the Brethren has had to meet, none has been more perplexing than that of slavery. At this time it is most difficult to realize the wisdom and devotion to duty that was necessary to keep the church clear of it and yet remain a united people. Upon this breaker few, very few, church organizations with a membership so widely distributed through the North and the South were able to ride. It is to the undying honor of the Brethren then living that they continued a firm, united people in opposition to this national sin until it was erased from the statutes of the American nation.

Although less than a half century has elapsed since the colored race was considered chattel for the white man in the South, very few persons can recall the spirit of that time. Furthermore, at the present, when the colored man has freedom throughout Virginia and when the State provides for the education of his children and when asylums are maintained by the public treasury for the unfortunate of his race, it is difficult to realize how the negro was bought and driven to market as so many beasts of the field, less than two generations ago. Every true citizen would readily wish that the records of this evil could be eliminated from the annals of our fair State, but it must ever remain in evidence of the fester spot of that time.

From the year 1620 to the surrender of General Lee

in 1865, the black man was held in bondage in Virginia. At first, however, little encouragement was given the slave-traders, and many of the leading citizens stood in opposition to it. More than one hundred petitions and protests were entered by various organizations of the

"I was once a slave."

Virginia people against the institution of slavery and the Colonial Assembly enacted laws against it, but this availed nothing with England's greed for the gain to be derived from this hateful traffic. George Washington, the father of our country, said that it was "among his first wishes to see some plan adopted by which slavery in his country (Virginia) might be abolished by law." He further wrote that his suffrage should never be wanting to this end. James Madison and Patrick Henry reprobated the principle of slavery. On account of this institution, Thomas Jefferson declared that "he trembled for his country when he remembered that God is just." This last-named statesman, at the Constitutional Congress on March 1, 1784, offered a measure tending to restrict the slave traffic, but this was defeated.

However, the lucid climate of Virginia, together with the invention of the cotton gin, made slavery far more profitable to the Virginians than to their brethren living in the more rigorous climate in the North. As the result of this the trader found a lucrative market for his human chattel in Virginia, and in the year 1790 there were 200,000 slaves in the State. The traffic extended beyond the mountains into the Valley of Virginia, and many of the Germans, who at first opposed slavery, yielded to its seductive influence. In time the traffic became extensive in this section also, and the slave-driver under the laws of the State plied his unmerciful vocation to his heart's content.

That the reader may see more clearly the nature and extent of this traffic in the Valley, the following advertisements as they appeared among others of a similar kind in the Rockingham *Register* in 1858 are here appended.

A well-known dealer located in Harrisonburg, Virginia, inserted the following:

A Few Negroes Wanted.—Whilst some of my Augusta friends are advertising largely for their hundreds and thousands of Negroes, I beg to state that I shall be satisfied to purchase A FEW valuable negroes, of both sexes, for which I will pay as HIGH PRICES as are paid by my neighbors. While I will be content to get a few Negroes, I wish it to be understood that I have money enough to pay for all that may be offered. I am always ready to act upon commission for my friends.—*Harrisonburg, Va.*

An Augusta County buyer makes use of printer's ink in this wise:

1,000 Negroes Wanted.—I wish to purchase one thousand LIKELY NEGROES, of both sexes for the Southern market, for which I will give the highest cash prices.—

Other dealers likewise called attention to their special claims for patronage. One more, reproduced from the Rockingham *Register and Advertiser* of July 30, 1858, is given here:

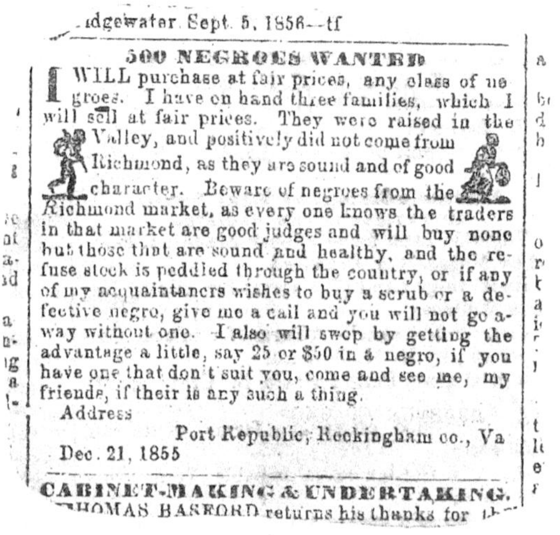

..idgewater Sept. 5, 1856--tf

500 NEGROES WANTED

I WILL purchase at fair prices, any class of negroes. I have on hand three families, which I will sell at fair prices. They were raised in the Valley, and positively did not come from Richmond, as they are sound and of good character. Beware of negroes from the Richmond market, as every one knows the traders in that market are good judges and will buy none but those that are sound and healthy, and the refuse stock is peddled through the country, or if any of my acquaintancers wishes to buy a scrub or a defective negro, give me a call and you will not go away without one. I also will swop by getting the advantage a little, say 25 or $50 in a negro, if you have one that don't suit you, come and see me, my friends, if their is any such a thing.

Address

Port Republic, Rockingham co., Va

Dec. 21, 1855

CABINET-MAKING & UNDERTAKING.

THOMAS BASFORD returns his thanks for th...

Of the traffic as it appeared then and as to the present condition of the colored man, Eld. Jonas Graybill gives the following interesting observation.

" I lived on the main road leading from Winchester, Virginia, to Knoxville, Tennessee. In the fall of each year large droves of slaves were taken south along this thoroughfare. The men were handcuffed on the sides of a chain forty or fifty feet long. Each one was just given room enough to walk and to lie down at night to sleep. Frequently, they had to leave their wives and children and go south never to hear from them again.

" In slavery times marriage among the slaves consisted of a simple ceremony without license. Very often the husband belonged to one slave-holder and the wife to another. When one was sold, not being able to write, they would seldom hear from each other. I was at a sale where two boys were sold to a slave-dealer. When they were led away their mother cried and prayed the Lord to take care of her boys. I saw one young man sell for $1,100 and another for $1,400.

" In time of the war a colored minister, who was also a slave, asked me what I thought of the war. I told him that it was an awful thing for a Christian nation to be engaged in. He said, ' This is true, but there are thousands of us poor slaves who are praying that the Lord will so overrule this war that we may be free.' When I look at the Negro today with the opportunities placed before him and as I see him in school and college with the privilege of the Sunday school and church, I am made to think that God certainly answered these prayers."

For various reasons, many citizens of the Valley would contract from year to year with the East Virginia slave-owners for the service of their slaves. This

Elder Jonas Graybill. See Biography, Chapter VIII,

was usually done at New Year, and so extensive was this custom that "slave-hiring day" was an event of no little importance in the different towns of the Valley.

Inherently opposed to this enforced servitude, from

the very earliest date the Church of the Brethren stood uncompromisingly in opposition to this human traffic in any form whatever. Years before the organization of any abolition party in the North, the Brethren decided that slavery can not be permitted in any form among them. In 1863, a writer reviewing the church on this question said: " The Brethren always believed and still believe that slavery is a great evil and contrary to the doctrine of Christ."

This conviction seemed to be no less strong regardless of the section in which the Brethren lived. In Virginia, where the colored man was held in bondage, and where he was bought and sold with little regard to his wishes, and where few dared to question the right or wrong of it, the church stood unalterably opposed to these unrighteous acts. In every instance when the question was considered in their general council meetings, the decisions were strongly in opposition to it.

Furthermore, that the reader may more fully see the position the church has ever held on slavery, a few extracts from the minutes of Annual Meeting are here given. In 1782, more than a decade before any organized political movement in any part of the country against slavery, the General Conference said: "Concerning the un-Christian negro slave trade, it has been unanimously considered, that it can not be permitted in any wise by the church, that a member should or could purchase negroes or keep them as slaves."

Again in 1797, the following decision was made by Annual Meeting: " that no brother or sister should have negroes as slaves, and in case a brother or sister has such, he (or she) has to set them free." Another part of this resolution relates to a slave-owner who asks for admission into the church. The decision stands that such persons shall be informed of the council of the church, but in case where they could not emancipate them at once, they may be held so long as the nearest church may deem proper and then they shall go free with a good suit of clothes. In case of children of slave parents, they could be kept until twenty-five years old, but their owners were required to have them taught reading and writing, and to bring them up in the fear of the Lord, and, after presenting them with a new suit of wearing apparel, they were to go free. In the event a brother should be disobedient to this decision, the minute speaks as follows: "Further, it is considered, if a brother contrary to this conclusion, would purchase negroes and would not emancipate them, he would have to be considered as disobedient and we would have no fellowship with him until he sets them free."

In 1812, the Conference denounced slavery as "a grievous evil" and declared that "it should soon be abolished." The Conference of 1813 reaffirmed the decision of 1797, with the exception that the children of slaves should be set free at twenty-one in case of males and at eighteen in case of females. This Conference also urged the members to be diligent in restraining their children, who are not members of the church, so far as possible, from buying, selling, and holding slaves.

The abuses arising from the Fugitive Slave Act, together with various laws enacted by slave States, brought slavery again before the Annual Conference of 1853, to be considered from a new view-point. Seeing that the efforts of the church were being frustrated by kidnappers, some Brethren thought it useless to make such great sacrifice to set their slaves free only to be sold into worse servitude. However, the church was unwilling to tolerate slavery even from this apparently reasonable standpoint. Concerning this, a query was presented to the Annual Meeting of 1853, which reads as follows:

How shall any branch of the church proceed in case an individual wishes to become a member who is in possession of a slave or slaves, and the law of the State in which they reside is such, that they cannot manumit them in safety without transporting them beyond its (the State's) limits, and as we are aware that the several States where slavery does not exist are contemplating and passing strenuous laws prohibiting their emigration thither? It seems indispensably necessary for us to adopt some other plan than hitherto practiced, in order that the church should be kept clear from the evils of slavery, and that such persons may be enabled to come into Christ's kingdom.

There was quite a difference of opinion how best to answer this query. This, however, was not because any of them favored the admission of slavery into the church, but it arose in the different views as to what was best to do with them when they were set free. After a somewhat lengthy discussion, the matter was deferred one year and placed into the hands of Joseph Arnold and B. F. Moomaw of Virginia, John H. Umstad, Samuel Lahman, Isaac Price, and David Bosserman of Pennsylvania, and D. P. Sayler and Henry Koontz of Maryland.

There was likewise a difference of views among the members of the committee. So strong was this that there was a majority and a minority report submitted. The text of the latter can not be given, but it is known that some of the Virginia Brethren were much interested in the colonization of the colored man and they would have gladly secured the endorsement of the general Brotherhood. The majority report was adopted which reads as follows:

First. Under no circumstances can slavery be admitted into the church.

Secondly. In all cases, where a holder of a slave or slaves wishes to become a member of the church, he be required to manumit all his slaves before baptism upon the following conditions: the males to go out free at the age of twenty-one and the females at the age of eighteen years. All those over and above these ages when manumitted are to be paid by their former owner such a sum, either in money or goods, as may be judged right by the church in which the case may occur, and which is considered as the best judge, being acquainted with all the circumstances, as a compensation for their services over age. This will enable the manumitted to emigrate to a land of liberty, and relieve the conscience of the liberator from the burden of taking with him to the bar of God the wages of oppression.

Other decisions were made on the different phases of the slavery question, but to the one end that slavery can not be tolerated in any form because "it was wrong; it belongs to the iniquities of Babylon; and it was making merchandise of the souls of men."

Whatever may have been the individual views of the Virginia Brethren on the subject, they at once set about to carry it out in practical life. If proof were needed to show their loyalty to the general Brotherhood, the reference to this one question alone should settle it forever. Yet how little we can realize the trial it cost to maintain them under the then existing conditions and

Linville Creek Church.

at the same time carry forward an aggressive missionary movement. At this time, it requires no philosopher to look back and pronounce slavery a most abominable curse. Even some that favored it then will now declare it an evil, but to stand in opposition to it amid the spirit of that time was widely different. Meeting its seductive influence from year in to year out, with the statutes of the State giving it full recognition, and an overwhelming sentiment in its favor, it required men of true conviction and courageous hearts to uncompromisingly stand in opposition to slavery. Beneath this influence, many men of less conviction fell and became disunited from their brethren in the North. Thus their religious bodies were rent asunder and were known as the churches of the North and churches of the South.

The Lord is truly to be praised for His guiding hand which brought the Brethren Church through these dark years, a united people. No North, no South, but all one—inseparably one in Christ Jesus. How easy it would have been to have lowered the standard for the sake of the missionary cause that burned so near their hearts! for the workers at almost every turn of the way came in contact with the slave-owners' interests. To the east it stood an unpassable barrier to all endeavor. Here, from generation to generation, slaves had been owned, bought and sold, and almost every one had come to think that the black man was created to become merchandise for the white man. Therefore it was not safe for the Brethren to preach in East Virginia at that time.

In some parts of the Valley of Virginia conditions were more favorable. The influence of the Brethren and that of the Mennonites and United Brethren, who held like views of slavery, strongly counteracted its influence. However, in other sections of the Valley, many slaves were held and the popular sentiment was strong in its favor. But these consecrated workers were willing to labor and wait. They were made to rejoice when some accepted the truth. Among the number at times were slaveholders. When the position of the church was fully set before them as to their slaves, not a few were like the young ruler in the time of Christ's ministry, they went away sorrowing, for their slaves represented much riches to them. Sometimes they were persons of wide influence and would have brought to the church prestige in the community in which they lived. However, a few were more noble in seeking after the truth and at the bidding of the church set their slaves free. In some instances they were valued at many thousands of dollars.

Furthermore, it was necessary that the church continue united in its opposition to this enforced servitude, for there were members who found it hard to comply with their promises they had made. To this end the churches would meet in their general council meetings to discuss and enact such measures as were best suited to carry out the decisions of Annual Meeting. Some of these measures appear to embrace even more than was contemplated by the decisions of General Conference. A meeting of this nature was held at the old Linville Creek church in 1855, the minutes of which are hereunto appended:

Rockingham County, Virginia, March 2, 1855.

We, the Brethren of Augusta, Upper and Lower Rockingham, Shenandoah and Hardy counties having, in general council meeting assembled in the church on Linville Creek; and having under consideration the following question concerning those Brethren that are holding slaves at this time and who have not complied with the requisition of Annual Meeting of 1854, conclude

1. That they make speedy preparation to liberate them either by emancipation or by will, that this evil

Rockingham County Va March the 2th day 1855

We the Breathren of Augusta upper and lower Rockingham Shanandoah and Hardy having in general Council assembled ourselfs in the Church on Linvils Creek and having under Consideration the following questing that is conserning those breathren that are holding slaves at ~~that~~ this time and have not complied withe the requisition of the anuel meeting of 1854 first may we have came to the following Conclusion that is that thay make speady preaparation to liberaten them either by emancipation or by will that this evil may be banish from amongst us as we look upon Slavery as dang-rous to be tolerated in the Church and is attended to Create disunion in the brotherhood and a great injury to the Cause of Christ and the progress of the Church so we ernistly exhort our breathren humbly yet Ernistly and lovingly to Clear themselfs from this principal of Slavery that you may not fail and come short of the glory of god at the great and notable day of the lord, and further more as considering Breathren hireing of a Slave or Slaves and paying wages to thare owners we dont approve of the Same and is attended with evil and combined with Slavery and taking hold of the same ~~[illegible]~~ evil which we can not incurage and Should we banish and put from amongst us and can not be tolerated in the Church

Brethren present

Benjamin Bowman	Abraham Knopp	Martain Garber
Daniel Yount	Martain Miller	John Neff
John Kline	Solomon Garber	John Wine
John Wine	Joseph Miller	
John Harshbarger	Jacob Miller	
George Shaver	Daniel Thomas	
Daniel Brower	John Brindel	
Jacob Brower	David Kline	
Selestine Whitmore	John Miller	
[illegible]	Christian Wine	

Minutes of Council Meeting, held at Linville Greek Church, March 2, 1855.

may be banished from among us, as we look upon slavery as dangerous to be tolerated in the church; is tending to create disunion in the Brotherhood, and is a great injury to the cause of Christ and the progress of the church. So we unitedly exhort our brethren, humbly, yet earnestly and lovingly, to clear themselves of slavery, that they may not fail and come short of the glory of God, at the great and notable day of the Lord.

Furthermore, concerning Brethren hiring a slave or slaves and paying wages to their owners, we do not approve of it. The same is attended with evil and is combined with slavery. It is taking hold of the same evil which we cannot encourage, and should be banished and put from among us, and cannot be tolerated in the church.

Brethren present:

Ordained Elders.	Ministers.
Benjamine Bowman	Abraham Knupp
Daniel Yount	Martain Miller
John Kline	Solomon Garber
John Wine	Joseph Miller
John Harshberger	Jacob Miller
George Shaver	Daniel Thomas
Daniel Brower	John Brindel
Jacob Brower	David Kline
Selestine Whitmore	John Miller
	Christian Wine
	Martain Garber
	John Neff
	John Wine

Despite these strong decisions, slavery continued to agitate the Virginia church. Not unlike the experiences of more modern times, there were Brethren who felt loath to part with their idol. Doubtless the difficulties in the way of manumitting them caused others to hesitate. Whatever the cause, they were not permitted to keep them as slaves. It became necessary to hold a similar meeting the 11th of September of the following year at the same place. This time the question considered was slightly different. It referred to what the church here in the slaveholding States should require of any slave-owner that desires to come into the church. Eld. John Kline in his notes says it is "a very delicate matter to act upon in the present sensitive condition of public feeling on slavery. But it is the aim of the Brethren here not to offend popular feeling, so long as that feeling does not attempt any interference with what they regard and hold sacred as their line of Christian duty. Should such opposition arise, which I greatly fear will be the case at no distant day, it will then be seen that it is the fixed purpose and resolve of the Brotherhood to 'obey God rather than man.'" "Life of John Kline," p. 382.

The minutes of the meeting are only preserved in part. The lower half is torn away. Enough is here to show how these Brethren handled this "delicate matter," as Eld. Kline called it. The part of the record which was preserved reads as follows:

"At a council meeting held at the Linville Creek meetinghouse the 11th of September 1856, the Brethren took into consideration the slavery question and came to the following conclusion:

That no members should be received by baptism into the church until they have first manumitted or set free all slaves, or slaves over which they have lawful control, which manumission is to be effected by putting on record in the clerk's office of the county a letter of freedom, with an agreement to assist them with

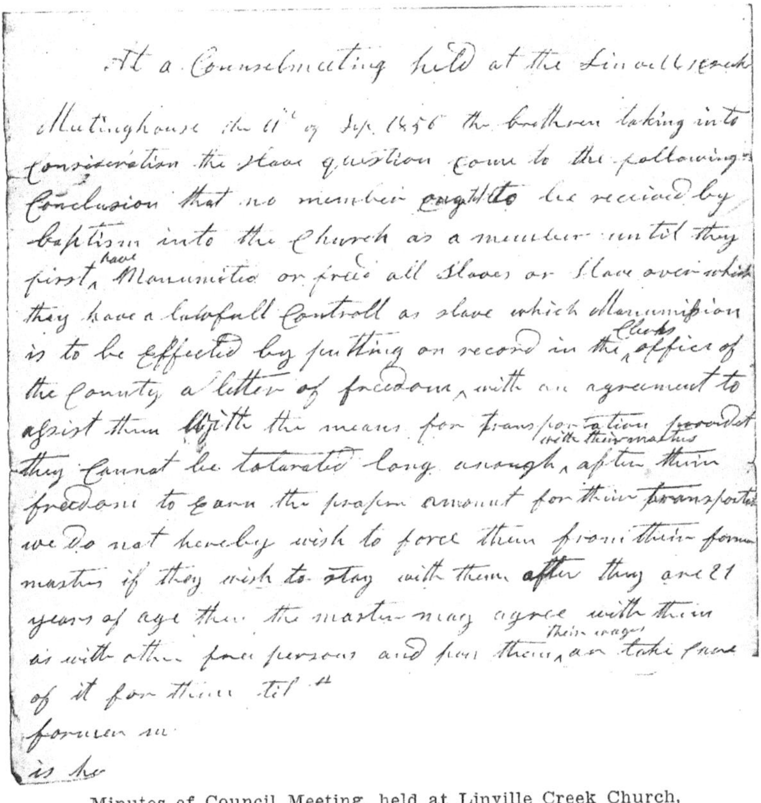
At a Counselmeeting held at the Linvills creek
Meetinghouse the 11th of Sep. 1856 the brethren taking into
consideration the slave question came to the following
conclusion that no member ought to be recieved by
baptism into the Church as a member until they
first have Manumited or freed all Slaves or Slave over which
they have a lawfull Controll as slave which Manumission
is to be Effected by putting on record in the Clerks office of
the County a letter of freedom with an agreement to
assist them with the means for transportation provided
they Cannot be tolarated long enough with their masters after their
freedom to Earn the proper amount for their transportation
we do not hereby wish to force them from their former
masters if they wish to stay with them after they are 21
years of age then the master may agree with them
as with other free persons and pay them their wages or take care
of it for them til
former
is ho

Minutes of Council Meeting, held at Linville Creek Church,
Sept. 11, 1856.

means for transportation, provided they cannot be tolerated long enough with their masters after their freedom to earn the amount for their emigration. We do not hereby wish to force them from their former master, if they wish to stay with them after they are twenty-one years of age, then the master may agree with them as with other free persons and pay them wages or take care of it for them.

Here the old paper is torn and it would only be conjecture to state what follows. Yet enough is given to show how persistently they labored to free the church from the contaminating influences of slavery.

It should be stated that some of these former slaves were much attached to their masters and gladly continued with them as long as they lived. The further fact should also be recorded, that not all slaves were unkindly treated by their masters as some have supposed. In many instances the opposite is true, but it could not be accepted as the rule. Whatever their condition, the Brethren were relentlessly opposed to this enforced servitude, which their records abundantly prove.

CHAPTER VI.

Period of Civil War—Oppression—Exemption Acts Passed.

For reasons that must be apparent to all, the years from 1860 to 1865 were the most eventful in the history of the Church of the Brethren in the South. The lamentable condition that befell any one section was not unlike that experienced in another. Yet, because of Virginia's geographical location, her soil was the constant ground of contention for the opposing armies. Therefore, the privations and sufferings of the Virginia churches was of a most unusual character throughout the unfortunate conflict.

The dark cloud that had been hovering over our national horizon for the past quarter of a century, at the beginning of this period began to grow more threatening and the mutterings of the distant thunders too plainly told of the approaching calamity. During the year 1860, the chasm between the North and the South rapidly widened. Reason was dethroned and the hearts of men, fired by designing politicians, were ruled by the wildest of passions. A friendly neighbor differing in his political views was not unfrequently taken for a foe. The election of Abraham Lincoln to the presidency of the United States was considered sufficient evidence that the rights of the Southern people would be trampled upon, and therefore, a sufficient reason for the rending asunder of the union of our country.

Thus the war between the North and the South broke forth in its awful fury in the spring of 1861, and our Southland of which we so delight to speak became gory with human blood. A Northern veteran in relating some of his experiences to the writer said, "I remember distinctly when we entered the Shenandoah Valley of Virginia, I thought it the most beautiful country my eyes ever looked upon, but before leaving it became a literal slaughter pen for human beings and the desolation of the country beggars description."

On the altar of this bloody war were offered six hundred thousand lives; more than eight billions of dollars in money and property; beside untold misery and woe to innocent and helpless women and children. All this could have been avoided and the results far more to be desired, if all men would have been governed by the teaching of the Prince of Peace. Yet, to the undying honor of many citizens of Virginia, strong efforts were made during the year 1860, to bring about an amicable settlement between the North and the South. Again in January, 1861, the Legislature of Virginia passed a resolution inviting all the States to a peace convention. This conference met in Washington, the 4th of February of the same year. After remaining in session for twenty-three days, it adjourned with but little result. Virginia hesitated but a few months longer and, like a deluded child, she left her moorings and cast her lot with the Southern Confederacy.

Throughout the year 1860, the church was quietly, yet earnestly, engaged in the Master's work. Because of the high tension of public sentiment, more fully inaugurated by the John Brown folly, the Brethren were derisively classed as Abolitionists, and the hand of persecution was already upon them. Through these conditions, the Lord quickly developed leaders that were able to present to the authorities and the public in general, the position of the Brethren Church on the questions that agitated the public mind. They were no less alert when an unjust attack was made through the public press or otherwise. In the early part of the year 1860, an article appeared in the Rockingham *Register* purporting to have been written by a brother against the enemies of the church, thereby putting it in an unfavorable light. The Brethren, in a general council meeting held at Millcreek, February 25, 1860, promptly repudiated the article in question and made endeavors to investigate the character of the writer. The minutes, somewhat lengthy, were signed by John Kline, Daniel Brower, John Wine, Solomon Garber, John J. Harshberger, Daniel Thomas, Martin Gerber, Christian Wine and Isaac Long. This alertness, the reader will see, was characteristic of the Brethren throughout the years that follow.

When suffering was necessary, they could do it with the bravery of the true hero. However, every opportunity that did not compromise principle was sought to present to the authorities the truths upon which the church stood, in order to avoid unnecessary embarrassment. During the whole of this time, no people were more solicitous for the peace and union of the country. At their conferences, their public meetings, and by special appointment, prayers were offered for the peace of the country. Nevertheless, the old year ended with much evil forebodings and the new was ushered in with an awful prospect in view. Of this, Eld. John Kline wrote on January 1, 1861:

The year opens with dark and lowering clouds in our national horizon. I feel a deep interest in the peace and prosperity of our country, but in my view both are sorely threatened now. Secession is the cry further south; and I greatly fear its poisonous breath is being wafted northward towards Virginia on the wings of fanatical discontent. A move is already on hand for holding a convention at Richmond, Virginia; and while its advocates publicly deny the charge, I, for one, feel sure that it signals the separation of our beloved old state from the family in which she has long lived and been happy. The perishable things of earth distress me not, only in so far as they affect the imperishable. Secession means war; and war means tears and ashes and blood. It means bonds and imprisonments, and perhaps even death to many in our beloved Brotherhood, who, I have the confidence to believe, will die, rather than disobey God by taking up arms.

The Lord, by the mouth of Moses, says: "Be sure your sin will find you out." It may be that the sin of holding three millions of human beings under the galling yoke of involuntary servitude has, like the bondage of Israel in Egypt, sent a cry to heaven for vengeance; a cry that has now reached the ear of God. I bow my head in prayer. All is dark save when I turn my eyes to him. He assures me in his Word that "all things work together for good to them that love him." This is my ground of hope for my beloved brethren and their wives and their children. He alone can provide for their safety and support. I believe he will do it.

With truly a prophetic eye, the horrors of a bloody war loomed up before him and every available means was put forth to assist in bringing about an amicable agreement. He urged public men in almost every station in life to use all their power to maintain the Union and avert the war.

On January 30, 1861, he wrote a letter to John Letcher, Governor of Virginia, commending him for the stand he had taken for the Union. In the same letter he very wisely made a plea for the Brethren, that they may be relieved from military duty in the event of the calamity he so much feared.

Immediately Gov. Letcher wrote him the following courteous reply:

Richmond, Virginia,
February 1, 1861.

My Dear Sir:

I received your kind letter this evening, and am gratified to find that our views upon public questions are so nearly in accordance. I have never doubted, that I would in the main, be sustained by the reflecting and conservative men, in all sections of our State, and I am now receiving numerous evidences, of the correctness of that opinion.

We have many men in the North and South, who are anxious to see the Union destroyed. By far the larger number, are reckless adventurers, without property, who have nothing to lose; and no revolution in the country or its business can therefore injure them. They think they may in a war better their condition, and they are therefore disposed to take chances, and run all hazards.

I would be glad to see the arrangement in regard to military service, suggested in your letter adopted. I think it entirely reasonable, that those who have conscientious scruples, in regard to the performance of militia duty, should be relieved by the payment of a small pecuniary compensation. There are enough of others who take pleasure in the performance of such duties.

It is gratifying to hear that my old friends in the Tenth Legion sustain me now, as in other days. I appreciate a compliment from such people most highly.

I have great hopes that the controversy now unhappily existing between the North and the South will be eventually settled, to the satisfaction of the conservative men of all parties.

I am truly

Your friend,
John Letcher.

Akin to the spirit that was shown in Eld. Kline, the church in Virginia throughout made noble efforts for peace. Appeals were made in person and by letter to public officials, but the spirit of war was upon the land and like a mighty avalanche it swept everything before it. No people more deeply deplored the unwise act of their own beloved State in withdrawing from the Union. It was plain now that nothing more could be done. The war was upon them. It is left to other pens to trace the awful suffering of the contending forces during these dreadful years.

With the consciousness of having done all they could to avert the fearful holocaust, they meekly bowed to the inevitable. In answer to a plea in behalf of some of the Brethren who had been indignantly treated by some of the soldiers, Col. John B.

Baldwin said: "The truth is, that war is nothing but a siege of violence, bloodshed and wrong. Whoever is responsible for inflicting such a curse on any people has a fearful reckoning to stand before the bar of a just God. It is to me a source of great and honest satisfaction, that I can, with a clear conscience, declare that I have never in my whole life said or done anything intended or calculated to stir up strife between the North and the South. I resisted to the last with all my might, the effort to break the old Union and bring on this war."

It should be here mentioned that Col. Baldwin afterward in the legislative hall of the Confederate Congress, became the great champion for the cause of the Brethren, whom he knew could repeat the sentiments of his words with equal emphasis.

With the war came a most trying condition for the church to meet. Their fidelity to the teaching of Christ against carnal warfare was now to be sorely tried. Prior to this, fines were imposed for non-appearance at time for military drill. In the spring of 1861, when volunteers were called, derision was heaped upon them. They were branded with a lack of patriotism and with cowardice. These were borne with a true Christian spirit. But one brother is known to have yielded to the military spirit of the time. In July of the same year, however, the State made a draft, calling for all able-bodied men between the ages of eighteen and forty-five years. Among these were many Brethren. They had always been law-abiding citizens, but in this they could not obey. God had spoken against engaging in carnal warfare, and they willingly obeyed Him rather than man. Some secured substitutes among those who were willing to go to the army and were not included in the draft, paying for their services from $800 to $1,500 each. Others were carried off to the army. A few were literally bound and hauled away from their homes. While there they were obedient to every command, save to shoot down their fellow man. It was at this time that Gen. T. J. Jackson made the somewhat famous statement: "There lives a people in the Valley of Virginia, that are not hard to bring to the army. While there they are obedient to their officers. Nor is it difficult to have them take aim, but it is impossible to get them to take correct aim. I, therefore, think it better to leave them at their homes that they may produce supplies for the army."

Immediately following the draft by the State, steps were inaugurated to free the Brethren held in the army. At first, all seemed destined to failure, but with a firm reliance in God, and a firm belief in the righteousness of their cause, they were persistent in their efforts. State officials were seen and army officers were written to and appealed to in person. It is definitely stated that Samuel Kline, a lay member living a few miles north of Staunton, made the trip alone to Richmond in behalf of his brethren. In Botetourt and Roanoke counties their cause was championed by Elders Benjamin F. Moomaw, Peter Nininger, Jonas Graybill and others. In Rockingham and adjacent counties there were many advocates of their cause. Here the Mennonite brethren, who held like views on war, joined them, and throughout the struggle for liberty, a most beautiful spirit for each other's welfare manifested itself. Hand in hand, they labored for those in bonds and for the exemption enactments recorded in these pages.

Yet none were more earnest in this than Eld. John Kline. His zeal is evidenced by the many records extant, a study of which will show a devotion to his brethren and the right that should inspire us to more noble deeds of love. Among the letters he wrote was one addressed to Col. Lewis, an officer in the Confederate Army. It is long, but of such interest that it is here given, omitting the part which refers to personal matters:

Bowman's Mill, Rockingham County, Va.
December 16, 1861.

My dear friend Col. Lewis:

I arrived home safe and have been looking to hear from you. * * * I now desire to approach you on another subject which I would like you to consider and use your influence with the generals and other officers in the army. The subject is this: We German Baptists (called Tunkers) do most solemnly believe that the bearing of carnal weapons in order to destroy life, is in direct opposition to the Gospel of Christ, which we accept as the rule of our faith and practice. To this we have most solemnly vowed to be true until death. Hence we stand pledged to our God to carry out that which we believe to be his commandment. By his apostles he speaks plainly in Romans 12: 17 to end of the chapter: "Recompense to no man evil for evil. Provide things honest in the sight of all men. If it be possible as much as lieth in you, live peaceable with all men. Dearly beloved, avenge not yourselves, but rather give place unto wrath: for it is written, Vengeance is mine; I will repay, saith the Lord. Therefore if thine enemy hunger, feed him; if he thirst, give him drink: for in so doing thou shalt heap coals of fire on his head. Be not overcome of evil, but overcome evil with good." In many other places also, the Lord has spoken on this.

We feel bound to pay our taxes, fines, and to do whatever is in our power which does not conflict with our obligation to God. Whenever God speaks we think we should obey Him rather than man. But in this unholy contest, both law and all former precedents of making drafts have been set aside. The privilege usually granted Christian people to pay a fine has been overruled and set aside, and they are compelled to take up weapons of carnal warfare to drill and if need be to shoot down their fellow man. This is not only revolting to them, but a positive violation to their solemn vow to their God. This is without precedent in a land of Christian liberty. Who the prosecutor of this outrage on our constitutional rights is I know not, but that it is so is clear. That it has been driven by some one is also clear. This state of things the much abused Abe Lincoln would have much deplored. For I am credibly informed that he issued a proclamation that no conscientious Christian should be forced to war or to take up arms.

Thus it should be in a land of Christian liberty. None but those who have a disposition or desire to rear up a hierarchy or despotic government could feel otherwise. None that have a spark of the spirit of Washington or Jefferson in their hearts would desire to compel their fellow countrymen to take up arms against their conscience, and to force them to kill their fellow man. Let any one look at and read the fifteenth section of the Constitution as before the convention: " Nor shall any man be *enforced, restrained, molested,* or *burdened* in his *body* or *goods* or otherwise *suffer* on account of his religious *opinion* or *belief.* This I understand is unchanged. Neither should it be.

Therefore, a great breach of the constitution has been practiced on us for we have been enforced, restrained, and molested because of our religious belief and opinion.

Please give this matter your earnest attention and tell it or read it to your fellow officers, and if expedient, to Gen. Jackson.

From your friend,
John Kline.

Although expressed in somewhat caustic language to a sympathizer of the Southern Confederacy, yet the letter was kindly received and Mr. Lewis in his return letter assured Eld. Kline that it would be a pleasure to do all in his power for his cause.

Influence was brought upon the legislature of Virginia during the session of 1861 to '62, in various ways. Some of the legislators from the Shenandoah Valley were well acquainted with the Brethren and did much for them. In this connection should be mentioned the names of Mr. Baylor of Botetourt County, and Mr. Gray of Rockingham County. Therefore the following act was passed which, through the kindness of Col. Mortin Marye, Auditor of Public Accounts, is here given.

ACT OF THE GENERAL ASSEMBLY OF VIRGINIA.

Chap. 25.—An Act providing for the exemption of certain persons upon religious grounds.

Passed March 29th, 1862.

1. Be it enacted by the General Assembly of Virginia, that whenever, upon application for exemption to the Board of Exemption, it shall appear to said Board that the party applying for said exemption is bona fide prevented from bearing arms by the tenets

of the church to which said applicant belongs, and did actually belong at the passage of this act, and further, that said applicant has paid to the sheriff of the county or collector of taxes for the City or town in which said applicant resides, the sum of five hundred dollars, and in addition thereto, the further sum of two per cent of the assessed value of said applicant's taxable property, then the said board on presentation of the receipt of said officers for said moneys, and after the said applicant shall have taken an oath or affirmation that he will sustain the Confederate Government, and will not in any way give aid and comfort to the enemy of the said confederate government, then the said board shall exempt said applicant; provided, that whenever such party may be unable, or shall fail to pay the said sum of five hundred dollars, and the tax of two per centum on their property, he shall be employed (when liable to militia duty) in the capacity of teamster, or in such other character as the service may need, which does not require the actual bearing of arms; and provided further, that the persons so exempted do surrender to the board of exemption all arms which they may own, to be held subject to the order of the Governor, for the public use.

2. The sheriff and collectors aforesaid shall account for all moneys received under this act as they now account for license taxes.

3. Said Board of exemption shall certify to the Auditor of Public Accounts lists of the persons so exempted, and copies of the sheriff's or collectors' receipts for such commutation money, in order that the Auditor may charge the officers with the amount so collected; provided the sheriff's commission shall be only two per cent upon the amount paid under this act.

4. This act shall be in force from its passage.

This act was a signal triumph, although in effect it was very short-lived.

During these months, there was much unrest among the Brethren. As previously mentioned, the State had already made a draft and there were strong rumors of the Confederate Government doing likewise. Apparently there was no relief for them. Therefore, they resolved to leave their country, homes and loved ones.

To the west of them lay a wide expanse of mountainous country through which they were compelled to pass. From this they naturally shrank, but urged on by hearts more brave, if possible, than theirs, under the shades of the night they bade the dearest objects of earth farewell to go—they knew not where. The experiences of these refugees were so varied and extensive that to fully relate them alone would make a volume. Some of these traveled in small companies; others in larger ones. The former could more easily elude pursuit. In time some of the people living along the way found it a lucrative business in conducting the refugees to "Yankeedom," as it was called. The fee usually charged was twenty dollars per person. Sometimes, however, they would need to hide in the mountains for days with little food or shelter, when pursued or when the Confederate Army was further north or west than usual.

The experiences of a company of eight are here given as an illustration. They had safely gone as far as Pendleton County, now in West Virginia, but the Confederate Army was then raiding the country, and these had to go to the mountains for safety. Here they were obliged to remain until almost famished with hunger before they could return to the settlement.

One of their number in relating their experience said, "We remained in our hiding place until we could endure it no longer. We then went to a farmhouse near the mountain to get something to eat. When we asked for food, they told us that the army took everything they had to eat, but a bit of buckwheat meal. This the good woman agreed to bake into cakes for us, which offer was thankfully received. However, the sight of food so intensified the pangs of hunger, that the half-baked cakes were snatched from the oven and eaten while the batter was dripping to the floor. So eager was one of our party that he presented an amusing sight when we left the house."

Some were captured and carried back to captivity. Notable among these were two companies taken in Hardy County, now West Virginia, in March, 1862. In one of these companies there were seventy-two and in the other eighteen. In each case they had gotten well on the way before being arrested. Bro. David M. Miller of Lima, Allen County, Ohio, who was one of the seventy-two, in a letter written at the request of the author, gives his experience during those eventful days in the following interesting manner:

Lima, Allen County, Ohio.
April 19, 1906.

D. H. Zigler,

Dear Bro.: I would like to give you a complete history of our experiences while in captivity, but it has been so long since it happened that I have forgotten some things. I know we started about five weeks before April 17, 1862, for we had a son born on that date. I was gone six weeks and when I got home, the boy was a week old.

There were sixty-two Brethren and Mennonites with eight or ten who were members of no church left our homes at the time stated above. When we got about a mile beyond Petersburg we saw some persons, we thought were soldiers, riding. They got ahead of us and stopped in a narrow place in the road. They took us back to Petersburg and searched us but found no weapon except one small revolver, but some of us had Testaments. They then started with us for Staunton, Augusta County.

The first night we fared very well. The next morning one man got away and also the next evening another man dodged out while we were on the march. The second night we were closely guarded. In two more days we reached Staunton and lodged in the courthouse. The next morning we were put on the train and sent to Richmond where we were put in a tobacco house and closely guarded. We were then moved to another house. Here some of the Brethren and some of the Mennonites were taken for examination. After this we were released by paying $500 and two per cent on what each one was worth. A Bro. Cline took the Augusta Brethren out and Bro. B. F. Byerly took us out who lived in Rockingham. They then sent us on the train to Waynesboro, and from there we went on foot. When I got home there was a boy about a week old.

I have written this to the best of my recollection.

Frat. Yours,

David M. Miller.

Beyond question the Exemption Act of the Legislature of Virginia was passed while these Brethren were in prison at Richmond. Their presence no doubt had much to do with its passage. Under its provisions and through the liberality of the Brethren at home, they were released. At a general council meeting

The "Old Courthouse" as it was in the Time of the Civil War.
(By Permission.)

held at the Middle River church, Benjamin F. Byerly and Christian Kline were appointed to go to Richmond to secure their release.

The other company mentioned above was approaching the town of Moorefield when overtaken by the pickets. Bro. Jackson Showalter, who was one of the number, said, "There were eighteen of us. We were leisurely passing along the road that leads to Moorefield when the pickets came up to us. After enquiring where we were going, they insisted that we should go back with them. The next day we were taken across the mountains to Woodstock. Here we were kept some days. Then we were marched south along the pike to Mt. Jackson. After remaining here a short time we were taken to Harrisonburg and put in the courthouse, which was used as a guard-house. In a few days Eld. John Kline was brought to prison also. He did much in many ways to cheer us up, for some of our number had become very much disheartened by this time."

Eld. Daniel Miller, who was also one of the captives, verifies the statement of Bro. Showalter and in addition thereto says, "When we were in prison the Exemption Bill, which permitted our release by the payment of $500 and two per cent on the assessed value of our property, was passed by the Virginia Legislature. The next day after its passage (March 30, 1862) a friend came from Richmond and informed us of the passage of the bill. In this time the authorities had also knowledge of it, and a quartermaster came to us and tried to induce us to enlist as teamsters, but none were willing to do so."

Although the Exemption Bill was passed as stated above, some time elapsed before the Brethren were set free. The account of this delay is not made clear. It is definitely known that the churches promptly raised the necessary amount of money, but, for some cause, the fines were not accepted when they were first tendered.

Eld. Miller adds, "I remember well when on April 16, we were ordered north from Harrisonburg. We marched with heavy hearts as far as the Judge Smith place, one mile on the way, when some of us were released. Why we were released at that place I never knew. Others were held longer. Among them were Elders John Kline, Joseph Beery and Gabrael Heatwole, Sr. I went to my home as quickly as I could, where my wife with a little baby girl awaited my coming.

"I can recall the names of all my companions when captured except one. The ones I remember are: John A. Kline, Joseph M. Kline, Christopher Miller, George Holler, Daniel Hert, Samuel Wine, John Swartz, Jacob Knupp, Martin Click, Hue Brunk, Henry Brunk, Henry Nisewander, Jacob Snell, Philip Hollar, George Wine, and Jackson Showalter."

While these Brethren were in captivity in Harrisonburg and the first named company were in Richmond, the Union Army made its first incursion through the Valley of Virginia. This was the cause of much agitation of the public mind and gave an opportunity to designing persons to make accusation against noncombatants. Therefore on the afternoon of April 5 Eld. John Kline was captured by scouts, taken to Harrisonburg, and cast into prison on the charge of communicating with the Union Army. When he was put in prison, he set about making their quarters as comfortable as possible. The following day he preached for them. In his notes, he said that the chief aim of the discourse was to encourage the captives. He was kept a prisoner thirteen days. On April 16 as mentioned above, the authorities attempted to move them north some eighteen miles to New Market. That day the guard with their prisoners, who were not released, went as far as the Bethlehem church. Here Eld. Kline preached in the evening. The next morning they started for New Market, yet about six miles distant, but on hearing cannonading to the north of that place, they retraced their steps to Harrisonburg.

On the 11th of April there appeared in the columns of the Rockingham *Register* an article at which Eld. Kline was much displeased. He therefore wrote the editor the following letter, a copy of which he kept in his own handwriting:

Large Jury Room,
Court House of Rockingham, Virginia.
April 15, 1862.

Mr. Editor of the *Register:*

In your issue of the 11th inst. I see an article headed Union Men Taken. In the article several names are mentioned who are known to have strong Union proclivities. Otherwise, the article made no nominal charge against us, which of course, it was out of your power to do, but the article carries with it a strong insinuation as though we had used our influence against the Confederacy. If this has been so, why not come out

Large Jury room

Courthouse of Rockingham Va April 15th 1862

Mr Editor of the Register

In your Issue of the 11th inst I see an article headed, Union men taken, in the article Several Names are mentioned, who ~~formerly had~~ was known to have strong Union proclivities, otherwise the article makes no nominal charge against us, which of Course it was out of your power to do, but the article Carries with it, a strong insinuation as though we had used our influence against the Confidaracy, if this has been so, why not Come out and point to the place where, or when, and what the act or deed, and if this Cannot be done which I know it Cannot, then why shut us up in the guard house,? Why make such false insinuations against good and inocent Citicens and Publish them to the world? why contrary to the Constitution, take up men without their accusers making affidavid that the thing charged was to their knowledge true? but all that is now nessessary is for some vague fiend to raise a falsehood and tel it to some of his Captains, who have no better principle then themselves, and law and Constitution is at an End, if this is the kind of laws that we are Contending for, then may the Lord save us from it, but I think by the quivilous movement so far transacted there has been more done to make Union men and int against the South, then all the influence of the Union men Ever did. because they were inactive this influence is active. first because near all those men that are taken are known to be Inocent. Second it shows to the world that those who are engaged of arresting such men on nothing but falsehood and misrepresentation, are acting under a Cowardly fear of being overcome, and thirdly, it is keeping all such out of Employ, and usefullness, at home preventing them from making provition both for man and beast, fourth it is keeping Just so many men out of the army as are engaged of guarding those, and weakening the army that much, and fifth it makes a Considerabl Expence upon the governent which all Could be avoided, besides many other privations and usefullness both to their families and neighborhoods

Letter Written to the Editor of Rockingham Register by Elder John Kline While He Was in Prison.

and point to the place where, or when and what the act, or deed, and if this cannot be done, which I know it can not, then why shut us up in the guardhouse? Why make such false insinuations against good and innocent citizens, and publish them to the world? Why contrary to the constitution take up men without their accusers making affidavit that the thing charged was to their knowledge true? But all that is now necessary, is for some vague fiend to raise a falsehood and tell it to some of his captains who have no better principle than themselves, and law and constitution is at an end. If this is the kind of laws that we are contending for, then may the Lord save us from it. But I think by the quivolous movement so far transacted there has been more done to make Union men and against the South than all the influence of the Union men ever did, because they were inactive. This influence is active.

1. Because near all those men that are taken are known to be innocent.

2. It shows to the world that those who are engaged in arresting such men on nothing but falsehood and misrepresentation are acting under a cowardly fear of being overcome.

3. It is keeping all such out of employment and usefulness at home, preventing them from making provisions for man and beast.

4. It is keeping just so many men out of the army as are engaged in guarding those and weakening the army that much.

5. It makes a considerable expense upon the government which all could be avoided, besides many other privileges and usefulness to both their families and neighbors.

On the approach of the Federal Army three days later, Eld. Kline was released, and friends were ready to assist him to his home.

The days the Brethren were in captivity were memorable to the church in Virginia. As one man they arose in behalf of the prisoners. Those in Harrisonburg were repeatedly visited by the membership near at hand. In these visits provisions were brought to

Elder Benjamin Miller.
See Biography, Chapter X.

break the monotony of the prison fare. Those in Richmond were not so fortunate in having the members near to them, but they were not forgotten. As previously stated, B. F. Byerly and Christian Kline were sent to Richmond to intercede for them, and secured their release.

OPPRESSION

The Brethren imprisoned in Harrisonburg were released under the provisions of the same act that gave those in Richmond their liberty. In order to raise the necessary amount of money, the different churches appointed receivers to take contributions for this purpose. Eld. Benjamin Miller, who now resides with his son Samuel, four miles north of Harrisonburg, was one of the number appointed. Eld. Miller in speaking of this experience says, "The liberality of the Brethren was remarkable. Within a short time thousands of dollars were placed in my hands to secure their release, but the authorities were not ready to receive the fines when it was first offered to them. The cause of this I do not know."

Their return from captivity was the occasion of much rejoicing, although their liberty was dearly bought by high fines. Yet it meant more to the church than simply their return. The exemption law meant the possible freedom of others as well. This however was but very short-lived. Before they were beyond the shadow of the prison walls "the Confederate Congress passed conscription laws levying on all persons between the ages of eighteen and forty-five years." This act was passed April 16, 1862, and shortly after the return of the Brethren it was being executed, regardless of the Exemption Act passed by the Virginia Legislature on March 29 prior. This subjected them again to the same influences and as Eld. B. F. Moomaw says in his Memoirs, Olive Branch of Peace, p. 57, "Later the conscript law was passed by the Confederate Congress. Then we had a repetition of the same work in part, to get Congress to recognize the exemption law as passed by the State Legislature."

The records indicate that this exemption was more difficult to secure than that from the Legislature. On April 21, 1862, there was an exemption passed by the

Col. John B. Baldwin, Who Was the Great Advocate for the Brethren in Halls of Confederate Congress.

Confederate Congress. In this, however, no one was relieved from military duty on religious grounds, but ministers of religion in the regular discharge of ministerial duties. As a natural consequence, the passage of this made it more difficult to procure the enactment of additional exemption. However, the Brethren set about with much energy to secure it.

Eld. John Kline again took his pen in behalf of the Brethren. Among others he wrote the following letter to Col. John B. Baldwin, who was a member of Congress:

Bowman's Mill, Rockingham County, Virginia.
July 23, 1862.

Much esteemed friend Col. John Baldwin:

I seat myself in behalf of my Brotherhood, the German Baptists, so-called Tunkers, to drop a few lines in order to give you a correct view of our faith toward our God, and, in consequence of that, our unpleasant standing in and under our government which we now live.

As there is now a session of Congress of the Confederate States on hand of which you are a member and the special representative of our immediate district, I wish to enlist you to advocate our cause in that body. I wish to be short as possible. I will, therefore, at once inform you that we are a noncombatant people. We believe most conscientiously that it is the doctrine taught by our Lord in the New Testament which we feel bound to obey. Having made in our conversion a most solemn vow to be faithful to God in all his commandments, it is and should be regarded by us as the first in importance and above all made by man to man or to earthly government. Hence we feel rather to suffer persecution, bonds, and if need be death than break the vow made to our God.

Yet, as touching things and obligations, which in our view do not come in conflict with the law of God, in whatever way our government may demand of us we feel always ready and willing to do. Such as paying our dues and taxes imposed upon us and assisting in internal improvements, our profession binds us to do. Paying unto the government that which is due it, but that which is due to God we wish to give to him. Through his Son and the apostles, he says "recompense to no man evil for evil." To him we feel to render obedience and therefore are bound not to take up carnal weapons to destroy our fellow man whom he teaches us to love.

We have noticed that those who have been made prisoners and paroled, their oath is regarded by the government. They are let alone and no one presses them into the army. This obligation is only made to man. Why then should not that solemn obligation be regarded by our government, which we have made to our God without any earthly interest whatever? Why not leave that class of men at their homes who can not, for conscience sake, make soldiers to kill others, that they may make provisions for the sustenance of life, which is as necessary to any government as soldiers?

It seems that the late Conscript law made by the Confederate Congress, whether so intended or not, is made use of to overrule or nullify our state law. This law was made by our State Legislature to exempt us from military duty provided each one pays a tax of $500 and two per cent on all taxable property. This, though as oppressive as it is, we were willing to pay, hard as it went with some. Now as we are informed through the above cited conscript act of Congress, we are again to be troubled. Our rights given to us by our kind legislature, for which privilege we have paid so dearly, is to be made null and void.

Please use all your powers and influence in behalf of us, so that the Conscript law or all other Confederate laws be so constructed that Christian conscience be so protected that the south shall not be polluted with a bloody persecution.

We as a people try to be as little burdensome to the government as possible. We believe that all the precepts and ordinances of our Lord should be equally regarded and should be practically obeyed according as given to us by the Master. We believe it to be our duty, but of love, to contribute to the poor and needy, and consequently we maintain our poor members and let none of them become dependent upon the country parish. Yet we pay our parish levy as all other citizens. These are some of our tenets given in general terms. In brief, we take the New Testament for our guide and Jesus Christ the man of our religious faith.

Please give this, our request, a candid consideration. At least so much as to write to me your opinion. If we can not get protection of our Christian liberty in the south, the home of our nativity, we will be compelled to seek shelter in some other place, or suffer bonds and persecutions as did many of our forefathers. For we can not take up carnal weapons of warfare and fight our fellow man to kill him.

Yours with highest esteem,

John Kline.

This letter no doubt was written at the instance of the church or at least at the request of some of the Brethren, as indicated by the language used. Although a number of the Brethren had been imprisoned, including the writer, no mention is made of it in the letter. The arguments used were convincing and if anything was lacking in real sympathy on the part of Mr. Baldwin for the church, all was now removed. He wrote Eld. Kline and suggested that a petition be gotten up to present to Congress. Bro. Kline drew a petition that included the Brethren and Mennonite churches. The petition as it appears in the congressional print is as in the handwriting of Eld. Kline, with but slight changes. It reads as follows:

To the Senate and House of Representatives of the Confederate States of America.

The Undersigned members of the Dunker and Menonite, Churches, in the state of Virginia, respectfully and humbly represent, that at the late Session of the State Legislature of Virginia, that body passed a law Exempting from Military duty the members of our Churches upon Each member paying the sum of $500 and 2 percent upon all his taxable Estate. This Exemption was based upon the long established Creed, of faith, of our Churches against bearing arms, and is as we think, & we feel, the Command of God. While we know, there is a Strong popular feeling against such Doctrines, yet it is none the less dear and Sacred to us, who believe it. The question which we present to you, is not one of persecution, in favor of our peculiar Doctrines, but a prayer that you may Exercise that same charity, and respect for our Opinions, and faith, that we freely accord to others, There are many forms of Religious Creeds, and various are the Doctrines of Religious faith. but there is no arbiter on Earth; God alone is to Judge. But there is a coincidence in Civilized Society, in its Universal respect, for the Conscientious conviction, of all Christian Churches. With this feeling, and in this Spirit, we appeal to you to pass a law. Ratifying the act of the Legislature, of Virginia, on this Subject.

It may not be amiss to state here, that under the Excitement of the hour, indiscreet and inconsiderate persons, have preferred the Charge of Disloyalty, against our Churches, this Charge, has not the Semblance of truth in fact, and has doubtless originated from our faith against bearing arms. We would further state, that Most of our members, Embraced in said act of the General Assembly of Virginia, have already payd the penalty of $500 & 2 per cent, to the officers of the state, and thus fulfilled our contract, and have Complied with the law. We only ask Congress, so far to respect our rights, our Consciences, and the act of the State of Virginia, as to ratify the same. And we will ever Pray.

Petition to the Confederate Congress by the Brethren in Virginia, in the Handwriting of Elder John Kline.

OPPRESSION

To the Senate and House of Representatives of the Confederate States of America:

The undersigned members of the Tunker and Mennonite Churches in the State of Virginia, respectfully and humbly represent, That at the late Session of the State Legislature of Virginia, That Body passed a law Exempting from military duty, the members of our Churches, upon each member paying the sum of $500 and 2 per cent upon all his taxable Estate. This exemption was based upon the long established Creed or faith of our churches, against bearing arms. This doctrine is coequal with the foundation of our Churches, and is we think and feel, the Command of God. While we know there is a strong popular feeling against such doctrine, yet it is none the less dear and sacred to us who believe it. The question which we present to you, is not one of persuasion in favor of our peculiar doctrine, but a prayer, that you may Exercise that same charity and respect for our opinions, and faith, that we so freely accord to others. There are many forms of religious creeds, and various are the doctrines of Religious faith; but there is no Arbiter on earth. God alone is to judge. But there is a coincidence in civilized society in its universal respect for the conscientious convictions of all Christian Churches. With this feeling, and in this spirit, we appeal to you, to pass a law, ratifying the act of the Legislature of Virginia, on this subject.

It may not be amiss to state here, that under the excitement of the hour, indiscreet, and inconsiderate persons have preferred the charge of disloyalty against our Churches. This charge has not the semblance of truth, in fact, and has doubtless originated from our faith against bearing arms. We would further state, that those of our members embraced in said act of the General Assembly of Va. have already paid the penalty of $500 and 2 per cent to the officers of the State, and thus fulfilled our contract, and have complied with the law. We only ask Congress so far to respect our Rights, our Consciences, and the Act of the State of Virginia, as to Ratify the same, and we will ever pray.

Signatures of Males.	Signatures of Females.	Signatures of Non-members.
		We, the undersigned of this Column, not being members of the above Churches, yet pray Congress to hear the above petition, and respect the laws of the State of Virginia and State Rights.

These petitions were entrusted to the hands of Col. Baldwin.

Also in the counties of Botetourt, Roanoke, and Franklin, the church was equally alive to its interests. Elders B. F. Moomaw and Jonas Graybill, after securing more than one hundred signatures to a petition, went to Christiansburg and through George Baylor presented it to Hon. B. F. Anderson with the request that he, as a member of the Confederate Congress, do all he can to have an exemption law passed. As a consequence of this and other influences, there was a general exemption law passed by the Confederate Congress on October 11, styled AN ACT TO EXEMPT PERSONS FROM MILITARY DUTY, REPEALING AN ACT TO EXEMPT CERTAIN PERSONS FROM ENROLLMENT FOR SERVICE TO THE ARMY OF THE CONFEDERATE STATES, approved the 21st day of April, 1862.

The section of the act mentioned above, which relieved persons from military service on religious grounds, was copied verbatim from the Statutes at Large of the Provisional Government of the Confederate States of America, by Eld. Albert Hollinger, which is here given:

"Every minister of religion authorized to preach according to the rules of his sect and in the regular discharge of ministerial duties and all persons who have been and now are members of the Society of Friends and the Association of Dunkards, Nazarenes, and Mennonites in regular membership in their respective denominations, provided members of the society of Friends, Nazarenes, Mennonites, and Dunkards shall furnish substitutes or pay a tax of $500 each into the public treasury."

Of this act, the Rockingham *Register,* Harrisonburg, Virginia, in the issue of October 17, 1862, says: "While it is more carefully drawn up than the exemption of April 21st, it contains liberal provision and wise discrimination well calculated to secure its popularity of all classes of citizens." No doubt this was true of the many classes that were included in it, and for the church it eliminated the additional two per cent on taxable property. Yet, it was still quite a hardship for the church, as many poor Brethren were unable to pay. This deficiency the wealthier made good for them. In addition to this, some of the Brethren had made payment to the State and the quartermaster was trying to collect a second payment, or force them into the army. On November 17 Eld. Kline wrote him very plainly, calling his attention to his unreasonable demand. The following extract is taken from this letter:

"I take this opportunity to write you concerning a letter that I saw yesterday from your hand to Mr. Andes, on the subject of fines imposed on our Brethren in order for them to be exempted from military duty. There seems to be something wrong. Why press those who have paid to the State? Cannot the Confederate Government as well indulge the State until she will pay it over as the individual who paid? Why trouble and harass those who have paid their fines and have their certificates from the sheriff? Or, why trouble even those of our members who have not yet paid and are desirous to pay as soon as they can? Even before the government has designated a proper person to receive the fines this has been done by the scouts. It seems to me you could save yourself and us a great deal of trouble by telling the scouts not to bother those who could establish their membership by one or two neighbors or members until the proper arrangements are made. When that is made by the government, the State may be ready to refund and we may have the necessary arrangement to meet the difficulty. There are many who are not able to pay their heavy fines. Others have to make this up and it is not done in a few hours or even days. All we ask is to have a little time and to be let alone for a while. Why this running the people who have by law been exempt, the distance of from two to twenty-five miles to Harrisonburg and again to a justice to certify to that which every one knows to be true?"

Before the close of the year the government designated persons to receive the fines, and the Brethren, on their part, raised the necessary money to pay them. This was the cause of a deep feeling of gratitude throughout the churches in Virginia. In the full belief that this deliverance was from the hand of God, they felt to honor His name. Therefore the Brethren in Botetourt County designated January 1, 1863, as a day of thanksgiving. They likewise desired that all the churches unite in their respective places of worship. To this end, Eld. B. F. Moomaw wrote Eld. John Kline the letter here given:

Botetourt City, Virginia.
December 16, 1862.

Dear Bro. John Kline:

You may be surprised at my writing to you so soon again. The object is to inform you that the brethren here seem to be so deeply convicted of the duty resting upon them of making a public manifestation of their gratitude to God for his special providence in so overruling the hearts of the late Congress of the Confederate States of America, as to release us from military service. While we agree with those brethren who say that the heart of every brother and sister should be drawn out in secret to God, yet we think, inasmuch as it was a public exhibition of his special providence, we should make a public demonstration of our gratitude. We have, therefore, set apart New Year's Day as the time to attend to this duty and heartily invite all those churches that feel so disposed to coöperate with us. You will please, after you read this, pass it to the Shenandoah Brethren.

I will here inform you that our military authorities are so construing the exemption bill as to deprive those few brethren that are in the army under the conscript act, from its benefit. I have just written to the Secretary of War upon the subject. If his answer

Bot. Cy Va
Dec 16th 1862—

Dr Bro. J. H. Kline

You may be [illegible] at my writing to you this soon again, the object is to inform you that the [illegible] here seem to be sensible [illegible] of the duty resting upon them of making a public manifestation of their gratitude to God for his blessing [illegible] in so overruling the hearts of the late Congress of the Confed. S. A. as to release us from Military Service. While we agree with the brethren who say that the heart of every brother and sister should be drawn out in thanks to God, yet we think inasmuch as it was a public exhibition of his special [illegible] we should make a public demonstration of our gratitude. We have therefore set apart [illegible] day as the time to [illegible] and hereby invite all those others that feel disposed to cooperate with us. You will please after you read this send it to the Shenandoah brethren.

I will here inform you that our Military Authorities are [illegible] the exemption so as to debar those of our brethren that are in the [illegible] from the conscript act from it. [illegible] just written to the Sec. War upon the subject, if the answer is unfavorable, I will [illegible] Congress for an amendment, so far as it concerns us.

The cause of the Lord is still onward [illegible] by baptism [illegible]

[illegible] will thank [illegible]

May you be [illegible] the blessings [illegible] in Christ.

Bro. Jacob Crane of [illegible] is no more [illegible]

B. F. Moomaw

Letter from Church in Botetourt County, Calling for General Thanksgiving on Account of the Passage of Exemption Act by Congress. Written by B. F. Moomaw.

is unfavorable, I will petition congress for an amendment, as soon as it convenes.

The cause of the Lord is still onward. We received five members by baptism last Sunday. We are tolerably well. Thank God for his mercy! May you be sharing like blessings. Yours in Christ,

B. F. Moomaw.

In accord with this request, an appointment was made at the Linville Creek church and that all the members might be fully free to take part in this service, the Brethren of the Linville Creek congregation through Eld. John Kline on December 30 paid the fines of a number of Brethren, which represented a sum equal to $9,000. Eld. Daniel Hays in "Olive Branch of Peace," page 226, in the following manner refers to the payment of these fines:

In his memorandum book of 1862-3, Brother Kline records the names of those who paid the military fine in Linville Creek congregation, giving the amount received and the amount paid by him in each case; and where the amount received did not equal $500, he advanced the difference, or borrowed the money and squared the account agreeably to the following entry:

December 30th, 1862.

I paid to Mr. Woodward, the Receiver of fines, $500 for each of the following persons:

Harvey Fifer	George W. Ritchie
Philip Baker	William Ford
Samuel R. Wine	George Rodecap
Adam Ritchie	John A. White
George Smith	Adam Andes
James W. Fitzwater	John B. Kline
William Spitzer	Isaac Kline
Henry W. Moyers	George Kline
Jacob Fitzwater	Samuel Kagey

From personal knowledge, I can state that a number of these Brethren were unable to pay the amount levied upon them or any considerable part of it. In such case the amount was furnished by individual members or the church at large. As Eld. Hays says, in some instances Brother Kline furnished the deficiency by his own liberal hand.

CHAPTER VII.

War Period, Continued—Annual Meeting for Southern Churches in Botetourt and Franklin Counties—Eld. John Kline Killed.

Two years of the dreadful war had now passed and the prospects of the new year betokened its continuance with increased fury. Human blood now flowed as it never did before on American soil, and our once united and happy nation was passing through a death struggle with the spirit of secession. Each antagonist was striving with renewed energy to strengthen his army for future conflicts.

During this time the church in Virginia passed through a series of experiences as related in the preceding chapter, the like of which, possibly, had never befallen a people. In all this the Lord had sustained them with a never-failing hand and it was to Him that they turned with truly grateful hearts for His manifold deliverance. In response to this feeling, and in accordance with the appointment previously mentioned, the Brethren throughout the Virginia churches assembled on Thursday, January 1, 1863, at their respective places of worship to render unto the Lord thanksgiving and praise for His remembrance of them when so sorely tried. At the Linville Creek church, the assemblage was addressed by Eld. Kline. He said:

I have somewhere read that in the reign of one of

the sovereigns of Great Britain, when the outlook of the kingdom was very dark and threatening, one of the king's advisers proposed appointing a day for public thanksgiving in all the churches throughout the realm. The king answered the proposition by saying that he could see nothing for which either he or the nation had cause for special thanksgiving to God. The minister responded by saying that the king and the nation both had great cause to thank God *that things were no worse.* The king yielded and the day was set. The Christian people assembled; the preachers recounted the blessings still left in the nation's store, with the rich promises of God to provide for the future as things should be needed, and there was a day of thanksgiving in England the like of which is not often seen.

It has been my experience, Brethren, and I think I have heard some of you say the same, that prosperity does not always make people most truly thankful. Great success in business is apt to foster a feeling of independence. Men may forget God. It was in the days of Israel's prosperity in the goodly land of Goshen in Egypt that they forgot the name of the God of their fathers. When God appeared to Moses in Horeb, he had to tell him from out the burning bush what his name was, and also by what name he should make him to be known to his brethren in Egypt. Some of the deepest heartfelt expressions of gratitude break forth in times of misfortune. A brother once told me that he was away from home when his barn was struck with lightning and burned to the ground. At his return he beheld nothing but the smoking destruction of his gathered harvest. But when his children came running to meet him, and he saw them all safe, and their mother standing in the door unharmed, he burst into an expression of thanksgiving, which, he confessed to me, surpassed every other emotion of joy he had ever felt. Our best experiences come to us when we are made to realize properly the good that is still left us.

We must look upon our exemption from army service as one proof of those interpositions in behalf of his children which our heavenly Father has promised, and which he is constantly fulfilling. "The effectual fervent prayer of a righteous man availeth much." God has not called us to prayer in vain. He invites us to come boldly to a throne of grace. Does he do this otherwise than with a will to hear? And the apostle's exhortation is: "In every thing give thanks," for "all things work together for good to them that love God."

Let our offerings this day be from the heart; and probably the best proof we can have that they come from the heart is a willingness and cheerful readiness to give of our substance to the needy poor. We must divide out, Brethren, to those who have, on account of the war pressure, been unable to provide for themselves. Think of the barefooted, half-clad and half-fed children in our land! I do not undervalue what you have already done. I know you have done much; but we should not feel that the burden of duty has all rolled from our shoulders so long as there is one needy brother or sister or child in our land. Brethren, I speak from my heart when I say that the church has never before enjoyed such an opportunity to grow rich, as the present offers. I mean rich in good works; rich in treasures laid up in heaven; rich in her title to an eternal inheritance in heaven, which our Lord calls "*the true riches.*"—Life of John Kline. Page 459.)

This discourse, in the style of the true leader, on the one hand directed the minds of his auditors to reasons for thankfulness while on the other the speaker pointed out duties not yet fully performed. At some places, the author is credibly informed, the services continued all day. Part of the time was given to the thanksgiving service while the rest of the day was devoted to supplication and prayer in behalf of the Brethren yet held by the authorities.

The reader readily recalls that statement in Eld. Moomaw's letter which refers to such conditions existing in his part of the State. Likewise, in various communities, every pretext was used by the authorities to hold the Brethren. Bro. Henry Davis, whose home was near Broadway, was held on the pretext that he joined the church the same day that the Exemption Act was passed. Believing in his right to protection under its provision, he returned to his home but was carried back to the army again by the scouts. Therefore he threw himself liable to a trial by court-martial. In a letter to his wife under date of March 14, 1863, he acknowledges to her that it is likely that he will be court-martialed, but bravely expresses no fear whatever as to the result. Yet he adds, " My captain is an extremely contrary man and I think it is the hardest place on earth to get justice." He requested her to get one of the Brethren to intercede for him by writing to the Secretary of War. Bro. Davis was released from the army but, with his son, who had become old enough for enlistment, fled from the country and remained away until the close of the war.

Very near the entire summer there was that constant annoyance by petty officials and scouts. On July 18, 1863, the Confederate Congress passed a second conscript law, levying a draft on all males between the ages of eighteen and forty-five. By this time, however, the Brethren had more certainly learned their rights. Although at times much threatened, they had no fear of contending for them. Bro. Moomaw, in writing Eld. Kline, August 31, 1863, refers at some length to an experience he had in

Elder Harden P. Hylton.
See Biography, Chapter X.

Salem with a quartermaster. He said: "The Brethren in Roanoke have been until lately much annoyed by the quartermaster in that county, refusing to allow them the benefit of the exemption. At length, however, I reported him to President Davis. He sent the case to the Secretary of War. He ordered him (the quartermaster) to report to Richmond and give an account of his conduct. I afterward met him in Salem, when he made a furious assault on me, cursing and threatening violently. I calmly told him I disregarded him; dispised his threats; that he must understand that he could not intimidate me and when he interferes with our rights I will attend to him. Since that time the Brethren have been unmolested."

The heroic stand taken by the Brethren in every section had a salutary effect for a time. This gave to them a greater opportunity for the advancement of the cause of Christ. Their visits to the different sections to see the members and preach the Word were renewed as of old. However, they were attended with much danger.

During this short interval the welfare of the church throughout the South appealed very closely to them. The privilege of attending Annual Conference had been taken from them by the continuation of the war and the future was uncertain. They, therefore, concluded among themselves that it was to the best interest of the church to hold their general council meetings or annual council meetings with a broader purpose in view, as previously defined by the committee of 1859. They therefore decided to conduct it as the Annual Meeting was conducted and discuss matters of general doctrine. The first one of this kind was held in April, 1863. For reasons urgently demanding his professional service Eld. Kline could not attend although he was requested to do so. However, he received the following communication from Eld. B. F. Moomaw, giving an account of the meeting:

WAR PERIOD CONTINUED

Botetourt City, Virginia.
May 1, 1863.

Much Beloved Brother in the Lord:

According to promise, I this evening seat myself to write a few lines to you. And first I will inform you that by the kind providence of God, I arrived safely at home on Thursday evening after I parted from you at Harrisonburg. Found my family and also the brethren well for which I thank our heavenly Father. On the next day pursuant to appointment, we met the brethren in council meeting. The surrounding churches were generally represented, including the churches in Washington County, Tennessee, and I had to regret that the churches generally were not more extensively represented. We had truly a fine meeting. The two days set apart for council were entirely consumed in discussing Scriptural and doctrinal questions. And while we had animated debates on several subjects, entire harmony and love marked the whole meeting. So much so that the brethren assembled unanimously agreed that we of the South would (God willing) hold annually a general meeting of the kind. So long at least, as we were deprived of the privilege of holding general conference with the brotherhood at large. For the furtherance of this object, Brethren D. Thomas, A. Naff, D. B. Klipper, and myself were appointed a corresponding committee to arrange the time and place for the meeting next year, which I think probably the brethren in Franklin County will take. We had preaching each night at several places and also on Lord's day.

The question concerning putting members in bond occupied a considerable portion of the first day, discussed freely pro and con and decided that the exhortation of Paul to the Corinthian Church was a law with its penalties defined and still so stands to the church. Another question as to how long a gross offender should be kept separated was decided, until the honor of the church is vindicated; he gives satisfactory evidence of contrition and humiliation to all and redeems his christian character by an exemplary life. As to publishing hymn books, it was decided as you suggested. I hope that you may at an early day be able to procure a copy that we may get a supply printed. They are much needed.

Another question, whether the one baptism spoken of by Paul (Ephesians, 4th chapter) was the baptism of water or of the spirit. There was no decision formally called for, but I think it was decided in the mind of the church, as being that of water."

The spirit manifest was most noble. The welfare of the church in the South could not be neglected for a lack of the privilege of attending General Conferences. Yet it was plainly understood that this should only continue until the close of the war.

While the church was thus engaged, other events were transpiring that threatened their liberties. The Secretary of War stood firmly by the Exemption Act of October 11, 1862, and the Brethren were successful in their appeals to him. But the fall of Vicksburg and the general encroachment of the Union Army from the west, together with the defeat of Lee's army at Gettysburg and its retreat to Virginia soil, caused no little consternation. The governor called an extra session of the Legislature in the main for the creation of a Home Guard.

In his message to the Assembly he gave various recommendations. Among these was the abrogation of the Exemption Act on religious grounds. Such repeal would have been a repetition of their experiences of the year previous. Most likely it would have been more awful in its consequences. The Brethren, however, did not fail to realize the importance of prompt action on their part. The different churches conferred with each other as to what was best to do.

Eld. Kline, on August 13, addressed a letter to the churches in Botetourt and Roanoke, through Brother B. F. Moomaw, calling attention to the message of the Governor, stating that "it is fraught with mischievous designs toward the Brethren." On September 2, Eld. Moomaw wrote the following epistle, which is given verbatim and in full:

Botetourt City, Virginia.
September 2, 1863.

Much Esteemed Brother:

Yours of the 13th ult. was duly received, which like all such communications from brethren, was like a calm to our troubled souls, for there is nothing in these times of sorrow to make the heart glad except our spiritual associations and those messages of love from brethren whose spirits are congenial with our own. You speak of the Governor's message to the Legislature as being fraught with mischievious design toward the brethren. You and I discover from the expressions of some of the members of that body that they are fully prepared to carry out his inhuman recommendation, and thus inaugurate a system of persecution, the like of which is only known to the dark ages of the religious world. But this measure is not passed yet from latest accounts and I still hope in the kindness of an overruling providence who has hitherto so signally protected his people, and if it be the will of God that we should be protected, he will still find instruments in the councils of the country to disappoint the intention of our enemies. I hope that there are still enough who cherish the blessings of religious freedom to control the final action of the Legislature. May God in his mercy so order it.

But the question that I would ask is if the Legislature be so lost to every sense of Christianity as to require our brethren to go into the army, what is to be done? I will here give you the reflections of my own

Elder Samuel Driver.
See Biography, Chapter IX.

mind upon the subject and await an answer. We have in every case complied with the requirements of the government, because we could do so without a departure from our principles, but if they now require us to go into the army without any alleviation, what shall we do? What can we do? Shall we not unanimously petition for permission to leave the country with, or without our property?

I forgot to say to you in the proper place that I think that our friend, J. T. Anderson of Botetourt, is chairman of the Committee on Military Affairs, if so I hope that he will exert a salutary influence in our favor.

I suppose you have before now heard of the melancholy death of poor John A. Bowman of Tennessee. He was killed in his own stable some three weeks ago under the following circumstances. A man was discovered about to take his riding horse. He approached toward him and when coming pretty near, the man ordered him not to approach but John still advanced expostulating with him and finally took hold of the horse when he shot him through the abdomen and then clave his skull with the butt of his gun. So ends his eventful life and it is thought will end his church.

It was not convenient for me to attend your meetings as proposed. You doubtless have seen my son, Daniel. I forgot to send by him for the minutes but I hope you have sent them by him.

It is likely that business will call me to Rockingham shortly, if so I will hope to see you and spend some time in your company.

There has been, and still is a number of Refugees in the county from East Tennessee. But the Federals are falling back towards Knoxville and some of the refugees are going back. I see in the minutes of the Yearly Meeting that there is a committee appointed for the Shenandoah Church. What is wrong there? Where are the picket lines now and what the chances for passing?

This leaves myself and family well. Thank God for his mercies! Brethren M. Graybill and Jonas Graybill have both been very sick with fever and indeed are yet in doubtful condition. The rest of the brethren are well as far as known by me.

B. F. Moomaw.

The correspondence at this juncture indicates more nearly a loss as to what course to pursue than at any time previous.

It should be stated in this place that the Military Bill before the Legislature was quite lengthy. It was composed of thirty-seven sections and covered twenty-seven pages. Although, by a vote of that body on September 22, it became the order of each day, yet it required much time for its consideration. The first section provided for calling into military service all male citizens, who were not exempt, between the ages of sixteen and sixty years of age. To this there was a strong opposition on account of the extreme ages mentioned. According to the order, the consideration of the bill, section by section, was begun on September 23, and the whole of that day was devoted to the first section without any indication of a disposition to vote upon it. This caused some delay, but in time the Substitute Bill was repealed. This affected many who had hired substitutes and paid heavily for them. The Exemption Law was also sorely threatened.

At this time the church resolved to make a formal request to the Government for permission to leave the State if no exemption would be allowed them. B. F. Moomaw and B. F. Byerly were appointed to go to Richmond in behalf of the church. Bro. Byerly had been on a similar mission in April, 1862. He was an eloquent speaker and convincing in his argument. Therefore, he was a strong assistant in presenting the claims of the church. Of their appointment and their intention of going, Eld. Moomaw wrote Bro.

Kline. This letter, which is also given because of its general interest, reads as follows:

Botetourt City, Virginia.
December 27, 1863.

Much Beloved Brother:

Through the mercy and grace of God, our kind and heavenly Father, myself and family and the brethren generally are well for which we return our grateful thanks for his unmerited favor, and hope that when this comes to hand it may find you enjoying the same blessing. The object of my writing at this time is to inform you that by the appointment of the brethren, Bro. B. F. Byerly and myself intend, God willing, to start to Richmond tomorrow to try to coöperate with those friendly to our cause to make some arrangements to help our brethren out of the military service. We intend to present before the authorities the manner that we have lived, as loyal citizens complying with every requirement of the law; paying our commutation, our tax in kind; what we have done for the destitute and suffering soldiers and the quantity of produce that we are making, according to the number of hands employed, etc., giving some instances. Such, for example, as this: one farm employing one substitute, one exempt on religious grounds, and their boys, has listed to the commissioner 1100 bu. of wheat, 1200 bu. of corn, 200 bu. of oats, 100 bu. of potatoes, 4500 lbs. of pork, 4500 lbs. of beef, etc. If nothing can be done in this we are authorized to request a peaceable passport out of the country, constantly averring that we cannot nor will we fight. If you have any thing that you think will favor the cause or wish to communicate with me, you can address me at Richmond. I should be glad to hear from you.

We held an election yesterday for two ministers. The lot fell upon Bro. Jonas Graybill and John C. Moomaw. While we are thus engaged, be engaged yourself and exhort the brethren to be engaged with the Lord for us, that we may still lead a quiet and peaceable life in all Godliness and honesty.

In haste, yours in the bonds of the Gospel.

John Kline. Benj. F. Moomaw.

In addition to the Governor's recommendation to the Legislature, the Congress was showing a disposition to repeal various parts of this Exemption Law. More especially was this true of the privilege granted to persons who had secured substitutes. Finally, on December 30, this law was annulled and all who had hired substitutes were therefore subject to military duty. However, the Exemption Act, on religious grounds, was not repealed.

On his return from Richmond, January 1, 1864, Eld. Moomaw wrote at some length concerning his recent trip. In this he was not altogether complimentary, as to the condition of things there. However, he gave expression of much praise to the Lord for the remembrance of His people. He referred to a conversation he had with Col. John B. Baldwin and Gen. Sparrow. The former, especially, pledged his support on behalf of the Brethren. He also made mention of Messrs. Staples, Goode and Anderson, as being favorable to maintaining the exemption on religious grounds.

Yet, in the ever-increasing straitened condition of the Confederacy, efforts were made by the general government to secure recruits from every available source, and exemptions from time to time were narrowed down to a very close margin. An effort was made to have the draft include all ages from sixteen years to sixty, and at the same time a movement sorely threatened the law under which the Brethren secured their liberty. Despite the assurance given by Eld. Moomaw on his return from Richmond, this new effort, to repeal the exemption on religious grounds, caused no little alarm.

Again Eld. Kline took his pen in defense of the church. He wrote various members of Congress concerning the threatening danger. However, a letter received from Col. Baldwin on January 28 gave a forecast of the sentiment of Congress. This, he declared, was favorable to the exemption, as it stands. About a fortnight later, a letter was received from Judge John T. Harris, who was a member of Congress. Mr. Harris, in concluding his remarks on this subject, said, "The exemption on religious grounds stands firm in Congress." The information thus received, besides other assurances, caused much thanksgiving among the churches. One writer gave expression to his gratitude in the following words: "God has again blessed His people. We are still permitted to enjoy religious freedom. May all His children praise Him and all be humbly thankful for this signal favor." In response to this gratitude for God's continued protection, as stated in the correspondence, "Saturday before Easter is set apart as a day for general thanksgiving unto God for His overruling hand in the late Congress, in assuring us continued religious liberty."

It is generally conceded that this was the last attack on the liberty, which was so highly prized by the church. However, lawlessness was on the increase, and the Brethren were subjected to many indignities by men of the "lewder sort." These were meekly borne, and with the consciousness of doing God's will, happiness was their lot, though fraught with trials.

The time was fast approaching for the meeting to convene in Franklin, as agreed upon the year previous. On February 21, Eld. B. F. Moomaw, a corresponding secretary, wrote to the churches in Rockingham concerning the proposed meeting. Through some misunderstanding, an appointment had been made at Flat Rock on the same date, April 15 and 16. By request, this meeting was changed in order to have as full representation at the Franklin general council as possible. Eld. Moomaw in a letter under more recent date, acknowledging this kindness, said, "We are thankful to the Brethren for changing their appointment and hope that the churches from the lower valley will be liberally represented in the general council in Franklin. It is intended as a general council meeting for the whole southern arm of the church; it is to be conducted just like the regular Annual Meeting and the minutes published. I am sorry that Bro. Thomas, as corresponding secretary, did not make it known at an earlier date. The Brethren from Tennessee promised to be with us." Eld. Moomaw in his communication invited the Brethren of Rockingham to present questions for discussion at the meeting. Unfortunately, the proceedings of this meeting are not now available, but it is known that the advisability of laying on of hands in setting apart deacons to their office was warmly discussed. Thus for a second and the last time there was an Annual Meeting held for the benefit of the Southern churches while isolated from the main part of the Brotherhood.

Depraved by the continuation of a heartless war for so many years and little restricted because of a lack of stability of the government, the lawless element of the country ran rife in evil conduct and deeds of violence. For this reason, public worship at times was abandoned and the church held its devotions secretly. Especially was this true of love-feast occasions.

The climax of this atrocity seems to have been reached when on June 15, 1864, Eld. Kline was shot by an assassin hidden in the timber. He had been to the blacksmith shop; had his riding horse, faithful Nell, shod; made a call at a home in response to a summons and was returning across a wooded ridge, about two miles from his home, when the dastardly deed was committed. His death was the result of a deeply laid scheme. He had been repeatedly warned by his friends, but his noble heart was devoid of fear. In response to these warnings, his repeated reply was, "They can only kill the body but they can not destroy the soul." His death was deeply felt throughout the Brotherhood, and much lamented by those who knew him best. It was then thought that the church had suffered an irreparable loss, but now, as we look back through the years that have intervened, we see the wisdom of the Lord in permitting his departure through the evil designs of these men, after his noble work in behalf of his Brethren was done. How fitting that such a life of unselfish devotion should be crowned by a martyr's death, and the doctrines he so strongly proclaimed should be sealed with his own blood. In truth, though he be dead, yet he speaketh. During life he was held in high esteem by men of authority in every calling. His benevolence was marked; a feeling of charity was ever extended towards the erring, but he rebuked sin in every form. Therefore, the evildoer hated him with a bitter hatred. On the 17th, a simple but impressive service was held at the Linville Creek church by Eld. Jacob Wine, assisted by others, after which his body was laid to rest in the cemetery near at hand. The grave is marked by a humble slab, with the simple inscription reproduced below:

Tombstone of Elder John Kline.

In sadness, the concourse returned to their homes with a desire that the mantle of charity should cover the act that took away his useful life.

A strong illustration of the deplorable condition to which Virginia had been brought by the war, lies in the fact that no effort was made to punish the perpetrators of the vile crime, although it could easily have been ascertained who did the act.

Shortly after this, the Confederacy received a blow in the Valley of Virginia from which it never recovered. Grant in his campaign before Richmond became aware of the amount of supplies the Southern army received from there and was annoyed by the raids made by the soldiery of that section. He therefore, in the beginning of August, summoned an army of 40,000 men, placed P. H. Sheridan in command, and gave him orders to spare nothing in this yet remaining great storehouse of the Southern Confederacy, upon which an army could subsist. The ruinous work in the once beautiful and fertile Shenandoah Valley but too plainly showed how fearfully the command was executed. With torch and axe and sword there was nothing left between the Blue Ridge and Alleghany Mountains worth fighting for. In his report he says, "I have destroyed a thousand barns filled with wheat, and hay, and farming implements, over seventy mills filled with flour and wheat, have driven in front of the army over 4,000 head of stock and have killed not less than 3,000 sheep. So entire has been the destruction that a crow flying across the valley must carry its own rations." Possibly there was a bit of boasting in this report. The two armies had been so long in the Valley of Virginia, that no one would think so many supplies could still remain. But the destruction that followed his track of fire and blood was most terrible. The Rockingham *Register* in its issue of November 11, 1864, gave an account of the losses sustained in Rockingham County alone, which was procured by the court appointing a committee of thirty-six magistrates and thirty-six reliable citizens, who visited every part of the county. The report is represented as having been carefully and accurately made, which appears as follows:

Dwelling houses burned	30
Barns burned	450
Mills burned	31
Fencing destroyed (in miles)	100
Bushels of wheat destroyed	100,000
Bushels of corn destroyed	50,000
Tons of hay destroyed	6,233
Cattle carried off	1,750
Horses carried off	1,750
Sheep carried off	4,200
Hogs carried off	3,350
Factories burned	3
Furnaces burned	1

In addition to this, the report continues, "There was an immense amount of farming utensils of every description destroyed. Many of them were of great value, such as McCormick reapers and threshing machines; also, household and kitchen furniture, money, bonds, plates, etc., etc. The whole loss being estimated at the enormous sum of $25,500,000. This estimate is in Confederate prices and should be reduced, we think, about one fifth, in order to bring it to government standard."

The above report is given chiefly because the Brethren were a dominant class among the farmers of the county and with their neighbors were reduced to poverty. However, this was not, by far, the greatest loss sustained. The morals of the country became polluted from the very conditions that prevailed and the return of young men after years of soldier life added a great menace to the purity of the homes.

Finally, the war practically came to an end by the surrender of Gen. Lee at Appomattox Courthouse on April 9, 1865. Thoroughly glad the desperate struggle was over, they now had an opportunity to look around to see the condition of things. This, as previously recorded, was beyond description. On every hand was desolation. As never before, the widows and orphans appealed for help. The Brethren bravely joined in every worthy effort to bring order out of chaos. During the war they had the courage to suffer for the teachings of the Master. Now they followed His example in assisting the destitute and suffering whenever possible. Throughout the churches in Virginia, the same benevolent spirit and generous disposition to assist in the betterment of the communities at large, was shown.

A few reasons are not out of place, why the Brethren needed to suffer so much during the war from a people who, as a class, are especially noted for nobleness of spirit. They may be included under three general heads.

1. Their long opposition to slavery caused them to

be classed among the Abolitionists, who were much disliked by the slaveholders.

2. Their uncompromising stand for the Bible teaching. Therefore, their refusal to go to war at any cost seemed little understood for a time.

3. The lack of a stable government, together with the excited condition of the people during the unequal contest, gave the man of evil designs an opportunity to execute his hellish schemes.

Through all of these trials, the Lord brought them a united and trustful people. With this heritage, they started anew to conquer in His name.

CHAPTER VIII.

Division of State into Districts—First District of Virginia —Church Organization.

In a preceding chapter the general council meetings have been traced until their development into the District Meeting, and the recommendation by Annual Meeting, that the States be divided into districts was also noticed. However, the war came before this was definitely agreed upon by the Virginia churches. Therefore, these meetings were held in various parts of the State from time to time during the war.

It has also been seen that the Tennessee and North Carolina Brethren united with them in these meetings, and especially is this true of the one held with the Botetourt church in 1863, and the one with the Franklin Brethren in 1864, which were virtually Annual Meetings for all the Southern churches during their isolation from the general Brotherhood. Yet, these conferences held during this time had the tendency to thoroughly prepare the churches to effect a division immediately at the close of the war. The churches in Franklin, Botetourt, Roanoke, Floyd, and Montgomery counties were the first to act, and designated their organization the First District of Virginia. As a natural consequence, when the churches in the north Shenandoah Valley effected their organization, they designated it the Second District of Virginia. The Tennessee churches were likewise organized, but it is not within the province of this volume to notice their history.

At first, the wide intervening territory was a sufficient line between the newly-formed Virginia districts. In time, however, it became necessary to have a definite line. To this end, a committee was appointed by the District Meeting of the Second District, in 1891, consisting of Elders Levi Garber, John A. Cline, and Levi A. Wenger to meet a like committee from the First District. This committee did not complete the work until 1893, when their report was accepted by the conferences of both districts. By this agreement, the James River became the line from its mouth to the confluence of the north and the south forks, and thence by the North Fork to Lexington. From here the line continues by a very indirect course to the northern limit of Greenbriar County, from whence it extends westward by that line, and on through the State of West Virginia.

New conditions in missionary endeavor in the two districts gave rise to a general revision of the division line in 1905. By this agreement, although it is not yet fully confirmed by the District Meeting of the First District, about twenty counties in southeast Virginia are transferred from the First District to the Second District in exchange for territory in West Virginia. The accompanying map of Virginia shows this line through the State.

In order that the development of the church in the different parts of the State may be more clearly seen, a chapter is separately devoted to each of the two districts.

FIRST DISTRICT OF VIRGINIA

THE FIRST DISTRICT OF VIRGINIA is here considered. This occupies the southwestern part of Virginia, the eastern half of North Carolina, and a number of counties in West Virginia. In this large territory, the Brethren first made but the three settlements in Franklin, Botetourt, and Floyd counties mentioned in a preceding chapter. By the time of the organization of the district in 1866, there were nine churches located in Botetourt, Roanoke, Franklin, Floyd, Montgomery, Monroe, Fayette, Alleghany, and Fraternity, North Carolina. At this time, according to the District Meeting minutes of 1907, there are forty-one church organizations in the district. Of this number, thirty-two are in Virginia, seven in West Virginia, and two in North Carolina, with a total membership according to last census of 3,585.

The absence of direct early records has made it very difficult to trace the development of all these churches from the first three settlements, but by the appointment of Eld. T. C. Denton by the District Meeting to collate data, and the coöperation of well-informed Brethren whose names appear in connection with their articles, this has been successfully accomplished. However, the lack of definite early dates must be admitted and is much regretted.

These writings are given as presented by the authors, except in some instances they have been abridged.

THE FRANKLIN BRETHREN.

By Eld. Daniel Peters.

[Eld. Daniel Peters was born June 5, 18—. He married Mary Brubaker January 17, 1850; united with the church in 1852; elected deacon in 1859; elected minister in June, 1872, and shortly after was ordained elder. He traveled much in the mission territory of the Franklin church. He was among the first ministers to preach in Patrick County, which was subsequently turned over to the Floyd Brethren on account of its being more convenient. In addition to the duties in the home church, he continued to labor in the adjoining counties of Henry and Pittsylvania even after the loss of his eyesight.]

The date of the organization of the church in this county is not known; but it must have been before the Revolutionary War, for my father, who was born in 1782, told me that he heard his father say there were Brethren here subject to that war. He also said that Brethren Jacob Miller and William Smith were the two first ministers. Both were located in the upper part of the county. They usually had meetings together. Bro. Miller preached in the German language and Bro. Smith in the English. Bro. Smith was a native of England. They preached about their homes and eastward for twenty miles. The membership at this time was small. A dwelling house served the purpose of a church, even on love-feast occasions. These Brethren took their staff in their hands and walked ten or twelve miles on Saturday evenings to the place of meeting. On Sunday morning at nine o'clock they would assemble and spend a while in reading Scripture and asking questions. After this the ministers would open the meeting and call on a deacon brother to lead in prayer.

The manner of living at that time was quite simple. They manufactured their own goods and made their own clothing.

Isaac Naff was elected to the ministry and later ordained elder. He also spoke the German language. The church seeing the necessity of English preaching, called Bro. John Bowman to the ministry, who became an efficient worker. He was able to speak in both the German and English languages with ability. In stature he was large and portly, yet very energetic and seeming never to tire in the work of the church. He traveled extensively and preached in several States. He always made the long trips on horseback and at his own charge. He was called to preach funerals and solemnize marriages long distances from home. In this he did more than any minister in the history of the Franklin church.

A man by the name of Jacob Faw in North Carolina, hearing of him but not knowing his name nor postoffice, addressed a letter to Preacher Bowman, Rocky Mount, Virginia, the county seat of Franklin. After receiving a reply from Bro. Bowman, he came to his home on Friday evening and talked with him on Saturday concerning the doctrine of the Brethren Church. On Sunday morning he went with Bro. Bowman to preaching. After services he was baptized. I was one of the witnesses to this impressive scene. After Bro. Faw's baptism he returned to his home in North Carolina and soon afterward the Brethren of this county began preaching there, going two or three times a year on horseback. In a short time a number of others were baptized. They were soon organized into a congregation. At this time Bro. Faw was called to the ministry and soon thereafter was ordained elder. During his administration and with the assistance of others, the church in North Carolina prospered. At the time of his death there were sixty or seventy members. It is still prospering under the care of Elders C. R. Faw and J. F. Robertson with an assistant minister. There are now one hundred and fifteen members and two houses of worship.

After this Abram Naff and Abram Barnhart were called to the ministry and later to the eldership. Eld. Naff attended a great many funerals also and often accompanied Eld. Bowman on the long preaching tours. By this time the membership had so increased in Franklin that the communions could no longer be held in dwelling houses. They were now held in barns and meadows. Therefore it was necessary to have a house of worship. One, in size forty by one hundred feet, was built in 1848. At this time Isaac Naff was an assistant elder with Abram Naff and Abram Barnhart in charge of the church.

In 1870, it was decided to divide the Franklin church into three organizations. Two houses of worship, Antioch and Bethlehem, were built in 1873, and the division was made. Two years ago the Snow Creek church was organized with about twenty-five members. It is also in Franklin County. With this there are four congregations in this county with about seven hundred members, and twenty-five ministers, eleven of whom are elders. Many members have moved to different parts of the West. The churches are united in faith and spirit. We have our coöperation meetings and work together in supplying our mission points in Henry and Pittsylvania counties. Through the preaching of the Franklin Brethren, a church has been organized in Campbell County, with Bro. W. I. Hall, a resident elder. Present elders of the congregations of the county are: Germantown—Abram Barnhart, Henry Ikenberry, and R. L. Peters; Bethlehem—Daniel Peters, Daniel Bowman, D. A. Naff, and George Bowman; Antioch—Riley Flora, Isaac Bowman, Samuel Ikenberry, and L. E. Brubaker.

The church in Franklin owns four meetinghouses and the ministers preach at twenty-two different points; the Sunday-school workers conduct four Sunday schools with an enrollment of three hundred and three scholars and an average attendance of two hundred and twenty-five.

The Swan Creek church in Campbell County was the outgrowth of mission endeavor of the Franklin ministers. Chief among these were Daniel Peters and Henry Ikenberry. When the church was organized in 1894, there were fourteen members. Now there are forty. Eld. W. I. Hall has charge of this church at present.

The time the Brethren first settled in Botetourt County can be more definitely fixed than that of Franklin County. The following concerning the Botetourt church is from the pen of Eld. Jonas Graybill.

[Eld. Graybill was born November 18, 1834, of Graybill, Crumpacker, and Kline ancestry. Owing to poor schools, long illness, and early death of his father, his education was meager. He married Catherine Snider December 18, 1856; joined the church October 15, 1857; was elected minister in 1863 and ordained elder in 1887. Although comparatively young, Eld. Graybill took an active part in behalf of the Brethren in time of the war. In company with Eld. B. F. Moomaw, he visited Congressman Walter A. Staples at Christiansburg and went to see Col. John T. Anderson of the Virginia Legislature. In addition to serving the Botetourt church, he has been closely identified with the Roanoke City church since the Brethren first preached in that city. He is now senior elder of the Botetourt church.]

After considerable investigation, I forward the following with reference to the Botetourt church. Botetourt County was taken from Augusta County in 1769, and in 1780 my great-grandfather, John Graybill, came from Berks County, Pennsylvania, with his wife, four sons and three daughters. Also in the same year a number of Brethren settled at Amsterdam, now Daleville. Among the number were the Gishes, Kinzies, Snyders, Niningers, Wingers, Lemons, Stoners, Bukners, Harshbargers, Ammons, Noffsingers, Huffs, Peters, Rifes, Arnolds, Fishers, Mangus, Moomaws, Cronses, Murrys, and Bonsacks. From this to the close of the eighteenth century, there were three or four ministers here and the church was organized during this time. My grandfather Crumpacker visited Botetourt shortly after 1800 and found an organized church here. David Rife, Henry Snider, and Jacob Peters were the first ministers. From the time of the organization to the present, the church has been presided over by Elders Abraham Gish, Abraham Crumpacker, Joel Crumpacker, Peter Nininger, Peter Nead, B. F. Moomaw, Jonas Graybill, Samuel Crumpacker, T. C. Denton, C. D. Hylton, G. H. Graybill, D. N. Eller, and J. A. Dove. The seven last named together with Lewis Skeggs, J. T. Layman, J. W. and

C. S. Ikenberry, E. C. Crumpacker, D. P. Hylton, and L. C. Coffman constitute the present ministry, who hold meetings at twenty-one different places. There are at this time five Sunday schools with an enrollment of four hundred and forty-two and an average attendance of two hundred and eighty-five. The church is large in area and membership, having a diameter of nearly twenty-four miles and a membership of five hundred and forty-eight.

The Botetourt church is splendidly organized and with its present efficient ministry much aggressive work is being done for the Master. The report of this church for the year 1907, as given in the *Gospel Messenger,* shows that there are twenty-one preaching places, thirteen of which are mission points under the special care of a minister. Their fourteen ministers preached two hundred and seventy-nine sermons in the home congregation and one hundred and ninety-nine in other congregations. Four series of meetings were held by the home ministry in their home church and nine in other churches. Twenty-three members were received by letter. Twenty-five were baptized and one reclaimed, making a total of forty-nine. Twenty-eight letters were given. Six members were lost by death, and three disowned. The total amount contributed for all purposes for 1907, was $4,324.68.

From the first the Botetourt church has had many earnest ministers, who have labored for the Lord here and in the surrounding territory. As a consequence of this, a number of other churches have been built up, of which mention is made in the succeeding pages.

The Mt. Joy church is also in Botetourt County. This organization is under the supervision of Eld. A. F. Pursley, who gave the following history of his charge:

The Mt. Joy church is in the northern part of the county. The first Brethren to preach here came from

Brother and Sister Ross, Who Are Supported as Missionaries in India by the Botetourt Memorial Missionary Society.

Rockingham and Augusta counties about the year 1857. Those first to come here were Brethren Miller, Thomas, Garber, Cline, and perhaps others I do not remember. Later the Brethren from southern Botetourt, Franklin, and Floyd counties came to us. The congregation was organized in 1859, with twelve members. We now have one hundred and thirty with A. F. Pursley and J. W. Pursley elders in charge. In our two Sunday schools there are eighty scholars enrolled with an average attendance of fifty-nine. The church owns three houses of worship and holds meetings at four other points.

At the present time there are three organized churches in Bedford County. Two of these, Geters Chapel and Saunders Grove, are under the supervision of Eld. Samuel Crumpacker, who gave the following information concerning his charges:

Geters Chapel church was the outgrowth of the mission endeavor of the Botetourt Brethren. Elders Peter Nininger and B. F. Moomaw did the first preaching. The church was organized in 1875 with about twenty members. At this time there are forty. There is no resident minister. The church has been under the care of the Botetourt Brethren since its organization.

Saunders Grove church was also established by the Botetourt Brethren and was organized in 1875. At this time there are thirty members with S. R. Saunders as their minister.

Concerning the Antioch church in Bedford County, Eld. J. P. Leftwich says:

About 1857, Abraham Brubaker and wife settled seven miles east of Bedford City. Ten years later Brethren David Plaine, Peter Nininger, B. F. Moomaw, John Brubaker, John Eller, Henry A. Beahm from Botetourt and Roanoke counties began holding meetings in this community. As a consequence of this, the Antioch church was organized with twenty members. At this time there are forty-five members. The elders in charge since the organization are Henry A. Beahm, John Davis, S. A. B. Hershberger, J. P. Leftwich and S. P. Beahm. The present ministry are J. P. Leftwich, S. P. Beahm, B. H. Funk, and J. R. Hughs.

The Patts Creek church in Alleghany County was also a plant of the Botetourt church. Eld. John W. Jamison states that Peter Nininger and Benjamin Moomaw began preaching on Patts Creek about fifty years ago and the church was organized shortly after that time. The membership at one time was about forty, but it has been reduced to twenty at the present time. In addition to those already mentioned, John B. Davis, George M. Jamison, and John W. Jamison have served this church as ministers.

Eld. A. M. Frantz writes concerning the Greenbriar church, that Elders Peter Nininger, David Plaine, B. F. Moomaw, John Moomaw, and others from Botetourt and Roanoke counties were the first ministers to preach there. Later Elders J. S. Flory, Andrew Hutchison, and others from West Virginia, did the preaching. The organization was formed about 1870. At this time there are sixteen members scattered over a wide territory. Eld. Frantz is the only minister and should have assistance.

There are two church organizations in Roanoke County. The accounts of these have been written by the senior elder in charge of each church. Both of them labor under the disadvantage of no early records being kept. Yet it is generally accepted that the

Brethren preached here soon after the settlement in Botetourt County.

Eld. C. E. Eller in giving a report of Peters Creek church says: "The number of members at present is one hundred and fifty. Beginning with our present ministry, I find that the following Brethren have had oversight of Peters Creek church: C. E. Eller, D. C. Naff, C. A. Williams, John B. Naff, John W. Eller, Moses E. Brubaker, Elias Brubaker, Christian Wertz, John Brubaker, John Eller, and Daniel Barnhart. The following Brethren constitute the present ministerial force: D. C. Naff, C. E. Eller, N. H. Garst, Levi Garst, J. S. Showalter, C. F. Webster, J. H. Garst, and J. H. Wimmer, who hold meetings at seven different places. Three meetinghouses are owned by the Peters Creek church, in which three Sunday schools are conducted, with an enrollment of one hundred and thirty scholars and an average attendance of one hundred."

The Roanoke City Church.

By P. S. Miller.

Elder in charge of the Roanoke City Congregation for 21 years, that is, from its organization until now.

[Eld. Miller was born in Augusta County, Virginia, April 30, 1849. His ancestors were closely identified with the history of the church in the county, from a very early date. His grandfather, Eld. Peter Miller, was one of the pioneer preachers and elders, and his father, Eld. John Miller, was the first elder of the Pleasant Valley congregation. Eld. Miller spent his early life on his father's farm, and was baptized by his uncle, Eld. Levi Garber, in

October, 1866. He was married to Elizabeth F. Click, in October, 1872; was elected to the ministry in 1878, and was ordained elder in August, 1892. Before moving to Roanoke City, he was identified as trustee and director, in Bridgewater College, to which he devoted years in aiding

Elder P. S. Miller.

the advancement of that institution of learning. Besides his work as preacher, and elder of the Roanoke City congregation, he has served his District on Standing Committee of Annual Meeting nine times, and has also served on a number of important committees, by appointment of both Annual and District Meetings. These various duties have made his life a busy one. He gives the following history of the Roanoke City congregation.]

Meetings were held in rented halls in the city from the beginning, in 1892, until the church was built, in 1894. The preaching was done by different brethren, from the beginning until the organization in 1893.

Roanoke City Church.

The church was organized the first Saturday in September, 1893, with thirty-two members, the following being the official board at the time of organization: P. S. Miller, elder; J. H. Graybill, Joseph Shickel, and W. P. Moomaw, ministers in the second degree, and Joseph C. Moomaw and Nathan R. Bower, deacons.

In the spring of 1894 a lot was bought on which to

build a church, which was done, and the house was dedicated in August of the same year. The entire cost of lot and house was about $2,000. In the succeeding years it was necessary to enlarge, in order to have room for the growing congregation and Sunday school; so the commodious house, as shown in the accompanying cut, was built and dedicated in the year 1906, at a cost of $4,600.

Since the organization, twenty-one years ago, about two hundred have been baptized, and about three hundred have been received by letter, making the total that have had membership about five hundred for the twenty-one years. The present membership is about three hundred, the other two hundred having been mainly (excepting some deaths and withdrawals) transferred by letter.

The following compose the present official board: P. S. Miller, elder in charge; J. H. Murray, elder; Joseph Shickel, D. R. Brubaker, and C. E. Trout, ministers in second degree, with Joseph C. Moomaw, F. E. Skeggs, Leland C. Moomaw, Peter Shilling, J. D. Bower, L. L. Layman, and James Mitchell deacons.

The Sunday meetings consist of two preaching services, Sunday school, and Christian Workers' Meeting. The Sunday-school enrollment is about two hundred and seventy-five, that of the Home Department and Cradle Roll one hundred and fifty each.

Of the workers among the membership, there are a number who are consecrated and active, constantly striving for the higher ideals of the Christian life, and always ready to aid in charitable, missionary, temperance and peace endeavors.

Since the above concerning the Roanoke city church was written, one hundred and fifty-five have been added by baptism, and fourteen were reclaimed, which added to the three hundred mentioned above makes the total membership about four hundred and seventy. The membership of the Sunday school has been increased also, from about two hundred and seventy-five to about three hundred and sixty. Many people other than our own membership enjoy the services at our church, which gives us much encouragement for many more additions to both the church and Sunday school.

The Brethren in Floyd County.

By Eld. C. D. Hylton.

[Eld. Chrisley D. Hylton, son of Eld. H. P. Hylton, was born in Floyd County, Virginia, June 20, 1859. Schools were few and he received such education as the old-time three-months-subscription schools afforded, until the institution of the public schools. On December 2, 1877, at the age of eighteen years, he was baptized into the Brethren Church. Seven winters were spent in teaching public schools. On December 22, 1881, he married Mattie E. Bowman, of Tennessee. On September 6, 1884, he was elected to the ministry and on the 27th day of the same month, he made his first attempt to preach a sermon, in the Flat Rock church, Ashe County, North Carolina. Two years later he began holding series of meetings and the Lord blessed his efforts to the saving of many souls. Twice Eld. Hylton in public discussions successfully defended the faith and practice of the Brethren Church against would-be assailants. On October 2, 1892, he was ordained to the eldership. In 1895, he with his family moved to Louisiana and spent one year. He was sent from there by the General Mission Board to take charge of the Florida Mission, where he resided for nearly three years. He was then engaged by the Mission Board of the First District of Virginia as district evangelist, where he spent two years constantly in the field. He is now located in the Botetourt church on a farm. During the fall and

Elder Chrisley D. Hylton.

winter he does considerable evangelistic work. His work has been confined mainly to Virginia, North Carolina, Tennessee, and West Virginia, with a few visits made to Maryland and Pennsylvania.]

When George III, king of England, sent his troops to the New World to force the United Colonies into submission to his demands, there was a young man on board one of the vessels whose name was William Smith. His genealogy is not known, neither is it known why he was transported with the troops, for in principle he was a noncombatant, and his sympathy was with the Americans. He refused to fight under the British flag.

After the struggle for independence had been crowned with success, young Smith decided to make his home with the Americans. Consequently, he settled down in life at the head of Daniel's Run, now in Floyd County, Virginia. At that time the country was very sparsely settled; ministers of the Gospel were scarce, and those who were religiously inclined traveled for miles to hear the Word of God preached. Young Smith being of a spiritual turn of mind naturally sought for a place to worship, and a people with whom he might worship God. He met Elder Jacob Miller of Franklin County and after learning of the faith of the Brethren decided to cast his lot with them. Smith demanded baptism at the hands of Elder Miller. (Tradition says that Smith had witnessed a baptismal scene of one who had demanded apostolic baptism of the king, whereupon the king caused him to be baptized by trine immersion.)

Not many years later, Bro. Smith was called to the ministry by the church. The Lord blessed his humble efforts; souls were gathered into the fold; and about the year 1800 the first Brethren church was organized in the territory which is now included mostly in Floyd County. William Smith was ordained elder by Eld. Jacob Miller.

On account of the Franklin County Brethren using the German language in their service and the Floyd Brethren using the English, the former for some time was known as the " German Arm " and the latter the

"English Arm." By constant mingling they worked harmoniously, and in course of a few decades all could understand English.

This new congregation was bounded on the north by the North Fork of Roanoke River, on the east by Franklin County, and on the south and west there were no limits. In 1845 this territory was divided and that part east of Floyd Courthouse was called the "East Arm" and that on the west was called the "West Arm." Services were held promiscuously over the territory in dwelling houses, barns, and groves. In 1857 the Brick church was built in the "West Arm" by the united and untiring energy of H. P. Hylton and Joseph Weddle at a cost of $1,300. Eight hundred dollars of this amount was subscribed by members and friends of the church. The remaining $500 was supplied by the builders.

In 1860 the "West Arm" was divided, and the territory north of Wills Ridge was called the Pleasant Valley congregation. About 1870 the "East Arm" built the Red Oak Grove church, and the Pleasant Valley congregation built their church called by the same name. In 1890 the Smyth's River congregation, in Patrick County, was cut off from the Brick church (as the West Arm was now called), was organized, and built a churchhouse. In 1892 the Burk's Fork church was taken from the Brick church and the same year the Union church was built. In 1893 the St. Paul church in Carroll County was organized and taken from the Brick church. In 1893 the Coylson church in Carroll County was organized and cut from the Brick church territory. In 1895 the old Brick church was torn down and a new wooden structure built on the same lot. It is now called the Topeco church. In 1897 again and perhaps for the last time, this old original congregation was divided and the Pleasant View church near the village of Hylton was organized and a new churchhouse was built bearing the same name.

The following parties have been elected to the ministry in the old Brick church congregation to the year 1907, viz.: Jacob Weddle, Austin Hylton, Archie Thompson, Joshua Thompson, Andrew Weddle, H. P. Hylton, Andrew Reed, John Weddle, Joseph Weddle, William Reed, Isaac Reed, J. B. Hylton, Cornelius Reed, J. H. Slusher, Harvey Weddle, P. N. Hylton, Joel Weddle, C. D. Hylton, Ananias Harman, Jacob Hylton, A. N. Hylton, and L. C. Weddle.

The following ministers were ordained to the eldership in the above church: William Smith, Chrisley Bowman, Austin Hylton, H. P. Hylton, Andrew Reed, John Weddle, J. B. Hylton, J. H. Slusher, Harvey Weddle, Thomas Reed, C. D. Hylton, Ananias Harman, and Jacob Hylton.

In addition to what Eld. Hylton wrote relative to the church in Floyd County, a brief account of the different local organizations is here given. These in the main are written by the respective elders in charge.

Eld. Harvey Weddle in writing of the Tropico church says: "We have been known by our present name since 1896. Prior to that time our name was the Brick church. The first ministers to preach in this community were William Smith and John Bowman. The church was organized in 1845 with ten members. All services were held in houses and barns until 1857, when the first house of worship was built. The present membership is one hundred and twenty. Also from the organization have sprung seven others and from them three more, with a combined membership of about one thousand members."

Elder W. H. Naff.

[Eld. William H. Naff was born April 29, 1845. On October 4, 1867, he united in marriage with Mary Jane Lampey. In September, 1877, he joined the church; was elected minister a year later and was ordained elder in 1887. He served as moderator, reading and writing clerk a number of times, and also was a member of Standing Committee at eight different Annual Meetings. Since his ordination in 1887, he has had charge of the Red Oak Grove church and for almost an equal length of time he has been in the same relation with the Elliot Creek congregation. In addition to this, he has served the White

Rock and St. Paul churches. As a school-teacher, he has been quite successful, having taught forty-three years and boarded at home all the while, with the exception of one session.]

Eld. Naff says: "Red Oak Grove church was organized about 1870. It was cut off from Pleasant Valley. At that time there were twenty-five members; now we have one hundred and five. The present ministers are W. H. Naff, M. J. Dickerson, S. G. Spangle, J. F. Keith, Asa Bowman, Charles Williams, and William Vest."

ELLIOT'S CREEK was organized in 1887 with about fifteen members. Now there are forty. The ministry of the Red Oak Grove church serve this organization.

THE ANGELS' REST CHURCH is in Giles County. Eld. M. J. Dickerson is in charge of the work. This organization was effected in July, 1905, and was the outgrowth of the labors of Elders M. J. Dickerson, W. H. Naff, and others.

THE BURK'S FORK CHURCH is in Floyd County and was organized in 1892 with sixty members; at present there are one hundred and fifty.

ST. PAUL'S CHURCH, Carroll County, at its organization in 1893 had twenty members. At present its membership is forty-five.

SMITH'S RIVER in Patrick County was organized in 1890 with twenty members and H. P. Hylton elder in charge. There are now one hundred and fifty members with W. A. Elgin elder in charge.

MOUNT JACKSON was cut off from Pleasant Valley with about forty members. However, adverse conditions have reduced this number.

THE PLEASANT VALLEY CONGREGATION in Floyd County has about two hundred members and is in a prosperous condition.

PLEASANT VIEW in Floyd County has about one hundred members with Owen Barnhart and S. P. Hylton elders, and Charles Hylton and Zion Mitchel ministers.

BEAVER CREEK has about one hundred members with two elders and three ministers.

WHITE ROCK is a small congregation in Floyd County with Washington Akers elder in charge.

THE CRAB ORCHARD CHURCH is in Raleigh County, West Virginia. The Brethren from Franklin and Floyd counties began preaching in this community about the year 1858, Christian Bowman being chief among them. The church was organized in 1868 or 1869, with twelve members. At present there are forty-five members with two ministers and one house of worship.

THE CHARLESTON CHURCH is in South Charlestown, Kanawha County, West Virginia. The Brethren from the Valley of Virginia began preaching here first, Jacob Thomas being chief among them. In 1885 the church was organized with fifteen members. At present there are twenty-one members with one meeting-house, but no resident elder.

THE CHESTNUT GROVE CHURCH is in Fayette County, West Virginia. Daniel Thomas from the Valley of Virginia preached here first in the year 1858. A few years later the church was organized with ten members and Bro. J. S. Flory was elected minister. At the present time there are seventy-five members, five ministers, and two houses of worship. The present Chestnut Grove meetinghouse is the third one built on the same site.

The author is indebted to Bro. J. M. Crouse, Stuart, West Virginia, for the information relative to the West Virginia churches.

The close organization throughout the district promises to be fruitful of much gain for the Lord. Of the present workings of the district, more is to be said in a later chapter.

A complete list of the ministry of the First District of Virginia would be lengthy. Among the churches are many very efficient workers for the Lord. Some names such as the Naffs, Moomaws, Hyltons and Crumpackers appear very frequently in the ministry of the different churches. A striking illustration of this is in the person of Daniel P. Hylton of the Botetourt church, son of Eld. C. D. Hylton. This young brother is the fourth generation of ministers in the Hylton family. He completed a course in the Botetourt Normal School and was called to the ministry at the age of nineteen years. He was born February 17, 1884, and at this time promises many years of usefulness in the church.

CHAPTER IX.

Second District of Virginia—Church Organization.

The northern and eastern portions of Virginia together with a number of counties in West Virginia constitute the Second District of Virginia. In area it is not so large as that of the First District, but the membership is much larger. At the time of the organization in 1866, the churches in northern Virginia were well prepared to carry forward the work of the district. At that time there were twelve local organizations with an outlying mission territory. Now there are thirty-three churches with a total membership of 7,430. Nearly all of these have an outlying mission field. In many places this mission territory should be organized into churches, and the strong churches doubtless would do more efficient work for the Master if they were subdivided.

At this time there is also a growing sentiment in favor of a division of the district. To this end a committee consisting of Elders J. M. Kagey, D. H. Zigler, E. D. Kendig, S. A. Sanger, and M. G. Early was appointed to investigate the advisability of such division and report to the District Meeting of 1908.

Of the thirty-three churches, three are in West Virginia. These were the outgrowth of early missionary endeavor of the church in the Valley of Virginia. The missionary, educational and charitable work of the district is considered in a succeeding chapter, together with that of the First District of Virginia. At this place the development of the churches from the three early settlements in Shenandoah, Rockingham and Augusta counties is here chronicled. In this it is not the purpose to repeat what has been said in previous chapters, only so far as is necessary for clearness of statement.

The settlements referred to early became known as the Lower Rockingham and Shenandoah Brethren, the Upper Rockingham Brethren and the Augusta Brethren. From each of these centers the ministers went forth proclaiming the Word of Truth, and churches were organized. They are taken up in the order as they appear above.

Elder S. A. Shaver

The churches north of Harrisonburg from the time of the first division in 1788 were considered under one regulation, with Benjamin Bowman as senior elder with Elders Martin Garber and John Glick assistants at first, with others succeeding in office of bishop as time went on. This continued without change until 1827, when the northern part of Shenandoah County was put under a separate organization. Eld. S. A. Shaver, who now has charge of this church, furnishes the following bit of interesting history concerning it:

" The Woodstock Church was organized in the year 1827 with twelve members. One half of them prior to the organization were, or belonged to the

River Brethren church. The names of those twelve charter members are: Abraham Hockman and wife, John Hockman and wife, John Gochenour and wife, Jonathan Gochenour and wife, George Shaver and wife, John Nihiser, and Magdalene Bronk. The territory extended from Stony Creek in Shenandoah County to the Potomac River.

"On the day of the organization, George Shaver was elected deacon, and a few years later became the first minister. The following is a list of the ministers from that time to the present:

"George Shaver, elected in 1834; ordained to the eldership, March 3, 1849.

"John Nihiser, elected in 1840; ordained elder in 1858.

"John Brindle, elected in 1856.

"Jonas Wakeman, elected in 1858; ordained elder in 1876.

"S. A. Shaver, elected in 1860; ordained elder in 1876.

"H. R. Mawery, elected February 25, 1888; ordained on August 27, 1904.

"J. M. Rymon, elected on May 21, 1892.

"D. H. Smith, elected on August 23, 1901.

"In the year 1857, James Tabler moved into the congregation and settled near Middletown. He was a minister at the time and soon thereafter the northern part of the congregation was organized into the Salem church and Bro. Tabler ordained elder. At this time Daniel Baker was elected to the ministry, and in 1866 ordained to the eldership."

At the present time, by information given by N. D.

Cool, a resident minister, the Salem congregation has sixty-three members, two churchhouses, seven meetings per month, two Sunday schools with about sixty scholars, and three ministers; viz.: N. D. Cool, C. H. Brown, and Lewis Detra.

In 1901, the eastern part of the Woodstock church was organized into the Powels Fort congregation. At that time William Peters and J. Clanaham were the resident ministers and S. A. Shaver chosen elder in charge.

In 1885, the Woodstock church was sorely rent by division, E. M. Shaver, a minister, uniting with the Progressive movement. With him a number of members withdrew from the church. At this time, however, there are one hundred and fifty members, four ministers, three churchhouses with eight regular appointments, and two Sunday schools with eighty scholars.

Returning to the division of territory as laid out by the line of 1788, the rest of the old district lying north of Harrisonburg remained in one organization until 1840. At this time a division line having Timberville as an objective point was agreed upon between Flat Rock and Linville Creek.

The history of the FLAT ROCK CONGREGATION is written by Bro. J. David Wine, who is a son of Eld. D. P. Wine and is an active deacon and Sunday-school worker of the Flat Rock church. He is also a member of the local mission board for the congregation. The author is indebted to him for other valuable information in the preparation of this volume.

" It was within the bounds of this church that the

New Flat Rock Church.

first settlement was made by the Brethren in northern Virginia. Here John Garber located in 1775. In 1783, Elders Martin Garber and John Glick also settled here. In 1800, John Kagey was elected to the ministry and ordained to the eldership in 1814. These brethren, assisted by others from Linville Creek, served the church until 1840, when an agreement was made to divide in two districts. For years, however, they continued to labor jointly in outlying mission territory.

"Isaac Myers was elected minister on April 8, 1845.

"Jacob Wine, elected April 8, 1846, ordained elder April 18, 1857.

"David Cline was elected minister on July 31, 1848.

"John Neff was elected minister, April 15, 1852.

"Abraham Neff, elected April 18, 1857; ordained elder, August 2, 1859.

"Daniel Hays was ordained to the eldership on April 23, 1881.

"Abraham J. Kagey was called to the ministry in 1889.

"John Ellis was ordained elder, April 23, 1881.

"S. H. Myers was ordained elder, March 16, 1882.

"M. J. Good was ordained elder, January 18, 1898.

"B. W. Neff was ordained elder, January 18, 1898.

"John F. Driver was elected minister, March 11, 1882, and moved to Linville Creek on October 17, 1890.

"D. P. Wine, elected January 3, 1885; ordained elder, August 22, 1905.

"B. Frank Garber was elected to the ministry, April 24, 1886.

"John W. Wayland was chosen minister in August, 1894.

"J. Carson Miller was called to the ministry, August 5, 1892.

"John H. Garber, elected minister on August 1, 1896.

"Charles Nesselrod was chosen minister, August 29, 1896.

"I. M. Neff was elected minister on November 20, 1896.

"L. D. Wakeman, chosen minister, September 16, 1904.

"Arthur B. Miller was called to the ministry on February 11, 1905.

"At the present time Flat Rock has four hundred and sixty members and eight ministers, two of which, B. W. Neff and D. P. Wine, are ordained elders. Twenty-two regular appointments are filled each month at eight different points. The church now has in prospect a subdivision of its territory into three divisions in the near future."

The present indicates many years of usefulness for this church.

The division line between Flat Rock and Linville Creek was laid out in 1840 and the boundary between Greenmount and Linville Creek in 1844. Prior to this each of these divisions were virtually independent of each other. From a very early date this was true, except in the election of ministers and deacons, and other questions of general interest, when they united in their choice. In such case the vote was taken separately at each place and the matter was decided by the sum total of all the votes cast. A notable example is given when Elders Benjamin Bowman and John Glick conducted the election of one minister and two deacons on May 31, 1818. The sum total of the votes cast for a minister in this election was sixty-five. Of this number John Wampler received fifty-seven. Daniel Miller, Samuel Coffman, and Benjamin Bowman were chosen deacons in the same way. At this time John Kline received a somewhat flattering vote, but his election to the deacon office was deferred until some years later and was conducted in the like manner.

At that time the southern part of the territory lying between the Flat Rock and the old Harrisonburg line was known as Upper Linville, and the northern part known as Lower Linville Creek. After the complete organization of these territories into churches, the name of the former was changed to Greenmount and the latter to Linville Creek. A brief history of the Linville Creek Church by Eld. John P. Zigler is here given.

[Eld. John P. Zigler was born January 10, 1845; was married to Sarah J. Driver October 20, 1868; united with the church in 1869; was elected to the ministry August 19, 1872; and was ordained to the eldership August 15, 1891. In a second marriage on November 2, 1890, he was united with Sallie E. Andes. To these two unions eleven children were born, all of whom united with the Brethren Church. He died October 15, 1907. He served the church on many important committees and was widely known as a minister of ability. Nearly his entire life was spent within the bounds of the Linville Creek church and it was here that the greatest work of his life was done. He was a grand-nephew of Eld. John Kline and partook of many of his noble characteristics. As an elder he was an example of unusual devotion to the welfare of his charge.]

Pencil Sketch of Elder John P. Zigler, from Memory, by Bro. C. E. Nair.

The following was written by him for this volume shortly before his death:

"The Linville Creek church is in the northern part of Rockingham County. Its northern border was agreed upon when the territory lying between Timberville and Harrisonburg was organized into Upper and

Lower Linville Creek. Its southern boundary was designated four years later when Greenmount was organized into a church. These churches continue to coöperate in important church work to the present, especially is this true in working the West Virginia mission territory.

" In 1830 the first Linville Creek meetinghouse was erected, which continued in use until 1868, when the present house of worship was erected. This congregation is well known as the home of Eld. Kline and the place where Eld. Peter Nead was married and made his home for a time. In 1830 John Kline and Samuel Wampler were at the same time elected to the ministry. They labored together in union and were advanced to the eldership in the same way April 13, 1848. Other ministers of the Linville Creek church were elected as follows:

"Abraham Knupp, April 5, 1845.
" Christian Wine, April 10, 1857.
" Samuel Zigler, February 27, 1858.
" M. B. E. Kline, December 13, 1861.
" David B. Rhodes, July 30, 1864.
" Joseph Wampler, ———, 1868.
" J. P. Zigler, August 19, 1872.
" M. J. Roller, August 29, 1878.
" Joseph Shickel, August 29, 1878.
" D. H. Zigler, August 22, 1890.
" J. S. Kline, August 20, 1896.
" J. S. Roller, August 20, 1897.
" S. D. Zigler, August 20, 1897.
" W. A. Myers, February 24, 1905.
" I. N. Zigler, August 1, 1907.

"John F. Driver moved into this congregation in 1891, and D. Hays in 1892.

"The Annual Meeting of 1879 was held at the Linville Creek church.

"In 1895, the western part of the congregation with about one hundred members was organized into the Brocks Gap church, which at present has a membership of one hundred and fifty, six ministers, two churchhouses, and one Sunday school with fifty-six scholars, which make an average attendance of thirty-four.

"At this time in the old church there are five hundred and thirty-three members and eight houses of worship owned as a whole or in part. There are six Sunday schools, four Christian Workers' meetings, and a Sisters' Aid Society. The church is in union and contends earnestly for the simple life as exemplified by Christ."

At the present, Daniel Hays, John F. Driver and D. H. Zigler are ordained elders, and with J. S. Roller, W. A. Myers and I. N. Zigler constitute the ministerial corps.

The Greenmount Church.

By S. L. Bowman.

[Bro. Bowman is an active minister of the Greenmount congregation. He is a descendant of the well-known Bowman family that appears so prominently in the early history of the Brethren in Virginia. In addition to his ministerial duties, he fills the important position of secretary of the Board of Trustees of Bridgewater College. Other valuable information furnished by Bro. Bowman is acknowledged at another place in this volume.]

"The Greenmount organization occupies an area of twenty miles in length by ten miles in width. Before the division of the territory north of Harrisonburg into the local churches, this was the extreme southern part and for many years it was known as Upper Linville. The present name was not adopted until after its organization into a church in 1844. Although this territory was a part of a much greater, there has been a resident elder within it from the time of the first settlement of the Brethren in Virginia to the present, save the few years intervening between the death of Eld. Benjamin Bowman, Sr., and the ordination of his son, Benjamin, in 1837.

"The following resident brethren were elected to the official position as indicated below:

"Benjamin Bowman, Jr., and Daniel Miller were elected deacons May 31, 1818. The former was ordained to the eldership in 1837 and the latter a few years later.

"Joseph Miller, son of Daniel, was elected minister, April 10, 1846.

"John Wine was elected to the ministry, April 9, 1851.

"Jacob Miller, son of Daniel, elected minister, April 13, 1849; ordained elder in 1859; and died in 1889.

"Jacob Spitzer was elected, April 19, 1855, and ordained in 1868.

"On November 5, 1863, William C. Therman and Benjamin Funk, who had officiated as ministers for years, united with the church and were received in their office. This addition, which at the first was considered exceedingly fortunate, proved to be the sorest trial in the history of the Greenmount and adjoining churches. William C. Therman, who was a man of much learning and rare argumentative ability, soon began to preach strange doctrines. Chief among these was a fixed date for the second advent of Christ. Through his apparent truthful interpretations of the prophecies, a number of the Brethren among whom were ministers were drawn from the faith. Some of these, however, returned to the church after the failure of the delusive prediction. About this time Benjamin Funk also became estranged from the church.

"Benjamin Miller was called to the ministry on December 6, 1866.

"George Wine was elected minister, April 13, 1867.

"Fredric Wampler, called to the ministry in 1868.

"Isaac Myers, elected minister, December 26, 1874; ordained, May, 1898. Jacob A. Garber was ordained elder in November, 1902.

"B. B. Miller was elected minister in 1889.

"J. W. Wampler was elected minister Mar. 31, 1894.

"John H. Kline, elected minister in April, 1897.

"S. L. Bowman was called to the ministry on August 5, 1899.

"William Miller, elected minister in November, 1902.

"Eld. Benjamin Miller is senior in office and the last seven ministers mentioned above are actively engaged in their respective duties. There are about three hundred and seventy-five members at this time, with six houses of worship and two additional preaching points. There are six Sunday schools with an enrollment of four hundred and forty scholars and an average attendance of two hundred and sixty-three. Two Christian Workers' meetings and a Sisters' Aid Society afford ample activity for the workers of this church.

"The Brush meetinghouse was built in 1843, Pine Grove about 1850, and Greenmount in 1859 and was rebuilt in 1898.

"In addition to the home work this church is actively engaged with the Linville Creek church in the extensive mission field in West Virginia."

From this joint mission territory of Linville Creek and Greenmount, the North Millcreek congregation in West Virginia was organized with sixty-four members, one minister and two houses of worship. In addition to this there are yet in this unorganized mission territory about ninety members with one church-house and another nearly completed.

Before the separate organization of any of the local churches in this part of the Valley of Virginia, the ministers succeeded in establishing the church on Lost River in West Virginia. There are at this time two organizations here. Eld. Siram May furnishes the following condensed information relative to these churches:

UPPER LOST RIVER has two hundred and fifty members, five ministers and two houses of worship.

LOWER LOST RIVER has a membership of one hundred and fifty, with five ministers and two houses of worship.

These Brethren carried the Gospel east as well as west. At the call of a lone sister, as early as 1835, they began to preach in Page County. Eld. Martin Rothgeb, senior elder in charge, gives the following very interesting account of the PAGE CHURCH:

"The first preachers of the Brethren came to this county in 1835. If there were any earlier than this it is not known. Among them were John Kagey, Samuel Wampler and John Kline. The members there were Sisters Gibbons, Farrey, Maggert and Rodecap. In 1850, the congregation was organized with twelve members. At that time John Huffman was elected minister and Isaac Spittler deacon. Nathan Spittler was elected minister in 1857.

"At this time we have eight ministers as follows: Martin Rothgeb, J. B. F. Huffman, John A. Racer, John A. Racer, Jr., Joseph S. Foster, Joseph Foster, Jr., W. D. Strickler, George W. Painter and David S. Bradley.

"At this time there are four hundred members in Page County, six houses of worship, and five Sunday schools are conducted with an enrollment of three hundred and eighteen and an average attendance of one hundred and ninety.

"In addition to the work in Page County, our Brethren have carried forward a missionary work in Rappahannock County, where there are sixty-five members and one house of worship. A minister should be located at this place."

The history of the churches in Rockingham County south of Harrisonburg is not unlike that in the valley north of that place. The first settlement here was made about 1785. As evidenced by the painstaking research of Bro. S. L. Bowman to whom the author is indebted for this information, among those early settlers was Eld. Peter Bowman, a brother of Eld. Benjamin Bowman. Little, however, is known of his work save that he was active in the ministry and that he was a writer of some ability. Closely associated with him are the names of Daniel Garber and John Flory. The former moved from his father's home at Flat Rock in 1790 and the latter married his sister, Catherine, the same year. They labored together for many years and under their ministration the church prospered greatly. Eld. Flory was born in 1766; married Catherine Garber in 1790; and died in 1845.

The names of John Wine, Daniel Yount, Isaac Long and Martin Miller are also closely connected with this period.

It is known that the Cooks Creek church was organized at an early date, but the exact time cannot be given. The boundary continued unaltered for years until 1907, when the southern portion was cut off and organized into the Bridgewater congregation. This new church has two hundred members, one church-house, one chapel, two Sunday schools with an enrollment of one hundred and seventy-five scholars, two Christian Workers' meetings, and a Sisters' Aid Society.

Eld. J. M. Kagey, who for many years has been a member of the District Mission Board and is also a member of the Board of Trustees of Bridgewater College, is the elder in charge of the Cooks Creek church. Eld. Kagey gives the following information concerning his charge:

" Since the organization of the southern part of

our district into the Bridgewater church, there are about two hundred and fifty or three hundred members in our church, five meetinghouses, and four Sunday schools with an enrollment of three hundred scholars. The present ministry are J. M. Kagey, P. S. Thomas, S. I. Bowman, and S. D. Zigler."

The old church and its latest offspring unite in working the West Virginia mission field, which territory has one hundred and five members and four houses of worship.

The Beaver Creek Church.

By Eld. H. G. Miller.

[Hiram G. Miller was born May 29, 1852; joined the church September 9, 1877; united in marriage with Julia A. Wright on November 7, 1877; elected minister April 4, 1885; and ordained elder on August 1, 1896. Eld. Miller has served the church as moderator of District Meeting and as a member of Standing Committee at Annual Meeting at different times. At present he is a member of the Board of Trustees for Bridgewater College and he also serves on the visiting committee for the same institution. The discipline of the Beaver Creek church, of which he is senior elder, is favorably known.]

"Doubtless the Beaver Creek and Cooks Creek churches were organized near the same time, but when the division was agreed upon is not known. Bro. John Brower was the first minister located in this section. He was followed by John Wine, Joseph Miller, Martin Miller, George Wine and the Thomases. Martin Miller was ordained to the eldership on April 5, 1855, and Daniel Thomas on December 5, 1862. Jacob Thomas was elected minister, April 5,

1855. George Wine moved from Highland County in 1863 and was ordained an elder in 1868.

"The Beaver Creek churchhouse was burned June 13, 1869, and a new building erected in October and

Elder Hiram G. Miller.

November of the same year. G. W. Wine was ordained to the eldership on August 5, 1893.

"From the southern part of this congregation, Elk Run was organized about the year 1870. At present there are one hundred and three members, two churchhouses, five ministers, one Sunday school with an enrollment of forty-five and an average attendance of forty-one, one Christian Workers' meeting with an enrollment of twenty, and one Sisters' Aid Society. The mission field is in Rockbridge and Bath counties.

"The Sangerville congregation was cut off from Beaver Creek, August 3, 1895. This church joins with the mother church in working the mission field, which comprises Highland County, Virginia, and Pocahontas and part of Pendleton counties in West Virginia.

Eld. Anthony A. Miller.

"From this territory there was organized in 1897, Crummets Run, now under the efficient care of Eld. A. S. Thomas, which at present has two hundred members, three ministers, one churchhouse and interest in one, and one Sunday school with seventy-five scholars. The church is unable to work its territory. Beaver Creek and Sangerville churches assist it.

"Also a few years later Thorny Bottom was organized with a membership of thirty and two ministers.

"In 1899, Anthony A. Miller, then a member of the District Mission Board, was placed in Highland County. On September 27, 1900, the Valley Bethel congregation was organized with forty-two members, with A. A. Miller minister in charge. He was ordained to the eldership, on August 22, 1902. At the present time there are thirty-six members, two ministers, one meetinghouse, and one Sunday school with an enrollment of forty-five and an average attendance of thirty-six. This church now has three outlying points in Bath and Highland counties with forty-seven members, making a total membership of eighty-three.

"In the remaining mission field there are one hundred and fifty members, six ministers, two houses of worship and five Sunday schools with one hundred and twenty scholars. Elders H. G. Miller and J. W. Wine jointly have oversight of this territory.

"The present membership of the parent church is three hundred and forty-six with seven ministers, who hold five meetings per month at two churchhouses, four Sunday schools with an enrollment of three hundred and forty-eight and an average attendance of one hundred and eighty-nine, one Christian Workers' meeting, and a Sisters' Aid Society."

When the Sangerville church was cut off from Beaver Creek on August 3, 1895, G. W. Wine became elder in charge. He was born February 24, 1834; united with the church in July, 1851; became a minister in 1869; and was ordained to the eldership in August, 1893. At this time he serves in the important position as counselor. His son, J. W. Wine, who was born December 21, 1858, united with the church in August, 1875; was elected minister, April 1, 1893; and was ordained elder on September 6, 1901. He is elder in charge and furnishes the following relative to this church:

"Sangerville was cut off from Beaver Creek congregation in 1895. At present there are three hundred and seventy-eight members, five churchhouses, five ministers, three Sunday schools with three hundred and seventy-seven scholars enrolled and an average attendance of two hundred and nineteen, two Chistian Workers' meetings, and a Sisters' Aid Society with forty-three members."

The following is the history of the MILL CREEK

Elder J. W. Wine.

CONGREGATION, much abridged from the writing of P. H. Showalter and J. P. Deihl. It stands as an evidence of the painstaking research of these brethren. The former is a minister and the latter an active deacon of this church.

"The Mill Creek congregation was organized in 1840. Some ten years prior to this time the Brethren from Cooks Creek began to preach here. Isaac Long and Daniel Yount moved here soon after this and labored earnestly for the upbuilding of the church. When the church was organized there were the following members present: Isaac Long and wife, Daniel Yount and wife, John Harshbarger and wife, Samuel Flory and wife, Daniel Miller and wife, Joseph Miller and wife, John Begoon, Sr., and John Yount's wife. Isaac Long became their elder and Daniel Yount faithfully stood by his side in the work of the ministry. During the same year, a house of worship, twenty-five by fifty-five feet, was erected.

" John Hershberger, Sr., was elected to the ministry on May 13, 1841.

" In 1845, Samuel Flory, who was among the charter members, was elected deacon.

" Isaac Long was elected minister on April 13, 1854.

" Christian Hartman and Fredric Miller elected ministers in 1855.

" In 1860, a new house of worship, thirty-five by fifty feet was erected.

" Isaac Long was ordained to the eldership in 1863.

" Henry Beahm was elected minister in 1865.

" John Hershberger was called to the ministry in 1867.

" Samuel Cline, elected minister in 1871.

" Noah Flory was called to the ministry in 1879.

" S. A. Sanger was elected minister in 1880.

"A. B. Miller, elected minister in 1883.

" P. H. Showalter, elected minister in 1883.

" In 1887, a new churchhouse, fifty by seventy feet, was erected.

" In 1889, H. C. Early moved into the congregation.

"I. S. Long, who with Effie Showalter Long are missionaries in India, was elected a minister in 1895.

"William H. Sanger, elected minister in 1899.

"D. B. Wampler was called to the ministry in 1900.

Isaac and Effie Long, Whose Home Was in the Mill Creek Church. They Are Now Supported by the Second District of Virginia as Missionaries in India.

"Samuel Pence was elected minister in 1903.

"C. E. Long was elected to the ministry in 1906.

"Joseph Pence was ordained to the eldership in 1906.

"Through the earnest efforts of some of the early Brethren, this church had a wide mission territory in East Virginia, extending over Green, Albemarle, Madison, and Orange counties. Finding the field too large, it was relieved of much of it by other churches. In 1901, Green County was organized into the Mt. Carmel congregation with about one hundred members. S. A. Sanger was chosen to preside over this, and Elijah Geer elected to the ministry. At the present time this church has about two hundred and fifteen members, one minister, five Sunday schools, and two Christian Workers' meetings.

"Mill Creek church at this time has four hundred and seventy-five members, four houses of worship, six Sunday schools with an enrollment of five hundred and an average attendance of three hundred, and a Sisters' Aid Society of about one hundred and fourteen members. This church has produced a number of earnest ministers. Among them were Isaac Long, Sr., Isaac Long, Jr., John Hershberger, Sr., and John Hershberger, Jr.

"The church is now presided over by Elders H. C. Early and Joseph Pence, assisted by Samuel Petry, P. H. Showalter, Samuel Pence and C. E. Long."

On account of prejudices arising from the position on slavery and war held by the church, the Brethren were a long time effecting an organization in East Virginia. At this time, however, there are seven organizations with many other members in various mission territories.

Bro. Dennis Weimer, an active minister and for many years a zealous worker in the mission field, furnished the following concise history of Midland congregation and adjoining territory:

"In 1881, Bro. Joel Garber, from Rockingham County, Virginia, settled near Midland Station, Fauquier County. Through his influence a number of other families located near him.

"In 1883, by appointment of District Meeting, Elders Isaac Long, S. A. Shaver and Daniel Baker met in the Midland schoolhouse with forty members and effected an organization with Jacob Hedric and Abraham Rickard as ministers. At the same time Solomon Snell was chosen minister and Isaac Long as elder in charge. Joseph Shaver and George Shaver were deacons. Measures were also adopted to erect a house of worship. This was built and dedicated the same year.

"The bounds of the congregation were wide and the increase in membership was rapid. This was mainly by immigration on account of the cheap land at that time. On November 10, 1883, G. F. Tabler, a minister, was received by letter. On April 23, 1884, Dennis Weimer moved into the congregation and Abraham Conner located near Manassas, both of whom were ministers. On September 8, 1886, the members in Madison County, ten in number, were annexed to Midland from Mill Creek church by mutual consent.

"Jacob Hedric and Dennis Weimer were ordained elders on September 12, 1886.

"In 1887, the Valley View meetinghouse, near Nokesville, was built.

"M. G. Early was elected minister on August 24, 1889.

"In 1890, reverses came to the Midland church, mainly from local trouble, and, as a result of this, Jacob Hedric and Dennis Weimer were deposed from the eldership. Now followed some dark days for this church, but in all this the members stood firm in the faith. Abraham Conner was made pastor and S. H. Myers of Timberville elder in charge.

"On March 10, 1892, S. H. Flory was elected a minister and in the same year J. E. Blough and J. F. Britton were received by letter.

"August 27, 1893, J. S. Holsinger, an elder, located near Nokesville and the following year was given oversight of the church. Andrew Chambers was received by letter in June, 1894.

"On December 26, 1894, the membership decided to divide the territory into three congregations and Abraham Conner, M. G. Early and Dennis Weimer were appointed to locate the division line. On March 9, 1895, the committee on lines made their report. At the same meeting, Dennis Weimer, by consent of District Meeting, was given charge of the Orange Mission.

"On August 1, a final meeting of the three churches jointly was held at the Valley View meeting-house, at which they agreed to erect a house of worship for the Cannon Branch church, near Manassas. The meeting was presided over by Elders E. L. Brower and J. P. Zigler; and the churches of Nokesville and Cannon Branch were fully authorized.

"On the following day at Midland, John Holsinger

was continued elder in charge of the Midland church and Andrew Chambers and Dennis Weimer ministers.

"On December 5, 1896, S. F. Sanger was received by letter and on May 22, 1897, was selected elder in charge.

"On July 22, 1899, the mission territory of Madison County was organized into a church by S. F. Sanger and Dennis Weimer. The latter was chosen pastor and Abraham Conner elder in charge. Since the organization, on July 31, 1900, F. Utz was elected minister. The Madison church has at present thirty-two members, and one churchhouse.

"In the Midland church on December 2, 1899, J. M. Cline and G. W. Chambers were elected ministers.

"About the year 1866, the Brethren from Mill Creek began to preach in Orange County, but no systematic work was done. Finally, the territory fell under the care of the Midland church, and, as stated above, Dennis Weimer became minister in charge. Through his efforts and the assistance of the District Mission Board, the work grew until November 21, 1904, when Orange congregation was organized with twenty-seven members. M. G. Early of Nokesville was chosen elder in charge and G. W. Chambers minister. At present the Orange church has twenty-eight members, one Sunday school with an average attendance of eight, one minister, and M. G. Early elder in charge.

"On December 2, 1905, in the Midland church, I. D. Byrd was elected minister. At this time the church has seventy-five members, three ministers, three churchhouses, three Sunday schools, and a Christian Workers' meeting with an average attendance of forty. The church today has a large mission field in Fauquier and Culpeper counties.

"In the original boundary of the Midland congregation there are about five hundred members, sixteen ministers, twenty-five deacons, six organized churches and eight churchhouses, with a number of other building used for services."

Elder M. G. Early.

The Nokesville Congregation.

By M. G. Early.

[M. G. Early, elder in charge of the Nokesville church was born in Rockingham County, Virginia, in March, 1856. He was married to Mattie A. Miller in 1878; united with the church in 1880; elected to the ministry in 1899; and ordained to the eldership in August, 1901.]

"When in March, 1895, the Midland congregation was divided into three districts, the middle portion, or that which embraced the southern portion of Prince William and the northern part of Fauquier counties, was designated the Nokesville congregation. In this territory were seventy-five members, with three ministers and two deacons.

"On the fourth Sunday of July, 1883, Jacob Hedric from Midland conducted the first services here, and from this time on regular services were held. For an account of the principal events as they transpire, the reader is directed to the history of the Midland congregation, of which this was a part.

"At the time of the organization, J. S. Holsinger became elder in charge and continued to serve the church in this capacity until March, 1898, when S. F. Sanger of Manassas was selected as elder. In May, 1900, Abraham Conner took charge of the church as elder. M. G. Early was ordained to the eldership in 1901, and from that time on the church was under his administration.

"D. W. Crist was elected minister in January, 1903.

"G. W. Flory, elected minister in October, 1903.

"J. F. Flory was called to the ministry in 1906.

"Other ministers who served the church are I. N. H. Beahm, 1897 to 1899; J. C. Beahm, from 1897 to 1904; E. B. Lefever, in 1899; M. H. Spicher, 1900 to 1904, and I. A. Miller, since 1899.

"At this writing there are five ministers and six deacons with a membership of one hundred and seventy-six, two houses of worship, two evergreen Sunday schools with an average attendance of thirty, two weekly Christian Workers' meetings, and a Sisters' Aid Society. The church has an active local mission board, which looks after the needs of the mission territory in Prince William, Fauquier and Stafford counties. The congregation furnishes funds in the support of the different places. At this time there are eighteen members in this mission field."

The Manassas Congregation.

By E. E. Blough.

[Bro. E. E. Blough is an active young minister of the Manassas church, but at present is pursuing a course of study at Bridgewater College. He is also a member of the District Mission Board.]

"This was originally a part of the Midland congregation and was organized into a church on July 31, 1895, by Elders E. L. Brower, J. P. Zigler and L. A. Wenger. At that time there were forty-seven members, with Abraham Conner, J. F. Britton and Jerome E. Blough ministers, Thomas Holsinger and J. T. Baker deacons, and John S. Holsinger elder in charge. Cannon Branch churchhouse was built in 1895.

"W. K. Conner was elected minister on November 13, 1897.

"E. E. Blough was elected minister on October 28, 1905.

"Other records previous to the church can be found under history of Midland congregation. At present the membership of the church is seventy-eight, with three ministers and five deacons. Abraham Conner, who is active and systematic in his work, is elder in charge. The congregation owns two churchhouses with three places of preaching, three Sunday schools, one of which is evergreen, and one Christian Workers' meeting. An outlying mission territory is worked in connection with the home appointments of the ministry."

The Fairfax Church.

By Lewis B. Flohr.

[Bro. Flohr is a young minister living in Vienna, Virginia, and was assistant District Sunday-school Secretary. He united with the church on October 15, 1894, in Adams County, Pennsylvania. In January, 1907, he was elected to the ministry by the Fairfax congregation. His wife was Elizabeth Kipe, of Frederick County, Maryland.]

"The Fairfax congregation was organized on February 7, 1903, from the territory belonging to the Manassas church and embraces Fairfax, Alexandria and Loudoun counties. The meetinghouse is located within the embankment of an old fort at Oakton, Fairfax County, in the vicinity where the greater part of the members live.

"The present ministers are Eld. S. A. Sanger, Eld. I. M. Neff, J. M. Kline, B. F. Miller and Louis B. Flohr. There are one hunderd and thirty-six members in the Fairfax church. Four Sunday schools are conducted with an enrollment of two hundred and twenty-four, which makes an average attendance of one hundred and twenty-five. The Christian Workers' meeting has an average attendance of forty and the Sisters' Aid Society has thirty members.

" Eld. S. A. Sanger has charge of the church. Besides the duties incident to his charge, he is zealously engaged in missionary endeavor at various points in East Virginia. He is a native of Rockingham County and was called to the ministry by the Mill Creek church in 1880.

" Elder Albert Hollinger, after serving the Washington City church for six years and where he was ordained elder in 1898, labored some years in the Fairfax church. His home now is at Gettysburg, Pennsylvania.

The first establishment of the church in Augusta County is so closely connected with the Middle River church that a history of this organization tells near the whole story. Therefore a short history of the Middle River Church by Eld. Levi Garber is here given:

[Eld. Levi Garber is senior in office in the Middle River church. He has long been a familiar figure in the councils of the church and has served on important committees. Born August 21, 1828, united with the church August, 1849; elected minister on December 21, 1860, and was ordained to the eldership in 1875.]

Absence of early records makes it difficult to definitely fix early dates. However, it was generally conceded that Abraham Garber was the first minister. According to the inscription on his tombstone, he was was born on November 10, 1760, and died February 16, 1846. He moved from his father's home near Flat Rock in 1790 and settled on Middle River. On the gravestone of his eldest son, John, is the statement that he was born July 14, 1792, and died July 16, 1854. This inscription states that he labored in the ministry for more than thirty years, which would place his election to that office in 1824, about the time the first meetinghouse was erected. Peter Miller was elected minister at the same time. It is known that these brethren were advanced to the eldership together, and that they labored in the church in the most cordial manner.

"In 1823, the first love-feast was held in an upper room of a private dwelling house. At this feast nine members communed. The following year the first churchhouse was erected as stated above.

"Some ten years later Daniel Brower was elected minister and a few years later Jacob Brower and Martin Garber were chosen ministers. Daniel Brower was ordained elder on April 20, 1850. John Miller was elected minister soon after this.

"The membership in Augusta County had now increased to more than five hundred members. However, they were much scattered. This necessitated the erection of two houses of worship. Therefore, in 1854 the Pleasant Valley churchhouse was built and the Barren Ridge meetinghouse was erected two years later. They were located with the view of dividing the Middle River congregation in the near future. In the year 1854, the two elders, John Garber and Peter Miller, died; the former in July and the latter in August. Their service in the church is worthy of special note. Elected at the same time, advanced to the eldership together, lived in the closest Christian fellowship, labored together in the ministry for more than thirty years in harmony, and closed their earthly conflict so near the same time. This is an example worthy of our study as laborers for Christ and His church.

"On March 31, 1855, A. D. Garber and John Brower were elected ministers.

"E. L. Brower and Levi Garber were elected to the ministry on December 21, 1860.

"Daniel Yount was called to the ministry in 1865. In the same year the congregation was divided. John Miller was ordained to the eldership and placed in charge of the Valley congregation, the northern division. John Brower was ordained and placed in charge of the southern division, Barren Ridge congregation. Eld. Martin Garber remained in charge of the old church.

"From 1865 to 1877, Brethren John A. Cline, Joseph M. Cline and John W. Click were called to the ministry.

"In 1875, Levi Garber was ordained elder.

"W. B. Yount was chosen minister on August 21, 1880.

"J. M. Cline was ordained to the eldership on April 23, 1885.

"Daniel C. Flory and A. B. Early were elected ministers on March 24, 1888.

"B. B. Garber was called to the ministry on August 25, 1899.

"D. C. Flory and A. B. Early were ordained elders in 1906.

"George Early was elected to the ministry in 1907.

"The Middle River church has two Sunday schools with an enrollment of one hundred and sixty-five, which make an average attendance of one hundred and thirty-five. There is one Christian Workers' meeting with an average attendance of twenty and a Sisters' Aid Society with thirty members. Two hundred and fifty members live in the home church, with seven ministers and two houses of worship.

"There are twenty-three members, one minister, and one house of worship in the mission territory in Albemarle County."

The Pleasant Valley Congregation.

By Eld. Peter Garber.

[Eld. Peter Garber, son of Elder Levi Garber, represents the sixth generation of the Garber family in Virginia and a direct line of ministers except one generation. He is a direct descendant of John, who was the first minister of the Brethren to settle in northern Virginia. He united with the church, became a minister in 1881, and was ordained elder in 1897. He served the church on the board of visitors for Bridgewater College and is active in the oversight of the Pleasant Valley church.]

"The territory of which the Valley congregation is comprised originally belonged to Middle River church. In 1854, the Pleasant Valley meetinghouse was built with a view of its being made a separate organization. This, however, was not fully effected until 1865. Then John Miller was elder and Abraham Garber assistant minister.

"In 1869, Daniel Miller was elected to the ministry.

"Samuel T. Miller was elected minister in 1874.

"J. W. Cline was called to the ministry in September, 1887.

Elder Peter Garber.

"Daniel Miller was ordained to the eldership in 1881.

"Peter Garber was chosen minister in 1881.

"S. D. Miller was elected minister in 1896.

"Peter Garber was ordained elder in 1897.

"B. F. Miller was elected minister in 1900.

"A. C. Miller was chosen minister in 1902.

"Perry J. Wenger was elected to the ministry in 1903.

"At present the Pleasant Valley congregation has four hundred members, ten ministers, four meeting-houses, four Sunday schools with an enrollment of four hundred and nine scholars and an average attendance of two hundred and seventy, three Christian Workers' meetings with an average attendance of thirty, and a Sisters' Aid Society with thirty-one members.

"In the mission field in Albemarle County, there are thirty-five members, one minister, one church-house with three meetings per month, and three Sunday schools.

"At the present time, this church is presided over by Elders Daniel Miller, Peter Garber and S. D. Miller, and, in addition to the ministry, have an active corps of deacons. None of the ministers elected since the organization have died. Moreover, A. D. Garber, who was elected on March 31, 1855, is the oldest in office in the State. Bro. Garber is yet hale and hearty."

The Barren Ridge Church.

By N. W. Coffman.

[Bro. Coffman is an active minister and school-teacher living in the Barren Ridge church. His life promises to be a very useful one for the Lord.]

"Barren Ridge organization was formed in 1865 from a part of the territory belonging to Middle River. Nine years prior to this, a meetinghouse was erected at this point with the above named object in view. At the time of the organization, John Brower was ordained to the eldership and placed in charge of the new church. After this, Elder Martin Garber moved into the Barren Ridge church, when he and Eld. Brower jointly presided over the church until 1884, when Samuel Driver and E. L. Brower were advanced to the eldership. Elders Driver and Brower presided jointly until the death of the latter in 1897. From that time Eld. Driver had sole charge until the ordination of Eld. George A. Phillips in 1904. Eld. Phillips now has the oversight of the church.

"The following Brethren were elected to the ministry in the Barren Ridge church:

"H. C. Early, about 1879 or 1880.

"J. C. Garber, on August 6, 1884.

"C. M. Driver and N. Walter Coffman, on August 12, 1898.

"H. L. Alley, on February 2, 1907.

"Four houses of worship have been erected, as follows: Barren Ridge second house in 1898, Jarman's Gap in 1897, and Blue Ridge Chapel in 1907.

"The present membership is about three hundred with the following ministers: Samuel Driver, George Phillips, J. C. Garber, N. Walter Coffman and H. L. Alley (at school). The first three named are ordained elders. In the home church there are eight regular appointments at three different points, four Sunday schools, one of which is evergreen, two Christian Workers' meetings, and one Sisters' Aid Society with fifteen members.

"The mission territory embraces Basic City and part of Albemarle County, which has a membership of thirty-five or forty.

"The increase in the membership of the Barren Ridge church during the year 1907 was fifty-three by baptism and five restored."

Eld. Samuel Driver has long been prominent in the affairs of the church in Virginia. He was born April 22, 1834; united with the church in 1867 and was elected to the ministry two years later at the private home of Bro. Jacob Zigler, near Churchville, Augusta County. The services were conducted by Elders Martin Miller and Daniel Thomas of Beaver Creek. In 1875, Bro. Driver moved to Barren Ridge congregation, where he was ordained elder in 1884. In 1904, he, at his own request, was relieved from the oversight of the church. In his younger days, he was closely identified with Bridgewater College. He died Jan. 18, 1908.

The Mt. Vernon Church.

By E. D. Kendig and S. I. Flory.

[Brethren Kendig and Flory are both active ministers in the Mt. Vernon church. The former, who served for a number of years on the District Mission Board, is elder in charge of the Staunton City church and associate in the supervision of the Mt. Vernon congregation. The latter is an enthusiastic missionary worker and is also Sunday-school Secretary of the Second District of Virginia.]

"In the year 1866, Eld. James R. Gish spent the summer preaching in what is now known as the Mt. Vernon congregation. When he left, there were about sixty members. From this time monthly meetings were held by Brethren from Barren Ridge church until 1870, when Bro. Gish came back again. This

James R. and Barbara Gish.

time he preached, canvassed the territory and built a house of worship. A church was then organized with E. D. Kendig minister. Samuel Forrer and John Forrer were chosen later. Other ministers were elected as follows:

"J. R. Kendig, on August 27, 1883.

"George B. Flory, elected in 1885.

"Samuel I. Flory and Justus H. Cline, on September 3, 1898.

"The Mt. Vernon church has a large mission territory extending over Amherst, Rockbridge and Nelson counties. From this territory the Buena Vista church was organized in 1905, which at this time has eighty-four members, one minister, two houses of worship, two Sunday schools with an enrollment of eighty scholars, and a Christian Workers' meeting.

"In the remaining mission field there are sixty-four members in Amherst, fifty-nine in Rockbridge, and twenty-five in Nelson. In the Mt. Vernon church there are ninety-six members with five ministers, four churchhouses with ten appointments per month, four Sunday schools, one Christian Workers' meeting, and one Sisters' Aid Society."

The Staunton Church.

Various individual efforts were made to establish a church in Staunton by the ministry of the adjacent churches during the years from 1890 to 1895. Chief among these were Elders Levi A. Wenger, Samuel Driver, Enoch L. Brower and E. D. Kendig. From this time, the work received the assistance of the District Mission Board and Eld. D. C. Flory, assisted by Sister Sauble, was put in charge of the work.

On May 20, 1898, a church was organized with thirty-nine members. Bro. Levi A. Wenger was chosen elder in charge and Bro. J. C. Garber pastor.

On October 6, 1906, under the supervision of Eld. E. D. Kendig, Eld. Noah Fisher took charge of the work as pastor. Under his ministration, the work has prospered. There are now seventy-five members, a Sunday school with an average of seventy-five scholars, one Christian Workers' meeting and a Sisters' Aid Society.

In addition to the mission fields mentioned in connection with the local churches there is a wide mission territory which falls directly under the care of the District Mission Board, which is noticed more in detail in the succeeding chapter.

CHAPTER X.

The Division of the First District of Virginia—Formation of New Local Organizations.

For a number of years many Brethren thought the interests of the church would be better served by a closer organization of our State Districts. Also, it was apparent that many local churches had grown too large to utilize all the forces to the best advantage in the Master's cause.

In time this led first to a division, in 1910, of the Second District into three separate Districts and a division of a number of the large local churches into smaller organizations; a full account of which is found in a succeeding chapter. Also, in 1913, the First District was divided into two separate Districts, a full statement of which is here given by Eld. P. S. Miller, a member of the committee appointed by the District Meeting of the First District:

"The District Meetings were held annually, but not so generally attended as it was felt they should be, because of the territory being very large, so that many of the members could not conveniently attend. It was therefore asked, through a query to District Meeting of 1910, that the District be divided by three. After a full discussion the paper was favored, and placed into the hands of a committee of five, whose duty it was to locate the most suitable lines for dividing the

District into three Districts, and to report to the next District Meeting. The committee's report was received by the District Meeting of 1911 and answered as follows: 'Deferred one year, to come before District Meeting of 1912 for general discussion, and to be decided by a two-thirds vote of both delegates and elders present.' After a full discussion of the question in the 1912 District Meeting, the following was given as the answer by the District: 'There being a very manifest difference of sentiment relative to proposed division lines, it was decided to divide the First District of Virginia into two parts as follows: The territory now known as the Roanoke and Botetourt sub-divisions to comprise one District, to be known as the First District of Virginia, and the territory now known as Floyd and Franklin sub-divisions to comprise one District, to be known as the Southern District of Virginia.' In consideration of the complete harmony in all District work, there was no desire to divide, other than with the view of the need of expansion, and doing the greatest good to the greatest number of people, therefore, the following as a memorial was passed:

" 'Memorial.

" 'Inasmuch as the First District of Virginia, assembled in District Council at Johnsville church, April 19, 1912, decided to separate into two divisions, to be known as the Southern District of Virginia, and the First District of Virginia, respectively, be it

" 'Resolved, That said division is the outgrowth of a demand for greater expansion in Christian endeavor for doing the greatest good to the greatest number, and for the training and encouraging of our young brethren and sisters to become more active in carrying forward the Sunday-school, missionary, educational and evangelistic work of our large territory; be it

"'Resolved, further, That, while a specific line has been established, separating our field of service and responsibility, we still continue, as formerly, harmoniously united in faith and practice, in purity of living, and in mutual bonds of Christian love and fellowship: and that the nearness of our respective fields of labor may afford us opportunity to meet with each other from time to time in worship and in praise to him who hath directed in this movement.' The Annual Meeting was asked to recognize the division in the following manner:

"'To the Annual Meeting of 1912.

"'The First District of Virginia, with a membership of fully four thousand one hundred and with seventy elders, and forty-three organized churches, embracing a very large territory, including portions of Virginia, West Virginia, and North Carolina, has, for the sake of convenience, and in order to do more efficient District work, agreed at its last District Meeting, held April 19, 1912, to divide into two Districts, subject to the approval of the Annual Meeting. The said division to go into effect fully about the beginning of the year 1913. The most northerly division has a membership of fully two thousand one hundred and retains the name, First District of Virginia. The most southern division has a membership of fully two thousand and is to be known as the Southern District of Virginia.' This was granted and the division fully effected.

"THE PRESENT FIRST DISTRICT.

"The present First District of Virginia has a membership of nearly two thousand two hundred. The territory is very large, embracing the counties of Roanoke, Botetourt, Bedford, Craig, and a part of Montgomery in Virginia, and Monroe, Mercer, Fayette, Raleigh, Greenbriar, and several other counties and parts of counties in West Virginia. The District is well organized for doing efficient and aggressive work. It has its Mission Board, of five members, its Temperance Committee of three members, its Program Committee of three members, its Sunday-school Secretary and two assistant secretaries, its Mission Secretary, its Treasurer, etc. In the District are twenty-two organized congregations with a combined ministry of about fifty, thirty of whom are ordained elders.

"The District holds, annually, a District Meeting, a Missionary Meeting, a Sunday-school Institute, a Ministerial Meeting, a Temperance Meeting, a Peace Meeting, etc. At Daleville College is held annually a Bible Institute, which is of great benefit and help to the ministers and other members of the District. Further reference to Daleville College and its workings will be found on another page."

In a previous chapter a brief mention was made of

a number of the churches constituting the original First District of Virginia. A more detailed account of these churches is here given. In some instances they were written by members of the committee appointed by District Meeting, while in others they were prepared by writers whose names are seen therewith. Slight repetitions may appear in a few cases. In the main the write-up appears as given by the respective authors.

The Peter's Creek Church.

By C. E. Eller.

"The Peter's Creek church is located in Roanoke County, six miles northwest of the city of Roanoke. The territory is twenty miles in extent. Roanoke River traverses it, and most of the membership lives on the north side of this stream. Three churchhouses are owned by the congregation. Two, Oak Grove and Poage's Chapel, are situated on the south side and one, Peter's Creek, on the north side of Roanoke River. The last-named house was built in 1845, and here in 1869 the Annual Meeting was held. The other houses were built at a much later date. Around each churchhouse members live who are interested in the work of the church and the study of the Scriptures. For a number of years Sunday-school work has been maintained, the three schools having an average attendance of one hundred and twenty-five. Two of them continue throughout the entire year. We have already witnessed results from the work, a number of Sunday-school scholars having united with the church and are being trained for Christian service. The entire offerings of all the schools are used for mission work at home and abroad.

"The church is under the care of Elders C. E. Eller, J. H. Garst, N. H. Garst, and D. C. Naff, assisted in the ministry by C. F. Webster, Levi Garst, J. H. Weimer, J. S. Showalter, and D. W. Roberts. These, with nine deacons, constitute the official board. Aside from the regular services at the three churches mission work is conducted at different points."

Brother and Sister Shaver, Copper Hill, Va.

The Copper Hill Church.

By N. P. Weimer.

"This church, a part of Peter's Creek, was organized in 1874 with twelve members. Two of these, John Shaver and Isaac Weimer, were deacons. There was no house of worship, but the cause prospered. J. H. Shaver was elected minister in 1888 and a church was built in 1892. N. P. Weimer was chosen minister in 1899, and in 1902 D. H. Shaver and J. H. Weimer were called to the ministry. C. E. Eller was chosen elder in 1905, at which time there were one hundred and ten members, of whom three were ministers and eight were deacons.

"In 1911 the three ministers were ordained elders, and C. H. Williams, G. T. Stump, and Eugene King were chosen ministers. At the present there are two hundred and ten members. Preaching services are held at seven places, and two Sunday schools are doing active work. Bro. John Shaver, one of the charter members, is actively in service for the Master.

The Johnsville Church.

[Eld. Jacob Grisso, who gave the very interesting history of the Johnsville church, has since died, which left the church without a resident elder, and at the present time there is no resident minister. Eld. John H. Garst, of Salem, Virginia, is elder in charge, and the preaching is done by him and the other ministers of the Peter's Creek church mainly. In addition to the regular services, they have Sunday school, and also a series of meetings each year. The total membership is from seventy-five to eighty-five.]

DIVISION OF FIRST DISTRICT

The Chestnut Grove Church.

By Virgie McAvoy.

[Sister McAvoy is a student of Bridgewater College and is an active church worker. The three following accounts were prepared by her at the request of the committee appointed by District Meeting.]

" The Chestnut Grove church is in Fayette County, West Virginia. Daniel Thomas, from the Valley of Virginia, preached here first in the year 1858. A few years later the church was organized with ten members, and Bro. J. S. Flory was elected minister.

" Now there are one hundred and seventy-five members, six ministers and two houses of worship, the Chestnut Grove and Pleasant View, respectively. Besides preaching at these two houses, seven other preaching points are filled regularly by the ministers of this church. Of these mission points, two, Kaymoor and Browns, are quite near Pleasant View church, and there is preaching at both every month. At Pack's Branch the Brethren hold forth interest in the church and have eight members. Also at Clifty a small churchhouse has been bought and the work seems to be in a thriving condition. There are five members at this place. Of the other mission points, there are eight members at Prince, eighteen at Shrewsbury, and six at Red House Shoals."

The Charleston Church.

" The Charleston church is in South Charleston, Kanawha County, West Virginia. The Brethren from the Valley of Virginia began preaching here first, Jacob Thomas being chief among them. In

1885 the church was organized, with fifteen members. At present the work has gone down considerably and at a recent District Meeting it was given into the hands of the District Mission Board."

THE CRAB ORCHARD CHURCH.

"The Crab Orchard church is in Raleigh County, West Virginia. The Brethren from Franklin and Floyd Counties began preaching in this community about the year 1858, Christian Bowman being chief among them. The church was organized in 1868 or 1869, with twelve members. At present there are fifty-six members, with two ministers and one house of worship."

SPRUCE RUN CHURCH, MONROE COUNTY, WEST VIRGINIA.

By Lena Fleishman.

"The first members baptized here were Joel Riffle and wife, Abraham Fleishman and wife and two others, in the year 1829 or 1830. Later a church was organized (the date not known), with Samuel Hutchison (father of G. W. and A. Hutchison) as elder, with about fifteen members. Elijah P. and Andrew L. Fleischman and A. Hutchison were elected to the ministry, and later ordained elders. James M. Hutchison and Geo. W. Hutchison were chosen to the ministry.

"The church prospered and in 1877 the Spruce Run churchhouse was built. At this time there were about sixty members of whom four were ministers. However, division in 1883 reduced this number to about fifteen. From this the church grew, until in 1890 there were about fifty members.

"The church is now in charge of Elders G. W. Hutchison and Alex. Evens. Through death and other causes some members have been lost, making the present membership thirty-six. The church is in good working condition now. Services are held at five preaching points and one Sunday school, with forty scholars enrolled, is working with good results."

The Botetourt church, of which mention is made in a preceding chapter, was one of the largest in the entire Brotherhood until divided into the three new organizations. The following account of these new churches is furnished by the committee appointed by the District:

The Cloverdale Church.

"This is one of the three congregations that formerly made up the Botetourt church. Its organization went into effect with the beginning of 1913. Eld. Samuel Crumpacker, Eld. J. A. Dove, Eld. E. C. Crumpacker, and John S. Crumpacker are the ministers who were in the organization. They have four churchhouses in this territory, the one at Cloverdale being a new brick house built and dedicated in 1913, besides a number of preaching points in other sections of the congregational territory. A prosperous Sunday school is in progress the entire year at the Cloverdale house."

The Daleville Church.

"This congregation is a child of the old Botetourt church, and occupies the territory where the old Valley church was built many years ago. It was organized January, 1913, with about two hundred members. Eld. T. C. Denton, Eld. D. N. Eller, Eld. J. W. Ikenberry, Eld. J. T. Layman, Eld. T. S. Moherman, C. S. Ikenberry, L. C. Coffman, J. M. Henry and G. O. Reed were the ministerial staff. Bro. Denton died before the end of the year.

"Daleville College is located in this congregation."

THE TROUTVILLE CHURCH.

"The Troutville congregation came into existence by the dividing of the Botetourt church into three separate churches January 1, 1913.

"This church was organized with about two hundred and twenty-five members. Eld. Jonas Graybill, Eld. George H. Graybill, D. Price Hylton, and C. D. Reed constituted the ministerial force. The first-named was chosen as elder in charge. Eld. C. D. Hylton and family moved into this congregation during the year.

"The directory for 1914 shows five ministers and seven deacons, eleven monthly preaching appointments, six church councils for the year, a quarterly mission circle, three evergreen Sunday schools, and a Christian Workers' Band.

"This church, in connection with Daleville and Cloverdale churches, is supporting Brother and Sister Ross at Vyara on the Indian mission field."

THE SOUTHERN DISTRICT.

The Southern District of Virginia formerly was a part of the original First District. As its name indicates, it embraces the most southerly portion of the State and a large part of North Carolina. The greater activity of the church, however, is in Franklin and Floyd Counties. But the workers are reaching out to other counties of the State and into the seventeen counties of the old North State, in which a few churches have already been established.

The work of the District is well organized in the different lines of church work. The Minutes of the District Meeting show a healthy growth. The membership at the present time is over two thousand. Brethren L. A. Bowman and Michael Reed were appointed by the District to present the various churches constituting it to the reader. Below is seen what is from their pen and that of others they have selected:

The Franklin Church.

By L. A. Bowman.

[Eld. L. A. Bowman, son of Eld. Isaac, was born February 13, 1875. He united with the church in December, 1891. He was married to Cora Anna Bowman, daughter of Eld. George, March 29, 1894. He was chosen minister June 13, 1903, and ordained elder August 11, 1911. He has engaged in evangelistic work and served his District on many important committees, and on Standing Committee at Annual Meeting. His life promises much usefulness.]

" In 1870 a decision was passed, asking for a division of the territory of the Franklin church into three separate organizations. Accordingly the division was made, and two houses of worship, Antioch and Bethlehem, were built in 1873. In 1910 a church was built in the southern part of the county, where a small body of members (about twenty-five) had previously been organized into a working body, and is known as Snow Creek church. These four churches have a membership of about eight hundred, including twenty-six ministers, sixteen of whom are elders. Regular preaching services are held at thirty-four different places. The ministry of Franklin County has made great sacrifices in traveling over

Eld. L. A. Bowman.

hills and valleys to preach the Word. Much of the traveling has been done on horseback, occupying two and three days to reach the appointments and return. They are now supplying the preaching at Spray, North Carolina, at Schoolfield, near Danville, at two points in Henry County, and one point in Pittsylvania County. A number of the ministers have engaged in evangelistic work, holding series of meetings at different preaching points in this and the adjoining counties of Floyd, Henry, Pittsylvania, Roanoke, Patrick and also in North Carolina. The names

Eld. Henry Ikenberry and Wife.

of Naff, Flora, Bowman, Peters, and Ikenberry have been prominent in the history of the church in Franklin County.

"The church in Franklin County owns eight houses of worship, three of them having been built in the last six years. Six Sunday schools are conducted by the Sunday-school workers, with an enrollment of four hundred and forty-six and an average attendance of two hundred and eighty-nine. Sister Rebecca Skeggs Wampler, missionary to China, is supported by the Sunday schools of the First and Southern Districts. Bro. E. E. Bowman, the Secretary of the Southern District, is alive in the great Sunday-school movement. Missionary sentiment is growing.

"The Brick church has a membership of a little more than two hundred. Of the elders of this congregation since the division of territory the following have gone to their reward: Abram Barnhart, Wm. Robinson, and Lee Angle. The elders at present are: Henry Ikenberry, R. L. Peters, Geo. B. Flora, and J. W. Barnhart. These are ably assisted in the ministry by Brethren G. A. Barnhart, H. W. Peters, and J. B. Peters.

"The Bethlehem church has a membership of about three hundred and sixty. Abram Naff was elder at the time of organization in 1870. He and his son, Eld. Joel Naff, have since gone to enjoy the fruits of their labors. The present eldership is composed of Brethren D. A. Naff, Daniel Bowman, Daniel Peters, George Bowman, B. T. Naff, J. T. Cummings, Preston Peters, and L. A. Bowman. These, with Brethren A. S. Montgomery, N. C. Peters, E. E. Bowman, and C. B. Boone, constitute the ministerial force. The ministry is ably assisted by a number of faithful deacons in looking after the affairs and needs of the church.

"In the Antioch church there are about two hundred and ten members. The elders, since its organization in 1870, are: Jeremiah Barnhart (deceased), Riley Flora, Isaac Bowman, S. M. Ikenberry, and L. E. Brubaker. The last four named are active at present and are assisted in the ministry by the earnest labors of Brethren Joseph Bowman, J. A. Naff, and Zion E. Mitchell. All of the ministers in this congregation have held series of meetings, except Eld. Isaac Bowman. He has never consented to conduct a meeting of this kind, but he has three sons in the ministry and two in the deacon's office.

"Mt. Hermon church, in Henry County, has about twenty-five members. It is the outgrowth of the labors of the Franklin churches. Eld. Riley Flora, of Franklin County, is in charge. In caring for the church he is assisted by two deacons. This congregation has a churchhouse of its own.

"Snow Creek church has about twenty-five members, including Bro. J. O. Boone, a resident minister. He is assisted in the ministry by the ministers of the Bethlehem congregation, Eld. D. A. Naff being elder in charge.

"Walkers Well church, in Pittsylvania County, is the result of the labors of the Franklin brethren. This church also has about twenty-five members, and is under the care of Eld. L. A. Bowman, of Franklin County.

"The Swan Creek church, in Halifax County, is under the care of Eld. W. I. Hall, a resident minister. This church is isolated from the other churches and is therefore hindered from mingling with those of like precious faith."

Pleasant Valley Congregation, Floyd County.

By R. T. Akers.

[Eld. R. T. Akers was born in Floyd County, Virginia, in 1858. He received such education as the common schools and academies of the country would afford. He taught school for five years, studied medicine, and began its practice in 1882. He married Lucy Reed November 23 of the same year, and united with the church in January, 1884. He was elected minister in 1894 and was ordained elder in 1904.

His duties as physician prevented a wider field of activity in the church, although he served for a time on the District Mission Board. He was always active in Sunday-school work.]

"In the year 1860 the Pleasant Valley church was organized from the then Brick church, but now Topeco, and comprised all the territory north and west of Wills Ridge. The war coming up between the States, building a house of worship was delayed until about the year 1868, when a rude framed building, forty by sixty feet, was constructed (this has since been taken down and a new building erected). As the territory on the north and west was unlimited, and as there were quite a number of members in the now Red Oak Grove congregation, a churchhouse was built about the year 1870 and an organization effected. There are to my knowledge no data as to the number of members in those days.

"About the year 1895 Mount Jackson church, in Montgomery County, was cut off from this congregation, with about forty members.

"In the year 1896 White Rock church was built

and a few years later the Brethren were organized with about one hundred and ten members.

"In the year 1899 Beaver Creek church was built, and the succeeding year an organization with ninety-six members was effected.

"Thus four congregations have been organized from Pleasant Valley, with an approximate membership of two hundred and seventy-five.

"The congregation now numbers one hundred and forty (estimated) members, with two churchhouses with a fourth interest in a union house; four ministers (all elders) and six deacons.

"The following parties have been elected to the ministry in this congregation (organized with Andrew Reed, elder, Cornelius Reed and Isaac Reed, ministers): Thomas Reed, Humphry Duncan, Noah R. Booth, Griffeth D. Reed, Henry Reed, S. P. Reed, Noah Reed, Wyatt Reed, R. T. Akers, Isaac A. Reed, and Michael Reed.

"The following ministers have been ordained to the eldership: Isaac Reed, Humphry Duncan, Noah R. Booth, Griffeth D. Reed, S. P. Reed, Wyatt Reed, R. T. Akers and Michael Reed."

Red Oak Grove Church.

By Eld. Michael Reed.

"This church was organized about 1870, Eld. Christian Bowman being in charge. It was formerly a part of Pleasant Valley congregation. At the time of its formation as a distinct organization there were twenty-five members, while at the present time there are about one hundred. The following elders, in the order given, have had care of the church since Christian Bowman: H. P. Hylton, John B. Naff, and W. H. Naff. The present ministers are W. H. Naff, M. I. Dickerson, S. G. Spangler, J. F. Keith, Asa Bowman, C. E. Williams, and W. F. Vest.

Eld. Michael Reed.

[Eld. Michael Reed, son of A. J. Reed, was born Dec. 23, 1868. He united with the church on Oct. 15, 1887. He taught school for six years. On March 30, 1893, he was united in marriage with Mollie E. Akers. He was called to the ministry Aug. 17, 1901, and ordained elder September, 1909.]

"The Beaver Creek Church was organized in 1900, with about one hundred members. While a number have united with the church, the loss of members going into other fields of labor leaves the membership about the same. Brethren H. R. Booth,

Henry Reed (died Sept. 26), J. F. Mannon, Jesse Booth, Richard Reed, and N. S. Mannon serve the church in the ministry.

"BURKS FORK CHURCH was organized in 1892 with sixty members. At present there are eighty. Eld. J. B. Hylton was put in charge of the new organization, with Joel Weddle assisting him in the ministry. The present ministers are A. J. Weddle, Austin Hylton and S. E. Hylton.

"THE MT. JACKSON CHURCH, in Montgomery County, was formerly a part of the Pleasant Valley congregation. It was organized about 1890 with forty members. This membership, however, has been reduced by adverse conditions. L. C. Scaggs, Preston Duncan and A. J. Akers form the ministerial corps.

"THE WHITE ROCK CHURCH also was a part of Pleasant Valley. It was organized in 1896 with about one hundred members, the membership at this time being about the same. G. W. Akers and Wallace Akers are the ministers.

"THE PLEASANT HILL CHURCH was organized in 1897. At this time there are ninety-five members, but no resident minister. Eld. A. N. Hylton has charge of the church.

"THE TOPECO CHURCH has one hundred and forty-five members at present, with A. Harman, A. N. Hylton, L. M. Weddle, G. W. Hylton and W. L. Jennings as ministers."

The Southern District of Virginia has a number of faithful workers for the Master. An entire list of this would grow lengthy. However, a few sketches are given below.

BIOGRAPHICAL.

ELD. HENRY IKENBERRY was born in Franklin County, Virginia, September 16, 1842, united with the Church of the Brethren April, 1862, and was united in marriage to Catharine Frances Hirt October 10, 1865. He was elected to the ministry in May, 1873, and ordained to the eldership August 29, 1885. He is at present senior elder of the Brick church. He has also served the Mt. Hermon church in Henry Country as elder for a number of years, as well as the Walkers Well congregation, Pittsylvania County. He has done much traveling and preaching in adjoining counties, served on Standing Committee one time and twice as Reading Clerk of District Meeting. Three of his sons—L. D. of North Manchester, Indiana, J. W. and C. S. of Daleville, Virginia--are ministers of the Church of the Brethren, and one son is in the deacon's office. Of his two sons-in-law, one is a deacon and the other is a minister. All the children, eight in number, are members of the Church of the Brethren.

ELD. RILEY FLORA is an able preacher and has given much of his time to the ministry. He is a wise and efficient elder, holding the church together when different views are agitated. He is at present elder in charge of the Antioch congregation and also the Mt. Hermon congregation. He is conservative in his views and always ready to defend the doctrines of the church.

ELD. JOEL NAFF was born May 20, 1833, near Boone Mill, Virginia. He was married to Mary E.

Boon in May, 1865, elected to the ministry in 1863 or 1864, and ordained to the full ministry about 1873. While his education was limited, his natural gifts were abundant. He was one of the most powerful preachers that the Southern District of Virginia has ever produced. Although his labors were highly appreciated he was called to his reward in November, 1885.

DANIEL A. NAFF, brother of Joel and son of Eld. Abram, was born June 27, 1848. Was married to Hannah Bowman July 22, 1869, elected to the ministry June 22, 1872, advanced to the second degree January 23, 1875, and ordained to the eldership November 27, 1886. He is at present elder in charge of the Bethlehem congregation (which is the largest in Southern District), is continually being called on to preach funerals and solemnize marriages, has served his District on numbers of important committees, as moderator of District Meeting, and has served his District three times on Standing Committee.

CHAPTER XI.

Division of the Second District into Three State Districts —the Newly-Formed Districts—New Local Organizations Formed.

For a number of years there was a growing feeling among many of the leading workers of the Second District of Virginia that this District should be divided into two or more State Districts. The membership in nearly every church had increased. New organizations were formed in the territory under the supervision of the District Mission Board. It was evident better work could be done by a division of the forces. This increased membership and delegates representing the local churches made District Meeting a burden except in the stronger churches.

In the Shenandoah Valley there were many members of the church. Especially was this true in Rockingham County, where at the present time there is the strongest membership of the Church of the Brethren to be found anywhere. East of the Blue Ridge Mountains, for reasons mentioned in preceding chapters, there were few strong churches. Here, too, was a large territory under the care of the Mission Board. It can easily be seen that it was a difficult matter to divide the District in a satisfactory way. The first committee appointed by District Meeting failed to recommend a division line. But in all this time the sentiment became more and more favorable to dividing the District.

In 1907 the Fairfax church petitioned the District Meeting in the following manner:

"1st. That a division of the District be effected by the creation of a new District east of the Blue Ridge.

"2nd. That a committee of five be appointed, two from east of the Blue Ridge and three from west of the Blue Ridge, to report to the District Meeting of 1908 the bounds of such new District, together with a plan whereby the territory in the new District will retain its interest in mission funds, college, Old Folks' home, Orphanage, etc., as at present.

"3rd. That the final action of the District Meeting shall be ratified by a majority of the organized churches embraced in the new District before becoming effective.

"Answer.—Petition granted, and J. M. Kagey, D. H. Zigler, E. D. Kendig, S. A. Sanger and M. G. Early were appointed as the committee."

After a careful investigation the committee made the following report to the District Meeting of 1908:

Report of Committee.

Your committee after taking under advisement the creation of a new State District in East Virginia, do not think that the interests of the church can be best served by such organization without a further division of our State District being effected. Therefore we would recommend that the Second District of Virginia be divided into three districts as follows:

(1) That the territory east of the Blue Ridge Mountain and lying north of the James River be designated the Eastern District of Virginia.

(2) That the Shenandoah Valley and the adjacent territory west of the Blue Ridge be divided into two State

Districts, the southern portion of which shall be known as the Second District of Virginia, and the northern portion shall be known as the Northern District of Virginia. That the line making the division of the two last-named districts shall correspond with the present established line running east and west and leaving Cooks Creek and Mill Creek to the north, and Beaver Creek, Bridgewater and Pleasant Valley to the south. Any territory not included in the above districts shall be termed mission territory.

(3) That the interests of the Old Folks' Home, Orphans' Home, and Bridgewater College, and the missionary endeavor of the various congregations shall not be affected by the establishment of the aforesaid division lines; and that the general mission work of the three districts shall be placed under the supervision of a Church Erection and Missionary Committee composed of nine members, three of whom shall be appointed under the provision made by the District Meetings of each of the three districts named above.

(4) That this report be spread upon the minutes for one year, and on its final passage by District Meeting it shall be ratified by churches representing a majority of the membership of each of the newly-formed districts.

J. M. Kagey, D. H. Zigler, S. A. Senger, M. G. Early, E. D. Kendig, Committee.

This report was accepted and spread on the Minutes for final action of the District Meeting of 1909. The report was adopted by this meeting and ratified by the local churches by practically unanimous vote.

The District Meeting of 1910 convened under most unusual circumstances. The District, by the plan of division, was divided into three Districts, but there remained unfinished business. A portion of this was the report of the vote of the churches on division. This situation was relieved by a recommendation by Standing Committee, which was adopted by the open conference, which reads as follows:

"Because of the unusual conditions under which the present District Meeting is convened, it is the sense of the Standing Committee that it is the duty of the present representation of the respective churches,

" (1) To transact all unfinished business of the Second District of Virginia.

" (2) That it is their privilege, on the final acceptance of the report of the formation of the three State Districts, to separately organize, according to the division plan, their respective Districts they represent."

This gave rise to the most unusual occurrence of four District Meetings being held at one place without the final adjournment of the delegate body of either until all of the meetings had completed their work. Each of the newly-formed Districts was represented by delegate on Standing Committee at Annual Meeting the same year.

Thus the story of the creation of the newly-formed Districts is briefly told. The work of the respective Districts continues according to the plan of division, except the mission work, which is conducted by a committee in each District instead of a joint board. An account of the various activities is given separately.

THE SECOND DISTRICT OF VIRGINIA.

The more southerly part of the old Second District, west of the Blue Ridge Mountains, is embraced in the present Second District, as shown in the accompanying map. It has a membership of about three thousand eight hundred and is well organized for work. Bridgewater College, owned jointly with other Districts, is located within its bounds. The Sunday-school work is under the supervision of a District Secretary, who is given two assistants. The record shows forty-one schools in the District, the greater part of which run throughout the year. The District Mission Board is composed of five members and is doing aggressive work. An account of the local churches is given by writers appointed at District Meeting, and whose names appear in connection with their writing.

The Bridgewater Church.

By J. S. Flory.

" The Bridgewater congregation was organized in 1907 from territory formerly belonging to the Cooks Creek church. The new organization began with a membership of two hundred and one, with Emanuel Long as elder and a corps of four other ministers and ten deacons.

" In 1908 a portion of the Beaver Creek congregation was added to the Bridgewater church. This brought an addition of sixty-eight members, including Eld. Hiram G. Miller, who has, since that time, been the active elder of this church.

" The present force of resident ministers consists of three elders, E. Long, H. G. Miller, and S. N. McCann; three ministers in the second degree, S. L. Bowman, J. S. Flory, and O. S. Miller; and D. H. Hoover in the first degree. Besides these there is a considerable number of student ministers in the college, who have their membership temporarily in the

Bridgewater church. During the session of 1913-14 there were seventeen of these.

"The deacon body is as follows: John S. Garber, J. A. Wenger, S. C. Smucker, D. S. Thomas, A. M. Miller, Marshall Garst, J. R. Click, S. B. Miller, John T. Miller, C. C. Wright, S. W. Long, D. C. Craun, W. N. Gordon.

"The congregation has three preaching places: the church on the Warm Springs pike, just out of town, the chapel at the college, and Stemphley Chapel at Stemphleytown. There is preaching each Sunday morning at the church, and each Sunday evening during the school session at the college; at Stemphley Chapel twice a month. A Sunday school is also maintained at each place. The total Sunday-school enrollment of the congregation is about four hundred and fifty.

"The congregation is building a commodious churchhouse at the college. Numerous Sunday-school rooms are being provided, and it will be equipped with modern conveniences so as to meet present day needs. It is expected to be ready for occupancy about January 1, 1915.

"The mission territory of the Bridgewater church is in West Virginia. A good churchhouse has been erected at North Fork in Pendleton County, and here a body of members, about fifty in number, has been secured. They have two ministers and two deacons and maintain a Sunday school.

"Another mission field, lying further west and chiefly in Pocahontas County, is worked jointly by the Beaver Creek and the Bridgewater congregations."

Beaver Creek Church.

"The division of the Beaver Creek congregation in 1908, which placed Eld. H. G. Miller in the Bridgewater church, left Abram S. Thomas as elder of Beaver Creek. The next year Jacob D. Glick was ordained to the full ministry, and Ernest B. Coffman was added to the ministerial force in 1914 by election.

"In 1912 this congregation built a new churchhouse at Mt. Bethel. M. J. Cline has been put in immediate charge of this work, and, with the able assistance of Sister Mae Albright, is doing an excellent work here. During this same year a strip of territory containing thirty-two members was added to the Beaver Creek church from the Cooks Creek territory.

"A new church was erected at Montezuma in 1913. This is provided with Sunday-school rooms, and is modern in structure.

"The congregation has four churchhouses, and a Sunday school at each. The membership is about four hundred.

"The territory of the Valley Bethel congregation was divided in 1914, the southern part being organized into the Chimney Run church. The parent organization has three ministers: A. A. Miller, elder, and C. B. Gibbs and A. H. Miller in the second degree. There are also three deacons. This congregation has four preaching points, with five appointments a month, and maintains one Sunday school and one Christian Workers' Meeting.

" Eld. A. A. Miller also has the oversight of the Chimney Run congregation, and is assisted by P. E. Ginger, in the ministry, and five deacons. They have two preaching places, with two appointments a month at each, and one Sunday school, with teachers' meeting, home department, and cradle roll.

" Crummets Run has an official body, consisting of three ministers and five deacons. George Puffenbarger is elder. They have two preaching places and maintain a Sunday school at each. The membership is about two hundred.

" At Thorny Bottom Josiah Beverage is elder in charge. He is assisted in the ministry by William Beverage. One Sunday school is in successful operation. They have about thirty-five members.

" The Hevener church has recently been organized into a separate congregation. John Hevener was ordained as elder of this body in 1913. They have about fifty members. Bro. Hevener keeps up appointments at three places. He is assisted officially by two deacons. They maintain two Sunday schools."

Elk Run Congregation.

By W. H. Zigler.

[Eld. W. H. Zigler is an active minister in the Elk Run congregation. He was born January 21, 1880, united with the church November 24, 1894, elected deacon March 11, 1899, chosen minister September 7, 1901, and ordained elder September 13, 1913. On September 30, 1903, he united in marriage with Sister Girtie M. Huffman. On election to the ministry Bro. Zigler took a special course in Bridgewater College to fit himself for the work, and in addition to serving his home church he does evangelistic service. His life promises much usefulness.]

"The first brethren to move into the vicinity of the Elk Run congregation were Henry Snell, Joel Garber and Jacob Zigler. The last-named moved from Timberville, Rockingham County, May, 1841. This was then a part of the Beaver Creek church. Meetings were held in a schoolhouse near Mt. Zion, and in the home of Jacob Zigler. Love feasts and council

Eld. W. H. Zigler.

meetings were held in the home of Bro. Zigler until the Moscow church was built in 1854. This was then known as the Pudding Spring District, and became Moscow congregation in 1870. It was changed to Elk Run when the churchhouse by that name was built in 1884. The other houses in this congregation are Bells Valley, built in 1871, Griffin, built in 1911, and Little River, purchased in 1913.

"There are three Sunday schools in the congregation, with a total enrollment of two hundred and thirty-two. The largest one is at Elk Run, with an enrollment of one hundred and twenty scholars. The territory embraced is large. It covers a part of Augusta, Rockbridge and Bath Counties. The membership is two hundred and six. The official body consists of four ministers and six deacons. The present ministers are Jacob Zimmerman, D. C. Zigler, W. H. Zigler and C. W. Zimmerman."

J. W. Wright.

[Bro. J. W. Wright was born September 15, 1868. He had the advantage of the public schools of Augusta County, and later he took a course in Bridgewater College. In 1896 he united in marriage with Nettie D. Ecker, of Maryland. Two years later he united with the church and was elected minister in 1907. He has served his District as Sunday-school secretary for four years.]

THE MT. VERNON CONGREGATION.

By S. I. Flory.

"The Mt. Vernon church, situated three miles

northeast of Stuarts Draft, has a membership of about seventy-five, under the care of Eld. J. R. Kindig.

"There are four mission points in this congregation, with a total membership of one hundred and ten, thus making a grand total of one hundred and eighty-five members.

"The mission points are: New Concord, Rockbridge County, cared for by Elders J. R. Kindig and S. I. Flory, alternately; Montebello, Nelson County, in care of Eld. J. R. Kindig; White Hill, Augusta County, cared for by Eld. S. I. Flory; Meadow Mountain, Augusta County, in care of Bro. Wm. T. Pannell."

The Buena Vista Congregation.

"The first church in Buena Vista, belonging to the Church of the Brethren, was a small building bought from the Methodists in 1905, by Brethren S. I. Flory and S. D. Gilbert.

"In the spring of 1906, Sunday school was organized, and in August of the same year Eld. Noah Fisher, of Indiana, conducted the first series of meetings. May 1, 1907, with the help of the District Mission Board, Sister Cora Ringgold was secured as a missionary for this territory. She proved herself most efficient in the various departments of church work, and continued her services in the mission for over three years.

"On June 1, 1908, with the aid of the Mission Board, Bro. Saylor G. Greyer was secured to take charge of the pastoral work, which had previously been supplied by Brethren S. I. Flory and R. M. Figgers. Bro. Greyer had charge of the mission about four and one-half years. The work prospered well under his care, with an increase of from six to one hundred and twenty-five members. During the time Bro. Greyer had charge of the Buena Vista Mission he was absent a year and four months. Bro. H. L. Alley very capably took care of the work during his absence. The present membership is one hundred and fifty members, with Bro. J. C. Garber in charge since March 1, 1914.

" The Buena Vista church was organized in August, 1908, under the care of Eld. D. H. Zigler. After the division of the District, Eld. S. N. McCann had oversight of the mission. But owing to overwork and ill health Eld. McCann gave up the work in the spring of 1912. Since that time Eld. S. I. Flory has had charge of the work.

" Oronoco, Amherst County, a mission point in the Buena Vista congregation, has about forty members, under the care of Bro. R. M. Figgers."

Pleasant Valley Church.

In addition to what appears in another chapter with reference to the Pleasant Valley congregation Eld. Peter Garber gives the following:

" The southwestern portion, known as Lebanon, was organized separately in 1908 with one hundred and twenty members and the northwestern part, known as Summit, was organized in 1914 with one hundred and forty-five members. The mother church still has two hundred and five members, with Elders Peter

Garber and S. D. Miller, with Brethren P. F. Cline, elected in 1906, Arthur C. Miller, elected in 1912, J. F. Glick, elected in 1906, I. N. Glick, elected in 1908, and Minor C. Miller, elected in 1914, ministers. These, with ten deacons, constitute the official body of the church, Eld. Daniel Miller and Bro. A. D. Garber having died a few years ago. The ministers of the three congregations named continue their labors together, and in addition to the home work assistance is given Free Union and Locust Grove, which have been organized and fall to the East Virginia District. Also preaching services are conducted at South River and at Waynesboro. An evergreen Sunday school, with an enrollment of two hundred and forty, is doing good work at the home church."

Lebanon Church.

"The Lebanon church, organized April 4, 1908; was cut off from Pleasant Valley. Brethren P. J. Wenger, D. L. Andes and J. W. Cline were ministers and J. C. Garber was chosen minister. Eld. S. D. Miller was given the oversight of the new organization, and P. J. Wenger was ordained elder August 12. Preaching services are held twice a month at the Lebanon church, and a Sunday school runs the entire year."

The following account of the organization of the Summit church was given by Brethren J. W. Glick and D. L. Evers:

"The Summit church was organized February 28, 1914, with one hundred and forty-one members. Elders Peter Garber and S. D. Miller, of the Pleasant Valley congregation, were chosen elders for one year. Two ministers, J. T. Glick and Benjamin Crawn, and six deacons were living within the bounds of the new organization. On August 14, 1914, J. T. Glick was ordained elder and Marion Crawn chosen minister.

"There are two houses of worship where regular services are held and where Sunday schools are conducted. An active Sisters' Aid Society and Christian Workers' Meeting give additional means for Christian activity and development."

Eld. Walter Coffman gives the additional information about the Barren Ridge church:

"The present membership of this church is two hundred and sixty, with Elders Geo. F. Phillips, C. M. Driver, N. W. Coffman and Bro. W. F. Walters, ministers. Regular services are held at eight different places; four Sunday schools are conducted, three of which are evergreen. Two Christian Workers' Meetings and a Sisters' Aid Society are actively working.

"The mission territory is under the supervision of the local missionary committee. This territory includes parts of Waynesboro and Basic City and the adjacent country. A small but interesting Sunday school is conducted here."

The Middle River Church, in Augusta County, is one of the strongest organizations of the District Its activities continued much as previously given until the year 1914. In this year, within a few days, two of its widely-known elders died. Eld. Levi Garber, well stricken in years, was at home waiting for the change to come; while Eld. D. C. Flory, in the State of Indiana, was actively engaged in evangelistic work, and after a short illness was called to his eternal reward. Eld. B. B. Garber, well supported by an official staff, has oversight of the church at the present time.

The Sangerville Church, which lies part in Rockingham County and part in Augusta County, is one of the aggressive churches of the District. George Wine, who is senior elder, is hale and hearty at more than fourscore years.

The Staunton Church completes the list of churches of the District. The work here is moving on with reasonable progress, with Eld. Casper Driver in charge.

THE NORTHERN DISTRICT OF VIRGINIA.

As the name indicates, this District embraces the most northerly part of the State, and, like the Second District, it lies wholly west of the Blue Ridge Mountains. The adjacent counties of West Virginia also belong to it. In extent of territory, it is one of the smallest Districts in the State, but it has a larger membership than any of the others. At the present time there are eighteen organized churches with a membership of about four thousand.

The District is well organized in every line of Christian work. The Sunday-school Secretary is given two assistants, and aside from visiting the schools, division institutes are held among the churches each year. The mission work is in the care of a Board of three members. The Orphans' Home and

Old Folks' Home are located at Timberville. These institutions belong jointly to the three newly-formed Districts. There is a temperance committee of three members that is expected to join in every line of true temperance promotion. In addition to the regular District Meeting there is held each year a District Sunday-school Meeting and a Ministerial Meeting. These meetings give ample opportunity to discuss living issues in a more general way and afford an opportunity for the improvement of the workers.

With the division of the State District came an increased disposition to divide some of the local churches. The Flat Rock church had the matter of division under advisement for some years. The territory was large, but the very uneven distribution of the membership over it made it difficult to divide. Finally, after repeated reports by committees, the Flat Rock church was divided into three separate organizations. The story is briefly told by writers.

The Timberville Church.

By J. A. Garber.

"After about a year's work, the committee appointed by the Flat Rock church made a report that all the members south of the line between Shenandoah and Rockingham Counties be organized into a separate church. The new organization was effected, with a membership of about one hundred and fifteen, on December 3, 1910, and the name Timberville given to it.

"J. Carson Miller was chosen elder, D. F. Zigler, secretary, C. J. Smucker, treasurer, Austin Garber, correspondent, Steven Ullery, solicitor for the Timberville congregation, and Annie Knupp, solicitor for Mt. Olivet congregation. The local Sunday-school committee was J. A. Garber, A. C. Garber and D. F. Zigler. The local mission board was composed of D. S. Wampler, J. W. Andes and Benjamin Knupp.

"On January 6, 1912, D. S. Wampler, D. F. Zigler and C. J. Smucker were appointed to confer with a committee from the Linville Creek church on a line between the two churches. By the agreement, which was approved by both churches, about sixty-five members, with two ministers, were transferred to the Timberville church. By this transfer there were included one house of worship, a half interest in another, and an obligation to fill every alternate appointment at a free church.

"The membership at present is about two hundred. Bro. J. F. Driver has the oversight of the church, and W. C. Hoover is actively assisting in the ministry.

"Two Sunday schools, a Christian Workers' Society and a Sisters' Aid Society assist in good lines of work."

The Flat Rock church, much reduced in territory and in membership by the new organizations being cut off, is in a prosperous condition. Elders B. W. Neff, D. P. Wine, and J. Carson Miller, with Brethren John A. Garber and Charles Nesselrod, serve the church in the ministry.

The Pleasant View Church.

By B. W. Neff.

[Eld. B. W. Neff is a descendant of the well-known Neff family that is noticed in the early church in Virginia. He has been actively engaged in the ministry for a number of years. In addition to the many duties in his home church he has had oversight of the Pleasant View church from the time of its organization.]

" The northern part of the Flat Rock church, consisting of about eighty-four square miles, in which one hundred and twenty-five members live, was organized into a church January 21, 1911. Included in the membership were two ministers, J. O. Wakeman and Samuel Long, and four deacons. Eld. B. W. Neff was chosen elder for one year. Since the organization Brethren William Harpine and Charles Wakeman have been chosen ministers. There are three houses of worship owned by the church, with an interest in another one. The church is prospering, but the loss by death and emigration almost equal the gain in membership."

The Linville Creek Church.

The Linville Creek church has been the home of some of the most widely-known Brethren in Virginia. Chief among these are Elders John Kline and Peter Nead. The former spent his entire life here, and it is here he is the most fondly remembered and beloved. The latter spent a number of his most active years in the ministry in this church, and, because of his ready use of the English language, he became widely known as the " English preacher." This, in addition to his ability as a public speaker, made his services much sought after. He did much to win prestige in Rockingham and adjacent counties for the church.

Eld. Kline's tragic end, described in a previous chapter, made a lasting impression throughout the church. Especially was this so where he lived, and it was the desire to mark the place of his martyrdom

with a suitable monument. This feeling became more pronounced as the half-century anniversary of his death drew near. A committee was appointed, the necessary land was purchased and deeded to the trustees of Linville Creek church, and the monument was erected at the place where Eld. Kline gave his life blood for the cause he loved. The face of the stone bears the simple inscription: "AT THIS PLACE ELDER JOHN KLINE WAS KILLED JUNE 25th, 1864." On the reverse side we read, "ERECTED IN 1914 IN MEMORY OF ELDER JOHN KLINE, A PEACE MARTYR."

This church could be rightfully termed a mother of churches. In another chapter mention is made of the organization of the Greenmount and Brock's Gap churches. Since that time the North Mill Creek church, with about ninety members, and the South Fork church, with more than one hundred members, were organized from the mission territory in West Virginia, worked jointly with the Greenmount church. In addition to this, in 1911, sixty-five members were transferred to Timberville, to help strengthen that young church, and on the 28th day of December of the following year the eastern portion of the home church, with over two hundred members, was cut off for a new organization. This left the mother church much reduced in territory and in membership. Two ministers and five deacons, with about two hundred and fifteen members and with two churchhouses, constituted its numerical strength at that time. Since then two ministers have been installed and the membership has increased to two hundred and fifty.

Besides the regular preaching services there is an evergreen Sunday school at each meetinghouse. A Christian Workers' Meeting and a Sisters' Aid Society give opportunity to the membership for good work. The present ministry consists of Elders D. Hays and D. H. Zigler, with Brethren J. C. Myers and Andrew J. Fitzwater.

The Unity Church.

By C. E. Nair.

[Bro. C. E. Nair is one of the active young ministers of the Unity church, and is much devoted to its welfare. His labors are much appreciated.]

"In a council meeting, held on December 28, 1912, by the Linville Creek church, it was decided to organize the eastern part of the church into a separate organization. This was done on January 3, 1913, at Newdale, and the name Unity given the new church. There were over two hundred members, with four ministers, in the organization, and Bro. J. Carson Miller was chosen elder for one year.

"On August 2, 1913, J. D. Huffman was elected minister, and on August 1, 1914, J. S. Roller was ordained elder. The present ministers are J. S. Roller, W. A. Myers, I. N Zigler and C. E. Nair. Preaching services are held twice a month at each of the four preaching places. Four Sunday schools, two Christian Workers' Meetings and a Sisters' Aid Society are doing good work.

"Among those who spent useful lives within the bounds of the Unity church, and from whose labors we are now reaping a harvest for the Lord, are Elders Samuel Wampler, Samuel Zigler, John P. Zigler, Joseph Wampler and M. J. Roller. The prospects of this young church are good."

DIVISION OF SECOND DISTRICT

THE GREENMOUNT CHURCH.

This church has been closely associated with the Linville Creek church in missionary endeavor from the time of its organization. It has a strong membership, but it is so centrally located that the church could not easily be divided to advantage. However, it makes good use of its ministry and Sunday-school workers by assigning them duty at outlying points. Bro. P. I. Garber was chosen minister March 25, 1910, and Bro. Daniel B. Garber was elected June 13, 1912. These, with Jacob A. Garber, I. C. Myers, B. B. Miller J. W. Wampler, John H. Kline and I. W. Miller, make a strong ministerial force.

Eld. J. M. Kagey gives the following information regarding his home church, Cooks Creek:

" Since the organization of the Harrisonburg church and a portion of our territory falling to Beaver Creek church, we have two hundred and sixty members in the home church and about one hundred members in the West Virginia mission field. At each of the four houses of worship at home we have an active Sunday school, and we have preaching services at six different places in West Virginia.

" The present ministry is composed of Elders J. M. Kagey and S. I. Bowman, with Brethren B. S. Landis, J. H. Bowman and L. S. Miller."

THE HARRISONBURG CHURCH.

By P. S. Thomas.

[Eld. P. S. Thomas, son of Eld. Jacob and Elizabeth Swope Thomas, was born April 12, 1857. He lived in the Beaver Creek church, where he was baptized in August,

1889. On October 11, 1891, he married Elizabeth Ellen McLaughlin. In May, 1892, he moved to the Cooks Creek church, where he was elected deacon, chosen minister, and ordained elder. He assisted in the mission work of that church in the West Virginia mission field, and when the mission was opened in Harrisonburg he took an active part in it. When the Harrisonburg church was organized he was elected its elder, which position he has held to the present. In addition, he is a member of the Board of Trustees of the Orphans' Home, and its secretary, and also secretary of the General Child Rescue Committee.]

Harrisonburg Church.

"The Harrisonburg church is the child of three congregations—Cooks Creek, Greenmount and Mill Creek—each furnishing a part of the territory which forms the congregation. The lines and corners of the three congregations, within the town, were transferred to the corporate boundaries of the town, and the Harrisonburg church lies wholly within its corporate limits.

" In 1900 steps were taken to open a mission in the town. At that time there were ten members living in Harrisonburg. A building, used for a private school, on High Street, was secured, and the work was formally opened June 9, 1901. Eld. J. M. Kagey preached the first sermon. Sunday school was organized in July, 1901.

" Services were held at different places, pending the purchase of a lot and the erection of a building, and it was not until August 29, 1905, that definite steps were taken. A lot was purchased and in January, 1906, it was learned that the property that had been occupied could not be secured again after April 1, 1906. On March 26 plans were submitted, a building committee was appointed, and the work soon thereafter was begun.

" The church was completed and dedicated on December 9, 1906. Bro. George W. Flory preached the dedicatory sermon to a large audience.

" The work remained under the control of the three congregations until February, 1909. At this time it was organized as a separate congregation, and P. S. Thomas was placed in charge of the work.

" At the date of organization there were sixty members in the Harrisonburg church. The membership has gradually increased, and at the present time there are more than one hundred members.

" An active Sunday school is maintained and a practical interest is taken in all the endeavors of the church."

Bro. J. P. Deihl, who wrote the account of the Mill

Creek church in another chapter, gives the following additional information concerning it:

"On August 17, 1912, Brethren Samuel Pence and C. E. Long were ordained elders, and in the same year B. F. Miller, a minister, moved into the congregation. Bro. Saylor Greyer, who had charge of the Buena Vista church, moved into this church in 1914. On August 29, 1914, Walter Hartman was elected minister.

"The name of Samuel Petrie, who was elected to the ministry in 1871 and died a few years ago, was omitted from the list of ministers of this church. His long service demands the mention of his name in connection with the Mill Creek church."

The Page Church.

By J. M. Foster.

[J. M. Foster is one of the most active ministers of the Page church and has the distinction of being the youngest elder in the Northern District of Virginia. He took a special course in Bridgewater College to prepare himself for the work of the ministry.]

"This church embraces the entire territory of Page County. It formerly had a mission field in Rappahannock County, but it was organized into a church and it fell to the Eastern District of Virginia.

"The plan of distributing the work among the ministry of the church is through a committee appointed for the purpose. Each one is made responsible for the appointments given him. There are five active ministers who serve the twelve different places of appointment in this way.

"At present there are five hundred members, and among those who labored so faithfully in the past to establish the faith are Elders John Huffman, Nathan Spitler, Samuel Spitler, Martin Rothgeb, J. S. Foster and J. A. Racer."

In a number of the churches in Virginia, few marked changes have come in recent years. In some instances, however, very familiar characters have given place to younger men. In the Woodstock church, Eld. S. A. Shaver, well known for many years, was called away by death. In August, 1911, Joseph M. Grabill was elected minister, and on August 22, 1914, Bro. J. M. Ryman was ordained elder. Bro. H. R. Mawery is senior elder at this time.

The Salem church, in Frederick County, is under the supervision of Eld. N. D. Cool. He is assisted in the ministry by Brethren C. H. Brown and L. A. Detra. The condition of this church has materially advanced in recent years.

Upper Lost River church and Lower Lost River church are closely allied in their work. Their territory is much similar, and their opportunity in outlying Districts is very great. The former has about two hundred and fifty members, but has not fully recovered from the effect of division in past years. The latter has a membership of over two hundred, and it is increasing. Both these churches lie almost wholly in Hardy County, West Virginia.

North Mill Creek church and South Fork church are also in West Virginia. Both were organized from the mission territory worked jointly by the Linville Creek church and the Greenmount church. Therefore they are very similar in government and environment. Here we have a striking example of faithful men living in the hearts of others after life's labors are done. The list of the names of brethren, who rode on horseback from the Valley of Virginia to preach to those people, is too lengthy to give here, but they are not forgotten by those who heard them. Their names will be handed to generations yet unborn.

Lewis B. Flohr.

Each of these churches has a membership of one hundred or more. The field is large and should have a fostering care. The church first named is under the supervision of Eld. S. A. Sites, and the one last named is presided over by Eld. Jacob A. Garber, of the Greenmount church.

The Brock's Gap church has two houses of worship where Sunday school is held and a number of other places where preaching is done also. Elders Daniel Turner and George Fulk, with Brethren J. W. Lantz, B. E. Lantz and F. A. Yankey, constitute the ministerial force. The membership at present is about two hundred.

The Northern District is making fair progress and the opportunities are greater each year. These churches, including the Powel's Fort church and the mission territory south of the James River, jointly with the Second District, give a wide field for service in the Lord.

EASTERN DISTRICT OF VIRGINIA.

By Lewis B. Flohr.

The Eastern District of Virginia was organized in April, 1910, from that portion of the old Second District of Virginia lying north of the James River and east of the Blue Ridge Mountains. It includes the two Eastern Shore counties, and has for its eastern boundary the Atlantic Ocean and the Potomac River; the Potomac also forms the northern boundary.

This territory includes forty counties, covers an area of 12,080 square miles, and embraces a population of 695,013, or slightly over one-third of the population of the entire State. Of this population, 428,024 are white, 266,516 are negroes, and 473 are Indian, Chinese and Japanese. The District has a membership of 1,157.

The movement for a division of the former Second District took shape in 1907, when the Fairfax congregation sent a paper to District Meeting asking for the organization of a new District east of the Blue Ridge. The committee into whose hands this matter was placed for report did not deem it expedient to organize a District in the east without further subdividing the remaining territory, and so recommended the creation of the Northern District also. (See map, page 160.)

The old Second District had grown so that the District Meetings were almost too great to be handled and entertained by even the large congregations. Besides, there were many who were convinced that greater missionary effort could and would be attained if the District were divided. The members east of the Blue Ridge felt that the expenses incurred in attending District gatherings would be better expended in a more circumscribed field, where it would not only be sufficient to entertain a District Meeting if necessary, but also aid in carrying on the mission work.

As may be inferred from the description of the District, this is a large and needy mission field. There are only a few congregations in position to carry on their home work and aid in the general work of the field. The brethren of the Valley as early as Civil War times, and even before, began their mission work in this part of the State, the Mill Creek brethren being foremost in the work, as may be seen in the details of this section. This was mainly in Albemarle, Greene, Madison and Orange Counties, but later extended to others. The writer a few years ago found trace of some efforts in Loudoun County, near Ryan, of a Brethren minister from the Valley, who preached, and baptized at least a couple of converts about or perhaps before the war. This work, however, seems to have been abandoned without having produced permanent results.

This District conducted its business after the plan of the parent District until the adoption of plans for conducting the work, which was finally effected in 1912. The mission work was looked after by a Board of three members until 1914, when the joint arrangement with the Second and Northern Districts was dissolved. The members of the Board were Eld. S. A. Sanger, president; Eld. E. E. Blough, secretary and treasurer, and W. F. Hale. In 1914 the membership of the Board was increased to five.

The Sunday-school field work had been looked after by Lewis B. Flohr, as assistant secretary of the Second District, until the organization of this District, when he was made District Secretary. He tendered his resignation in 1911. This was not accepted, but he was given an assistant, Jesse J. Conner. In 1912 W. H. Sanger was appointed Sunday-school Secretary. He is still secretary, and has as assistant Jesse J. Conner and Sister Martha Click Senger, the three constituting the Sunday School Board of the District, which has general charge of the Sunday-school work. They prepare the programs for the Sunday-school Meeting, held in association with the Ministerial Meeting, annually, and designate the officers of the meeting.

The following table shows the status of the Sunday schools of the District at the end of the calendar year 1913:

Sunday-School Statistical Report for the Year Ending December 31, 1913

Name of Congregation	Name of Sunday-school	Months in Session	No. in Tea. Train. Class	Tea. Meeting	General S. S. Work and Benevolence	Total Collections for the Year	Officers	Teachers	Cradle Roll	Home Dept.	Main School	Total	Average Attendance	Membership of Congregation	Pupils Convert-ed During Yr.
Belmont	Belmont	12			$ 1.88	$ 23.10	3	3			43	43	32	20	5
Bethel	Bethel	9			1.17	9.58	5	3			43	43	18	47	5
Fairfax	Dranesville	7½			2.73	19.45	3	4	7		43	50	33	194	5
Fairfax	Oakton	12	8	*	26.39	98.49	8	8	12		150	162	72		2
Fairfax	Red Hill	8			2.00	13.75	6	3			41	41	27		1
Locust Grove	Lower Union	12				12.00	13	4	18		80	98	46	50	6
Madison	Madison	8				3.83	4	3			30	30	19	35	
Manassas	Bradley	12			3.50	15.10	7	4			30	30	18	65	5
Manassas	Cannon Branch	12	7		26.00	44.76	3	4	12	5	63	80	41		3
Midland	Midland	12	8		5.81	22.80	3	4			96	96	30	75	3
Midland	Mt. Hermon	12	2		7.70	18.02	4	4			40	40	30		3
Mine Run	Mine Run	12			1.50	8.17	2	2			14	14	9	16	
Mt. Carmel	Cedar Grove	12				1.50	1	1			18	18	7	225	
Mt. Carmel	Evergreen	12		*	8.50	23.55	12	8	41	2	110	153	60		3
Mt. Carmel	Haneytown	6				1.97	3	3	22		70	92	42		1
Mt. Carmel	Mountain Grove	12		*	2.70	8.50	9	5	60	10	98	168	67		12
Mt. Carmel	Shiloh	5			2.00	3.00	2	3			45	45	40		3
Nokesville	Auburn	6						3			60	60	26	300	
Nokesville	Hoadley	6			2.50	4.00	3	3			15	15	12		
Nokesville	Nokesville	12	19	*	69.75	120.61	7	8	16		100	116	66		
Nokesville	Valley	12			12.00	25.00	5	5	10	22	57	89	43		
Trevilian	Trevilian	12			1.49	31.74	3	4	12	30	35	77	40	40	6
(Buena Vista)	Oronoco	6				6.55	2	6			50	50	30	55	6
(Pleasant Valley)	Wayside	6			5.60	6.25					56	56	26	35	
		235½	44	5	$183.22	$521.72	108	95	210	69	1387	1666	819	1157	80

The various congregations have conducted Christian Workers' Meetings practically ever since their introduction. Aid Societies have been conducted by the sisters in a number of congregations for some years. They have a District organization and are accorded time during the District Meeting to reorganize and render reports and a brief program. These organizations have done much good in supplying clothes to the needy, both in this District and in others, and in making money contributions to various church activities.

Educational.

As a whole, the Brethren of this District are friends of education, and believe in educating their children where the influences are for good. Bridgewater College has an increasing patronage of our young people. Realizing the need of an educational institution to do work below that of college grade, the Brethren in 1909 opened

Hebron Seminary.

Hebron Seminary is the lineal descendant and rehabilitation of the school founded by I. N. H. Beahm at Brentsville, Virginia, 1897, as a private enterprise under the name of Prince William Normal School. "Its development demanded an organization, and hence a charter was secured and a board of trustees chosen, and the school continued successfully as Prince William Academy." In 1905 it was turned over to the county authorities as a county high school, which was operated for a time and then discontinued.

In 1908 the Brethren about Nokesville became enthused with a desire to rehabilitate and reopen the school. A canvass of the situation revealed the consensus of opinion as unfavorable to the old location at Brentsville; it was therefore decided to move to the railroad and erect a new buildinng to house the institution. A commodious three-story building, with part basement, was erected in 1909 on a site convenient to the depot at Nokesville, Virginia, donated by W. R. Free, Jr., and the school reopened in the fall of 1909. All subscriptions and donations were given outright, and no stock has ever been issued; none is provided for. The school and property are, to quote from the constitution of the seminary . . . "owned and controlled by the Church of the Brethren through a body of trustees acting for said church . . ." The institution is now entering on its sixth year's work at its new location, with all indebtedness provided for.

Belmont Congregation.

This is a newly-organized congregation and was first recognized by District Meeting in 1913. It embraces Spottsylvania County and has a membership of twenty-one. It has one Sunday school, with fifty-two enrolled. Eld. S. A. Sanger has the oversight.

Bethel Congregation.

This congregation is located in Nelson County, and has one house of worship located near Arrington, on the Southern Railroad. The membership numbers forty-eight; the Sunday school has a total enrollment of fifty-four. Bro. E. Jay Egan is pastor, employed by the District Mission Board. Bro. W. E. Cunningham, a resident minister, assists in the work. Eld. I. N. H. Beahm has the oversight of the congregation.

Fairfax Congregation.

This congregation now has a membership of one hundred and ninety-seven, and is presided over by Eld. I. M. Neff. He is assisted in the ministry by B. F. Miller, J. R. Leatherman, W. H. Sanger, E. E. Neff, D. H. Miller and M. M. Myers, who are at present attending Bridgewater College. A meeting-house was recently erected in the northwest part of Fairfax County, near Dranesville, thus making two. There are three Sunday schools, with an enrollment of two hundred and sixteen.

Locust Grove Congregation.

This congregation was organized in 1913. It is located in Albemarle County and has about fifty members. Eld. S. A. Sanger has the oversight and now lives at Free Union, within the congregation. Bro. Geo. A. Maupin is a minister here.

Madison Congregation.

Eld. S. A Sanger has charge of this congregation. It is located in Madison County and has one church-house. One Sunday school is conducted; it has an enrollment of thirty-eight, which corresponds exactly to the membership of the church. Bro. H. L. Yager, a young minister, whose home is in this congregation, has been doing some ministerial work there the last year or so.

Manassas Congregation.

Bro. J. M. Kline is now one of the ministers of this church, having moved here from the Fairfax congregation a few years ago. There are now two Sunday schools conducted, with an enrollment of one hundred and thirty-eight. The membership is seventy-five.

Midland Congregation.

Eld. M. G. Early, who is elder in charge of this church, moved here from Nokesville, Virginia, in 1913, as also did Bro. Geo. W. Beahm, a minister. Bro. John A. Hinegardner was elected to the ministry in 1913. Bro. Dennis Weimer died in 1912. There are now two meetinghouses, with a Sunday school in each; the total enrollment is one hundred and two. The members number seventy-five.

Mine Run Congregation.

Eld. S. A. Sanger has the oversight of this congregation. They are without a resident minister at the present. Belmont congregation was formed from a part of their territory in 1913, thereby reducing the number of members.

Mount Carmel Congregation.

This congregation is located in Greene County, and extends into the borders of Albemarle and Madison. Eld. S. A. Sanger, who has faithfully worked in this field for many years, even before moving from the Valley to the eastern part of the State, is elder and pastor in charge. The membership is two hundred and thirty. There are five Sunday schools conducted, with a total enrollment of five hundred and eighty-six. Sisters Nelie and Ellen Wampler have been working in this field for several years, teaching school in the winter, carrying on Sunday schools and all kinds of Christian work so much needed. There are six churchhouses within this congregation.

Nokesville Congregation.

Eld. I. A. Miller now presides over this congregation. Bro. A. K. Graybill was elected to the ministry in 1913. Bro. S. H. Flory was ordained at the same time. There are three houses of worship, and a total membership of two hundred and ninety-three. Three Sunday schools are conducted; they have a combined enrollment of two hundred and eighty-six. The ministerial force at the present consists of Elders I. A. Miller, I. N. H. Beahm, and S. H. Flory, and ministers, J. F. Britton, ——— Wells, J. T. Flory, Lewis B. Flohr and A. K. Graybill.

Rappahannock Congregation.

This congregation was organized in 1909 (or 1910), with Eld. R. A. Nedrow in charge. Eld. S. H. Flory now has the oversight, Bro. Nedrow having moved from the District. This was formerly a part of the congregation in Page County, and was organized as a result of the formation of the Eastern District. The membership is forty-six.

Trevilian Congregation.

This is a new congregation, situated in Louisa County. It was organized in 1912, is in charge of Eld. I. N. H. Beahm, and has a membership of fifty-one. Bro. A. B. Miller was ordained to the eldership in 1914. Bro. B. F. Glick is in the ministry. There is one meetinghouse, and a Sunday school having sixty-seven enrolled.

CHAPTER XII.

Biographical.

This history would be incomplete without some of the lives of the ministers who so earnestly labored for the development of the churches in Virginia. But when there are so many deserving names suggested, it becomes a matter for much reflection which to mention or where to draw the line. If the list grows too long it will in itself defeat the purpose of such a catalog. In addition to this, it is often the case and for various reasons, the examples that would be most helpful to us are little known. However, the following biographies are given with the hope that the reader may be inspired to more noble deeds for the Master. Wherefore, they are given for ensamples unto us.

The deeds of the earliest ministers are so closely interwoven with the records of the church that little more need be said of them. Jacob Miller, Peter Smith, John Bowman and John Garber have become household words. In addition to them other names are well known.

ELD. BENJAMIN BOWMAN, SR., who lived near Greenmount, Rockingham County, Virginia, came to the State about 1785. He served the church north of Harrisonburg as senior elder for a number of years. His name appears repeatedly among the old records. He was a well-known minister of unusual attainments

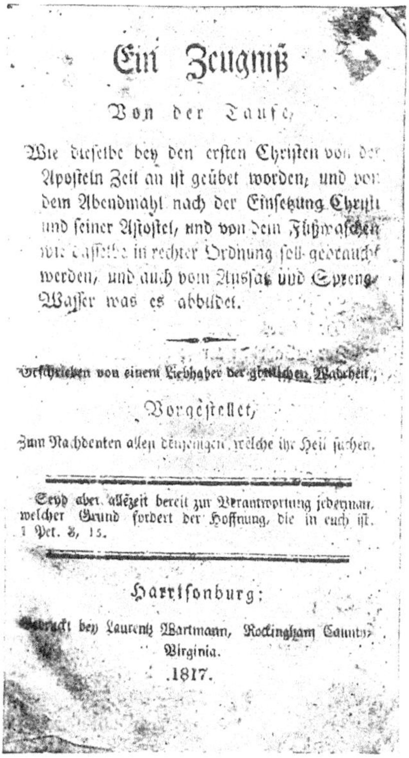

Ein Zeugniß

Von der Taufe,

Wie dieselbe bey den ersten Christen von der Aposteln Zeit an ist geübet worden, und von dem Abendmahl nach der Einsetzung Christi und seiner Apostel, und von dem Fußwaschen wie dasselbe in rechter Ordnung soll gebraucht werden, und auch vom Aussatz und Spreng-Wasser was es abbildet.

Geschrieben von einem Liebhaber der göttlichen Wahrheit,

Vorgestellet,

Zum Nachdenken allen denjenigen, welche ihr Heil suchen.

Seyd aber allezeit bereit zur Verantwortung jedermann, welcher Grund fordert der Hoffnung, die in euch ist. 1 Pet. 3, 15.

Harrisonburg:

Gedruckt bey Laurentz Wartmann, Rockingham Caunty, Virginia.

1817.

Title Page of Book, "Points on Baptism," etc., by Elder Peter Bowman. The Only Known Copy is Owned by Gen. John E. Roller, Harrisonburg, Va., by Whose Courtesy this Page is Presented.

for his time. He was born November 1, 1754, and his death occurred in 1829.

ELD. PETER BOWMAN was a brother of Benjamin and came to the State at the same time. His home was south of Harrisonburg. Doubtless these two took part in establishing the line in 1788 running east and west through that town. He was also a man of strong character and attainments. Some of his writings are still extant. A photograph of the title page of a book credited to his pen appears on page 217.

ELD. MARTIN GARBER, son of John Garber, lived near his father's home in Shenandoah County. He was associated with Eld. Bowman in charge of the church north of Harrisonburg. He was very active in the ministry and served the church on Standing Committee at different times. Like his father, he died comparatively a young man. His death, which occurred in 1814, was considered a great loss to the church.

JOHN GLICK, who came with Martin Garber to Virginia, was also an elder and served the church as an assistant for a number of years with commendable zeal. He survived Eld. Garber a number of years.

Mention has previously been made of Yohones Kagey as "Kagey the Good Man," but it should be remembered that his acts of benevolence in relieving physical suffering was not his only great work. He was a minister of unusual ability. With his high sense of duty toward his fellow men and great love for the church, he was a power for good in his community and in the surrounding churches. He served the church during the first half of the nineteenth century. Eld. Kagey was elected minister in 1800 and ordained elder in 1814.

DANIEL GARBER and YOHONES FLORY were distinguished elders in Upper Rockingham. They were brothers-in-law and labored in much harmony for the church. Associated with them were John Brower, John Wine, Joseph Miller, Daniel Yount, and Isaac Long, Sr. These Brethren laid the foundation for the strong churches of Cooks Creek, Beaver Creek, Bridgewater and Mill Creek.

ABRAHAM GARBER was born November 10, 1760, and died February 16, 1848. Fifty-eight years of his life were spent in Augusta County, Virginia. The first of these years he spent as a pioneer preacher. The latter years, he was the elder of the Middle River church, of which he was the founder.

Among the Brethren who made early settlements in southwest Virginia was Eld. Abraham Crumpacker. He was born in Carroll County, Maryland, in the month of November, 1767. His father was also a minister and died while preaching. His widowed mother moved to Rockingham County about the time the Brethren first settled in that part of the State. Eld. Crumpacker's opportunity for an education was limited. Yet he was able to read the Bible in both the English and German languages. He united with the church when he was nineteen years old; married Mary Rife on December 25, 1792. To this union twelve children, five boys and seven girls, were born. His ministerial labors began soon after his marriage. After serving the church for some years, he with two of his brothers moved to Bedford County, Virginia. Here he met with the misfortune of losing five of his children. Three of them died in the month of September, 1802. In this church he was ordained elder. In September, 1818, he moved to Botetourt County and served the church here forty years. His unusually clear memory, together with his thorough knowledge of the Bible, made a concordance unnecessary. Much of his time was devoted to the church. After the death of his wife on May 25, 1851, he lived with his sons-in-law, George Bair and Eld. Jonas Graybill. At his request, B. F. Moomaw was ordained elder in 1858.

During his long life he never took medicine from a doctor, but in his last illness he called for the elders, to be anointed. He died on April 22, 1859, at the ripe age of ninety-one years. The funeral services were conducted by Elders Peter Nininger, B. F. Moomaw and David Plaine. Two of his sons were ministers, and four of his grandsons and nine of his great-grandsons fill that important office at this time.

ELD. AUSTIN HYLTON was also one of the pioneer preachers of the Brethren Church in southwestern Virginia. He was called to the ministry in 1829 by the "West Arm" of the Floyd County church and was ordained to the eldership eight years later. At his request Chrisley Bowman was also ordained at the same time. About 1850, he moved to east Tennessee and located on Boones Creek in the Knob Creek congregation. Soon after this his wife died. In a second marriage he united with the widow Bowman, who was the mother of the late Eld. George C. Bowman. Eld. Hylton died in 1879, at the age of eighty-five years. All of his children went with him to Tennessee, except his oldest son, Hardin P., who remained in Virginia. Eld. Austin Hylton was not a very fluent speaker, but he lived an exemplary life.

The name Naff appears very prominently among the churches in southwest Virginia. Among them were some of the most noted preachers in that part of the State. Of this number, Eld. Abraham Naff was very distinguished in his day. He was born on February 25, 1806; married Hannah Peters, April 6, 1830; and died, February 6, 1873. In his time he traveled and preached much. He attended a number of Annual Meetings and served on important committees. Much of his time was given to the welfare of the church at home and also in outlying mission territory.

So much has already been written concerning Eld. John Kline and so frequently does his name appear on the pages of this volume, that it would seem almost useless to make further mention of him. Yet the service he rendered the Virginia church is of such unusual character, and he was so widely known throughout the Brotherhood, that at least a short biography of him should appear here. At no time has any minister appeared more prominently among the Virginia churches than Eld. Kline, and it is a matter of doubt if this statement does not equally apply to the entire Brotherhood. And it was not only with the church that his marked ability was recognized. Public men in almost every position had much regard for his superior judgment. Nothing that would tend to the advancement of the public good seemed too inconsiderable for his attention. As a physician he was successful, and he possessed the much coveted ability to adapt himself to the conditions that surrounded him and their needs. But it was for the church in much humility and earnestness of spirit that he devoted his powers, limited only by his endurance. On June 17, 1856, he wrote:

"This day I am fifty-nine years of age. When I was young my ambition led me to hope that I might some day attain to distinction in the world, and leave an imperishable name. I own with shame before my God, that my heart was full of vanity. I now thank him that he has led me to know and feel myself but a poor sinner redeemed. I am wholly dependent upon him for all that I am or ever shall be. Lord Jesus, may I live to glorify thee, and thee only. I believe thy truth. I trust thy love. May thy glory be the end of all my efforts in life, and thy love the propelling power in all I do. Hallowed be *thy* name, not my name. *Thy will* be done, not my will. Give me grace thus ever to pray and to walk humbly before thee." "Life of John Kline," page 374.

Eld. Kline was born in Dauphin County, Pennsylvania, June 17, 1797. About fourteen years later he came with his parents to Virginia. They settled in Rockingham County, near where the Linville Creek church now stands, and where he resided the remainder of his life. He united with the church while he was yet young as evidenced by old papers. On March 10, 1818, he was married to Anna Wampler. He was elected deacon in 1827, chosen minister in 1830, and ordained elder on April 13, 1848. In this office he served faithfully until the tragic end came on June 15, 1864, as stated elsewhere in this volume. Eld. Kline served the church under many important appointments. He was also moderator of Annual Meeting a number of times. But it was among the Virginia churches and the outlying mission territory that the greater part of his important work was done. During the Civil War his service to the Brethren was of an invaluable character and for whom he gave his life. His death was that of a martyr if there ever was one. However, these events are fully given in another chapter.

Closely associated with the name of Eld. John Kline is that of Eld. B. F. Moomaw. So intimately were the acts of their lives interwoven for a number of years, that to write the biography of the one would be to relate many of the experiences of the other. Although their homes were separated by nearly one hundred miles, their visits to each other were not infrequent and this distance was made on horseback. Their correspondence shows a most lively interest in each other's welfare and devotion to the church. Eld.

Moomaw was born in Botetourt County, Virginia, March 30, 1814, where he lived until his death on November 6, 1901. He was ordained elder in 1858 and for a number of years before this he was quite active in the councils of the church. For many years he was a prominent figure at the Annual Meetings and was well known throughout the Brotherhood. His service on a number of important committees is well known, but, like his associate, Eld. Kline, it was among the Virginia churches and the adjacent mission territory that his greatest work was done. During the Civil War his service in behalf of his Brethren was fruitful of much good for their welfare. Eld. Moomaw was a fearless, aggressive worker for the Lord and his church; and his name will be revered as long as the worth of a good name and memory shall last.

Eld. Benjamin Bowman, son of Eld. Benjamin Bowman, Sr., lived at Greenmount, Rockingham County. He was born on June 28, 1785. In his younger days Eld. Bowman is said to have been a wayward youth, but his father and mother were so solicitous for the welfare of their son that they made him an object of their earnest entreaties during their evening devotions. On one occasion young Benjamin chanced to hear these intercessions in his behalf and it so wrought upon him that it entirely changed his life. His service to the church during his long ministry was of a most distinguished character. He was elected deacon May 31, 1818, ordained elder in 1837 and departed this life on April 9, 1872.

ELD. DANIEL MILLER also lived near Greenmount and his election to the ministry was at the same time as that of Eld. Bowman, as shown in the records of the Greenmount church. He also served that congregation as elder for a number of years. Eld. Miller was an earnest worker, but labored under the disadvantage of not having the use of the English language. However, he did much good work. Yet the greatest record of his life is the gift of the noble family of nine boys and nine girls to the church. A number of his sons became prominent ministers.

ELD. HARDEN P. HYLTON, son of Eld. Austin Hylton, was born in Floyd County, Virginia, November 11, 1822. His parents were quite poor and he was never permitted to attend but three months of school. Although deprived of the usual opportunities, he secured education sufficient to meet the demands of the day. He was full of energy and was determined to see better days. On October 8, 1843, he united with the church and one year later was elected deacon. In 1846 he was chosen minister and was ordained elder in 1850. In 1844 he was married to Frances Bowman. To this union were born nine children, of whom three, John W. B., Chrisley D., and Solomon P., are elders in the church. Eld. Hylton was active in the ministry for about fifty years. He was aggressive in his undertakings, yet he regarded the wishes of others. During the war, he baptized many, and while some of his neighbors were forced into the war or to hiding in the brush, their wives and children shared his hospitality. He was a friend to the poor. Bro. Hylton did much to encourage the development of his country. He served on several committees in his State district and several times served on the Standing Committee. His companion died February 15, 1898. He married Sister Sarah Carter, who survives him. He died on December 24, 1905, at the age of eighty-three years, one month, and thirteen days.

ELD. DANIEL THOMAS, whose home was near Spring Creek, Rockingham County, was one of the most active ministers in his day. In the estimation of Eld. John Kline, Eld. Thomas had few equals as a public speaker. He was also prominent in the councils of the church although he died comparatively a young man.

ELD. JACOB MILLER, son of Daniel, lived in the Greenmount church. He was elected minister on April 13, 1849; ordained elder in 1859; and died in 1889. He was an interesting speaker, persuasive in manner and pleasing in person. For many years he was writing clerk of District Meeting and before the publication of the minutes a number of them appear in his handwriting.

The Yount family originated in the liberty-loving country of Switzerland. The ancestor of the American branch of the family emigrated to the United States in an early day and settled in York County, Pennsylvania. Later, in company with his two sons, he removed to the vicinity of Broadway, Virginia.

Of these sons, Joseph, grandfather of the subject of this sketch, again removed in 1808 to the neighborhood of Crimora, Augusta County. Their eldest son, Samuel, then six years old, on coming to manhood married Eliza Whitmore. Their second child was Daniel, in whose memory this is written.

Elder Daniel Yount.

ELD. DANIEL YOUNT was born near Crimora, Virginia, October 28, 1832. Reared on a farm, he was early taught habits of truthfulness, respect for religion, industry and economy. He received only a common-school education, but by observation, reading and some travel, he became possessed of a considerable fund of valuable information. He became a minister of the Brethren Church in 1872. On January 20, 1885, he was killed by a railroad train. In 1857 he married Margaret C., daughter of Daniel P. Bowman, deceased. She died at Bridgewater, Virginia, March 1, 1902. They had one child, Walter B.

In reading over the minutes and committee reports, a number of different names are seen appended. Among them are the names of John Harshberger, Sr., John Harshberger, Jr., Isaac Long, Sr., and Isaac Long, Jr. These were all ministers of the Mill Creek congregation, Rockingham County. All of these Brethren were deeply consecrated to the cause of the Master. They were in their time among the most enthusiastic missionaries in Virginia. They served the Mill Creek church jointly as ministers and elders for many years, as shown by the history of that church.

BRO. ABRAHAM GARBER was born December 19, 1824. He united with the church in 1847 and was elected minister on March 31, 1855. He has faithfully served the Pleasant Valley church, Augusta County, as minister for fifty-three years and bears the distinction of being the oldest in that office in the Second District of Virginia, if not in the entire State. At this writing he still enjoys good health.

ELD. DANIEL HAYS, the character of this sketch, is well known to many of the readers of these pages. He has frequently attended the Annual Conferences for a number of years and has been a member of the

Tract Examining Committee and the *Messenger* Advisory Committee. In addition to this he has at different times represented the Second District of Virginia at Annual Meeting and served under ap-

Snapshot, by Sister Sadie Zigler, of Elder Daniel Hays at His Desk Where He Wrote "The Olive Branch of Peace."

pointment on special important work of the church. At this writing he is senior elder of the Linville Creek church.

As a writer, Eld. Hays is well and favorably known. He has contributed valuable articles on Bible doctrine, history and biography to the *Gospel Messenger* and other periodicals from time to time. But as author of "The Olive Branch of Peace," he did his most far-reaching work.

He is a native of Hampshire County, now in West Virginia. He was born on May 16, 1839. In the year 1862 he united with the church, was elected minister in 1867, and ordained elder at Flat Rock, Shenandoah County, in 1879. On September 3, 1873, Eld. Hays was married to Sarah Myers. To this union have been born five children, two sons and three daughters.

ELD. BENJAMIN MILLER was born September 29, 1829. He united with the church in 1853, elected minister in 1866, and was ordained elder a few years after. He is at this writing senior elder of the Greenmount congregation, but is not actively engaged in ministerial duties. In time of the Civil War, while the Brethren were in prison, he took an active part in securing their release.

Eld. Miller was twice married. His first union was with Hettie Showalter, from which seven children are yet living and are active workers in the church. On November 28, 1899, he was married to Catherine Fitzwater. At this time he resides with his son, Samuel, four miles northwest of Harrisonburg.

ELD. JACOB WINE was elected minister on April 8, 1846, and was ordained elder April 18, 1857. During his long ministry, he served the Flat Rock church faithfully and was aggressive in every line of church work.

Although the space allotted to this catalog is rapidly taken, yet there remain many examples of sacrifice and devotion to duty untold. It is with regret that such lives as were lived by Peter Nininger, John A. Cline, Levi A. Wenger, Samuel Wampler, Samuel Zigler, Christian Wine, Daniel Baker, Jacob Thomas, Fredric Wampler, Michael Good, George Shaver, Daniel Miller, Joseph Wampler and others, and that the acts of such aggressive workers as Samuel Crumpacker, J. A. Dove, Martin Rothgeb, J. W. Wampler, Daniel P. Wine, John F. Driver, Jacob A. Garber, Peter Thomas, Benjamin Neff, Abraham Thomas and many others, whose names do not appear elsewhere in this volume, should not be used to exemplify Christian devotion for the benefit of the rising generation. But only an additional few in the activities of life can still be given.

Walter B. Yount, president of Bridgewater College since 1892, was born near Crimora, Virginia, June 22, 1859. He has been a student all his life and is a graduate of Juniata College, Huntingdon, Pennsylvania, and of the National Schools of Elocution and Oratory of Philadelphia. He was a student at the University of Virginia for six years; and also took special Bible work under Doctors Harper and Price, and Elocution under Dr. Clark in the University of Chicago. His services to Bridgewater College have been of a most unusual character, the limits of which can not be given in a biographical sketch. He has served the Brethren Church as a minister since 1892.

Pres. Yount has been twice married. The first union was with Minnie B. Andes. On July 10, 1907, he was married to Emma J. Eller, near Daleville, Virginia. Carl and Dee, two boys rapidly building up to manhood, bless their home.

ELD. H. C. EARLY was born on a farm in Augusta County, Virginia, May 11, 1855. In addition to the public schools in the community in which he lived, he attended the Shenandoah Valley Normal School two terms, but never completed a regular course. At an early age the study of medicine had special attraction for him and was only prevented by obstacles that seemed unsurmountable.

Bro. Early united with the church December 12, 1876; was elected minister November 6, 1880; and was ordained elder in August, 1898. He became active in the ministry and devoted much of his time to evangelistical work, but of late years other duties, much to his regret, interfere with that line of Christian work. At the present he is senior elder of the Mill Creek church.

Eld. Early is widely known as a speaker and writer of ability. He has been a regular contributor for the *Gospel Messenger* for twenty-seven years and now serves on the editorial staff of that periodical. He is a member of the General Missionary and Tract Committee and has served under other important appointments of both the District and General Conferences. At the present time his life promises much additional usefulness for the Lord.

On May 25, 1876, he was married to Mary A. Showalter. From this union have been given to them six children, five girls and one boy.

Eld. D. C. Flory was born on a farm near New Hope, Augusta County, Virginia, April 3, 1854. He united with the church in August, 1877; was married to Kate Driver December 23, 1880; elected minister in March, 1888; and ordained elder in 1906.

In his youth Bro. Flory had the benefit of the ordinary school of the community in which he lived and also the high school of New Hope. He studied for three sessions at the University of Virginia. During the session of '78 to '79, he taught in the Juniata College of Huntingdon, Pennsylvania. In 1880 he established the Spring Creek Normal School, which afterward developed into Bridgewater College.

Eld. Flory has been for some years engaged in evangelistic work, but at the present he devotes much of his time to the oversight of the Middle River congregation.

The valuable service rendered the church by Bro. G. B. Holsinger demands a sketch of his life here. He was born May 10, 1857, in Bedford County, Pennsylvania. He traces his ancestry to the founders of the Brethren Church, being the sixth generation from Alexander Mack. At the age of eighteen he united with the church.

The first twenty-five years of his life were spent on his father's farm, five winters of which he was engaged in teaching public school. Naturally fond of music, he gave it much self study from childhood. At the age of seventeen he became his own instructor in instrumental music, soon learning to play at sight any Sunday-school music, church tune or anthem. A year later he attended his first singing school, after

George B. Holsinger.

which he did some class teaching. In order to be thoroughly qualified to follow his chosen profession, he attended a number of musical normals conducted by the foremost teachers of the day. In two instances he was awarded first prize in musical composition.

At the founding of Bridgewater College, he became teacher of the department of music, which position he held for sixteen years. Having been elected musical editor of the Brethren Publishing House in 1898, he resigned his position in the college.

During these years he has edited or assisted in editing ten popular music books, some of which are "Psalms and Hymns," "Gospel Songs and Hymns No. 1," "Song Praises," "The Brethren Hymnal." etc. His more than two hundred musical compositions are found in over one hundred and fifty different music books. He has directed the music at nine successive Annual Meetings of the Brethren Church.

Since 1898, in connection with the editing of music books, he has been engaged in teaching vocal music classes in many of the churches of the Brotherhood. He is devoted to the church, and ever tries to inspire all with the true worshipful spirit of sacred song.

In 1884 he married Sallie A. Kagey of Bridgewater, Virginia. One son, Clyde, blesses the union.

BRO. JACOB A. GARBER, son of Eld. Levi Garber, was born in Augusta County, Virginia, Oct. 1, 1853, and was married to Mary E. Myers November 20, 1873. From this time he made his home in Rockingham County and united with the church at Greenmount in December of the same year.

Bro. Garber was elected deacon in March, 1874, chosen minister in 1877, and ordained elder in November, 1902. From the first he was active in the work to which the church had called him. He took an active part in the missionary endeavor of the Greenmount church and has served that church as elder for a number of years.

Eld. Garber, in his work of the ministry, has attended seven hundred and sixty funerals and officiated at some one hundred and sixty marriages.

Eld. S. D. Miller, who lives in the Pleasant Valley church, Augusta County, was born August 2, 1862. He united with the church in November, 1884; was chosen minister March 14, 1896. He is associated with Eld. Peter Garber as elder of his home church and also the Summit church. For a number of years Bro. Miller has been a member of the Board of Trustees of the Orphans' Home.

Among the most active ministers of the Second District is Eld. A. S. Thomas. He is a son of Eld. Jacob Thomas, and united with the church in 1879. He was elected deacon in 1885, chosen minister in 1892, and ordained to the eldership in 1903.

Bro. Thomas has served his District frequently on Standing Committee at Annual Meeting and other important committees. Besides home church duties he is engaged in successful evangelistic work.

Eld. S. I. Bowman is closely associated with the work of the Northern District. He fills the office of District Treasurer. In addition to the duties as associate elder of the Cooks Creek church he is engaged in evangelistic work with marked success.

William K. Conner, who for a number of years has been working under the supervision of the District Mission Board at Newport News, Virginia, was born at Royersford, Pennsylvania, March 28, 1873.

William K. Conner.

He received the degree of B. E. at Bridgewater College in 1899. He has taught in the Prince William Normal School and in Bridgewater College. He united with the church in 1893 and was elected minister in 1897.

BRO. J. CARSON MILLER, for a number of years Secretary of the District Mission Board, was born March 18, 1861, near Moores Store, Shenandoah County, Virginia. He completed the Latin-Scientific course at Mt. Morris College in 1882. He afterward studied at the same institution and at the University of Virginia. For nine years he was Professor of Mathematics and Science at Bridgewater College. He united with the church in 1887 and was called to the ministry

August 20, 1897. In September, 1889, he was married to Ida May Smith.

George W. Flory, with his wife, Abbie, has done very successful evangelistic work among the Virginia churches. He was born in 1870. In October, 1903,

Brother and Sister George W. Flory.

he was elected minister in the Nokesville church. He is now taking further studies at Bridgewater College and also serves the Board of Trustees in the important position of solicitor for that institution.

It is not only in Virginia that her children live earnest lives for the Master, but wherever they go beautiful examples of devotion to the truth and right are to be seen. The statement is made, that there are more native-born Virginians living outside the State than within her borders. It is not certain, however, that this would apply to the Brethren. Yet it is known that many have gone from their ancestral homes and they can be found as presidents and teachers in the literary schools and colleges, in the front rank of the work of the Sunday school, and in the important calling of the ministry. It is with a pardonable degree of pride that they who remain within the shadows of the sanctuary of their childhood look upon the successes of their kindred in other States and foreign climes.

CHAPTER XIII.

Missionary, Educational, Sunday School, and Charitable Work of the Church.—General Review—Conclusion.

More than forty-two years have passed since the surrender of General Lee at Appomattox, which virtually ended the dreadful war. During this time, a momentous struggle has been enacted by Virginia to restore her once proud position among her sister States. In this her bitter tears of sorrow and repentance for the unwise act of 1861 availed her nothing. With her public institutions broken down, her treasury bankrupt, and her people stricken with a poverty beyond the description of pen, the race with an unsympathizing world was an unequal one. However, true to the character of her people, these years have wrought wonders and her star is again floating over the Land of the Free with ever-increasing splendor.

Not unlike the struggle of the State, has been the experience of the Brethren in Virginia, as a church, against the evils arising from the influence of war, and the effort to extend the kingdom of Christ under adverse conditions. As truly as the pages of history show that all peoples have been affected by their environments, so surely have the Virginia churches had to meet problem after problem peculiar to the influences that surrounded them.

The period of privation and suffering had changed their position in the front rank for best methods in all good work to a struggle for self-existence, which was followed by years requiring the simplest and most inexpensive procedure for the Lord's cause. Wherefore, the application of these methods during this time caused them to crystallize in the public mind, and it required years of patient labor to introduce plans differing from them. This, however, was accomplished, and the Virginia churches have an organization in missionary, educational, Sunday-school and charitable work that could be studied with profit by more pretentious people.

Under the title of the different districts, the advancement of the church from the local organizations to the multiplication of others has been chronicled. In this chapter, it is the purpose to notice the development of some of the potent forces that augmented this work. In order to do this in a comprehensive manner, it is necessary to make mention of the work of each district separately.

The Missionary Work of the First District of Virginia.

By Eld. D. N. Eller.

[Eld. D. N. Eller, son of Eld. John W. Eller, was born November 16, 1862, near Salem, Roanoke County, Virginia. His early life was spent on his father's farm and he had the advantages afforded by the public schools of the county. At the age of eighteen, he began teaching school. In 1885, he entered Bridgewater College and graduated two years later in the English Course. Subsequent to this, he taught in the public school three years. In 1891, he entered Botetourt Normal College as instructor in English and Philosophy and became president of that institution three years later, which position he holds at this writing. Pres. Eller was elected minister in 1888 and ordained to the eldership in 1904. He has been secretary of the District Mission Board since 1898.]

The Mission Board of the First District of Virginia was organized on August 23, 1885, at the Valley meetinghouse in Botetourt County, when a constitution and by-laws were adopted. The board at that time was composed of B. F. Moomaw, Jonas Graybill, J. M. Hayslett, Joel Naff and H. M. Garst. For a number of years, little was done. However, some assistance was given in building meetinghouses and filling appointments among isolated members.

The board was reorganized in 1889 with some advancement in the work, but not much mission money could be raised. In 1899, the District Meeting decided that a district evangelist should be put in the field and the services of Eld. C. D. Hylton were secured for two years. Eld. Charles M. Yearout and others served subsequent to that time.

In June, 1902, a charter was secured from the Legislature by which the board can legally hold property. Since then several thousand dollars of endowment fund has been raised.

At the present time, a mission is supported at Charlestown, West Virginia, and at points in Mercer and Raleigh counties, same State. Beside these, there are a number of other points that receive a partial support.

The spirit of missions has grown much in this time. Our collection at District Meeting increased from $11 to $150 in five years. In 1890, the board raised and expended $172.13, and in 1907, the receipts and expenditures were $1,266.71. At this time the resources amount to $2,362.64. Aside from this, much individual effort is being put forth for the Lord and two missionaries are supported in India.

The Missionary Work of the Second District of Virginia.

It is most natural that the effort to secure an organization in missionary endeavor should meet the same obstacles in the Second District of Virginia as that in the First, as the conditions surrounding the churches were identical. Therefore, it required years to evolve a plan acceptable to all. During all this time, there were aggressive individuals and the subject was brought before District Meeting repeatedly in the form of queries, petitions, and plans submitted. This can be seen in the minutes of District Meeting very soon after the records were preserved. These plainly show that the sentiment was strongly favorable to congregational endeavor rather than central organization.

In 1878, the following query was presented to District Meeting, which was passed with the appended answer:

As there are many calls for preaching everywhere, would it not be advisable for this District to set apart or select two or four Brethren to go and preach the Gospel in those places, wherever they may be called or think it good to do so, and establish the doctrine of the Brethren; the District to have control of the Brethren in this matter, and they report to District Meeting, and the District bear the burden? (We ask a prayerful consideration of this important matter.)

ANSWER.—We make no change for the present, but earnestly request more perseverance under our present system. We do not desire, however, to prohibit any congregation from sending ministers as proposed in the query.

Later queries received much the same answers except that the congregations were urged to see that the families of Brethren do not suffer while they are away preaching the Gospel. In 1885, in response to a request that a missionary plan be adopted in accord with the recommendation of Annual Meeting of 1884, the District Meeting replied as follows:
"We urge each congregation to appoint a committee of brethren in their respective congregations to receive all calls, and see that they are filled by a minister, and pay the expenses if necessary. This plan is adopted."

The following year, a formal request was made for a District Mission Board. In response to this, a committee was appointed to look into the advisability of such a plan and in the meantime the churches were urged to carry out the recommendation of the previous year. For some reason, the names of this committee were not given, but it is supposed to have been composed of S. A. Shaver, John A. Cline and S. F. Sanger. To the District Meeting of 1887 they submitted the following missionary plan:

First. That the District be subdivided as follows: First Division: Mt. Vernon, Barren Ridge, Middle River, Pleasant Valley, Mill Creek and Midland. Second Division: Moscow, Beaver Creek and Cook's Creek. Third Division: Greenmount, Linville Creek, Flat Rock, Woodstock, Salem, Lost River and Page.

Second. That a Corresponding Secretary be appointed in each subdivision who shall serve for a term of two years.

Third. That each local church appoint solicitors to raise the required funds, and a treasurer whose duty it shall be to receive all funds collected by the solicitors of said local church, and report amount collected to corresponding secretary of the division quarterly. The above-named Treasurer shall hold said funds until called for by his corresponding secretary.

Fourth. It shall be the duty of the corresponding secretary, with the treasurer of his local church, to receive calls for preaching made within their territory, and if necessary see that said calls are filled by proper Brethren, whose expenses and other burdens shall be borne so far as they may think proper—out of the funds held by the local treasurers.

Fifth. It is understood that these arrangements shall not interfere with the arrangement of any local church in their efforts to spread the Gospel. But when assistance is needed they should confer with the corresponding secretary of their subdivision, whose duty it shall be to call for assistance from the other local churches, and when necessary call on the secretaries of the other subdivisions for assistance.

Sixth. It shall be the duty of the corresponding secretaries of each subdivision to make an annual report to the District Meeting of the number of calls made and filled, and the amount of money collected and disbursed by them.

Seventh. We earnestly request all our dear brethren and sisters to give this work their prayers and support and especially urge all our Elders to adopt and foster the above plans.

John A. Cline was appointed corresponding secretary of the first division, S. F. Sanger of the second division, and S. A. Shaver of the third division. Some good work was accomplished under its provisions; but its greatest usefulness was to prepare the churches for the reception of a plan submitted a few years later.

In the meantime, numerous requests were made for district evangelists to be put in the field and for a general revision of the missionary plan of the district. Finally, the District Meeting of 1894 appointed E. D. Kendig, H. C. Early and D. H. Zigler, a committee to draft a plan more nearly in accord with the request of Annual Meeting, which made the following report to District Meeting of 1895:

First. That this District Meeting appoint five Brethren sound in the faith, fully awake to missionary work, well acquainted with the needs of the District, suitably located, to be known as the Church Erection and Missionary Board of the Second District of Virginia.

Second. That said Board is to be composed of Brethren selected from the ministers, deacons, and laymen of the District, and that two of them be appointed for three years, two for two years, and one for one year. All vacancies by expiration of term of office or otherwise, be filled by District Meeting.

Third. That said Board have the right to effect her own organization, and enact such regulations as may be found necessary to carry on the work in harmony with this plan. It shall be the duty of the Treasurer of this Board to act as District Treasurer of the General Missionary Fund.

Fourth. That said Board secure one or more Brethren as District Evangelists, in sympathy with the doctrine of the Brethren, and keep them constantly employed, if possible, where they are most needed. And further, it shall be the privilege of the Board to engage suitable brethren for certain fields, as their judgment may direct.

Fifth. That all the local churches appoint solicitors to collect funds for the use of the Board in carrying forward the provisions of this plan. The establishment of a fund by donation, bequest, etc., is recommended; the interest of which shall be used for missionary purposes.

Sixth. That said Board shall build, or assist in building, houses of worship, where in their judgment is necessary.

Seventh. That said Board may coöperate with the different congregations in their evangelistic work, but shall in no way interfere with it.

Eighth. That said Board make a full report to each District Meeting of money received, how expended, results accomplished, and the condition of the field.

Under the provisions of this plan, J. M. Kagey, E. D. Kendig, Anthony Miller, George Miller and D. H. Zigler were appointed the first Board.

The following year, $302.30 was collected for district missions and about the same amount expended. In addition to this, $61.45 was received for general mission work and $500 endowment fund. In order to handle the endowment fund with safety, it was necessary for the Board to be incorporated, but in the application for a charter, unexpected difficulties were encountered. The Virginians in their struggle to throw off the State church, described in a preceding chapter, were influenced to the other extreme. Wherefore they adopted a constitution, a provision in which forbade the granting of a charter to a religious body. In the hope of a solution of the problem, the

Board appealed to District Meeting of 1896 as follows:

We, the Mission Board of the Second District of Virginia, respectfully request the District Meeting of 1896 to instruct us how to proceed in order to become a body capable of transacting business in a safe and legitimate way. Signed in behalf of the Board.
E. D. Kendig, Sec. J. M. KAGEY, *Chairman.*

ANSWER.—We authorize the District Mission Board to take such steps as are necessary to transact business in a safe and legal way.

Trustees were appointed and confirmed by the court to hold such funds. Subsequently, a constitutional convention assembled in Richmond and a charter was procured, which enables the Board to legally hold endowment, bequests and property of any kind.

In order to more fully secure the coöperation of all the churches and broaden the usefulness of the work in general, the Board made the following petition to District Meeting of 1899, which was granted:

In order to make our District Mission work more efficient, will not District Meeting direct that each church of the Second District of Virginia appoint a local committee whose duty shall be to coöperate with the District Mission Board in order to interest all our members in District Missions, and in looking up the needs of the respective fields, and securing suitable Brethren to work them.

A number of these committees have done excellent work in the respective fields of the local churches. In addition to this, they have proven a veritable bureau of information as to available workers, as well as the needs of the respective fields and the work in general. In this way, the District Mission Board becomes a medium through which every part of the district is brought in close touch with the rest and it has been enabled to render assistance in some way or other to every church in the district. Likewise, the congregations have contributed to the district work in general. Wherefore, since the organization of the Board in 1895, the receipts for missions have increased from less than $100 per year to more than $3,300, beside the various amounts placed directly in the hands of the local committees by the churches, which in some instances equals the amount given to District work in general.

The Board has been enabled to make appropriation in whole or in part toward the erection or purchase of twenty-four houses of worship and to push the work in various new fields, as well as assist in the older territory. In addition to this, it should be mentioned that in this time there have been many examples of noble personal devotion and sacrifice; but to enumerate all these would require much space. Also the churches of the district have contributed annually various sums of money to the work under the care of the General Missionary and Tract Committee and for the past five years directly support two workers in India.

While these statements give encouragement to the friends of missions, the writer is conscious of the fact that it would be possible for the churches of the Second District of Virginia to do many fold more work than what is being done at present, and it is hoped that the next decade will show far greater strides in the good work than has been made in the past.

Educational Work.

In all successful work for the Lord, the educational feature must be a companion in some form or other. It is true, our forefathers had no colleges to attend and they accomplished much good. Yet it should be remembered that they were real students of the Bible and nature. In this way some of them became learned men in their day and were powers for good. However, that which cost them a lifetime of toil to attain can be acquired in comparatively a few years under the method of instruction in a modern institution of learning. Therefore, the Brethren in Virginia see the importance of good schools under the care of the church. There are two such institutions in the State. The one is at Bridgewater, Rockingham County, and the other at Daleville, Botetourt County. Both of which are doing much for the church and their respective communities.

Just when and where the first institution of learning was established by the Virginia Brethren is not definitely known. That the early settlers were favorable to education is generally conceded, for a number of them were men of learning. Doubtless they united their labors with other people in educational work and honors alike belong to all. Yet, in 1859, near Broadway, Rockingham County, a school was established so distinctly associated with well-known Brethren of the time that special mention is made of it. What their full designs were will possibly never be known as the war with its destruction came shortly afterward. Yet it is plainly evident that the school was designed to be above the ordinary grade. Eld. John Kline in his notes ("Life of John Kline" page 409) says:

"Saturday, February 26. Attended a meeting which was held today to elect directors for the establishment of an Academy, to be known by the name of Cedar Grove Academy, near my place. John J. Bowman, John Zigler, and Daniel Miller were appointed."

A building was erected which was used for school purposes many years, and was torn down only a few years ago.

In the fall of 1880, Eld. Daniel C. Flory, assisted by Bro. James R. Shipman, established the Spring Creek Normal School. A year later it was expanded into the Spring Creek Normal School and Collegiate Institute. In 1882, the institution was moved to Bridgewater and was called the Virginia Normal School. Seven years later the charter was amended and the institution assumed the name of Bridgewater College, which title it has held with varying success to the present. In 1904, by action of the District Meeting of the Second District of Virginia the church took direct ownership and control of the institution. Since that time the addition to the equipment of the school has been very marked. The history of the Daleville School is fully given in a succeeding article. Therefore no mention of it is necessary here.

With this short introduction of the educational work of the Brethren in Virginia we have an account of each of the two schools written by an instructor in the respective institutions of learning.

Dr. John S. Flory.

Bridgewater College.

By Prof. John S. Flory.

[Dr. Flory was born on a farm near Broadway, Virginia. After spending his early years in the district schools, he attended the Broadway Graded School for three sessions, where he completed the high school course. In September, 1888, he entered Bridgewater College, where he remained two years. The session of 1890 to 1891 was spent in the Ohio Normal University. He was a student in Mt. Morris College during the next three years, where he received the degree of B. Lit. From the fall of 1894 to the spring of 1902 he taught English Literature in Bridgewater College, where he received the degree of B. A. in June, 1902. In the fall of this year he entered upon post-graduate studies at the University of Virginia. While at this institution, Prof. Flory won rare distinction as a student and writer, and was also honored with the degree of Doctor of Philosophy. His thesis on the early literary activity of the German Baptist Brethren shows much painstaking labor.]

The influence of Bridgewater College in the development of the Brethren Church in Virginia during the last quarter century must now engage our attention. With the nature of this influence and something of its extent, many of the readers of this book are already familiar. Yet, it may be doubted whether many of us realize the true significance of this influence, or appreciate the extent to which it has been exercised. This influence has been exerted, for the most part, silently, and has accomplished its work by transforming our ideals, broadening our interests, clarifying our views, elevating our standards, directing our aims, and cultivating our emotions and sympathies.

The college was not founded primarily as a religious institution. The principal aim of its founders was to provide a school home for the Brethren's children, where their moral and spiritual condition should be carefully guarded while they were acquiring their secular education. The need of this was felt when it became certain that the young people were going to be educated whether the church took precaution to provide means for their instruction or not. And the repeated example of young men from

Brethren families going off to State or undenominational institutions or to those of other sects, and thus being led away from the church and lost to her service, forced the conviction that the only way to save the young people for the church was to provide for their education and at the same time surround them with wholesome moral and spiritual influences.

This educational object was not peculiar to Virginia, but was practically the same in Pennsylvania and Illinois, the other two centers of early educational endeavor among the Brethren. The idea of adding to the curricula courses of Bible study was an afterthought and came as a process of development. No education is complete without religious instruction, and our people were not long in realizing this.

Consequently, our Bible courses are at present as definitely outlined and as carefully graded as any other department of our school work.

That we as a people are deeply interested in religious instruction is evident from the crowded condition of our Bible institutes year after year. The first of these institutes held at the college was during the session of 1891-2, and since 1894-5 they have been continued each year with increasing interest. For the last five years the average attendance has been about three hundred.

The establishment of courses of Bible study at the college met with many hindrances and discouragements. When a demand for this work first arose there was no one in the faculty specially prepared to teach it. And rather than do the work in an unsatisfactory manner the arrangement of courses was delayed until some one could be secured or prepared for the position. As the former seemed impossible, it was arranged that Prof. S. N. McCann should prepare himself for this particular work. Accordingly he entered the Southern Baptist Theological Seminary at Nashville, Tennessee, where he studied two years and would have graduated at the end of the third. This entire plan was broken up however, in the spring of 1897, when Prof. McCann was chosen by the General Missionary and Tract Committee to go as a missionary to India. This was against his inclinations, as he preferred to give his life to the cause of the Master in the homeland, yet as he felt this a call from God, after a conference with Prof. W. B. Yount, president of the college, he decided to accept the call and go to the foreign field. Of his work there many who read these lines already know.

This left the college again without a Bible instructor, and two more years were passed before courses of study were offered to the public. Since that time commendable interest has been shown in the work. A good number of persons have taken one or two years of the work, but up to this time only three have finished the complete course. Of these two are ministers of the Gospel and the third (a lady) is a missionary.

The chief influence of the college, therefore, in developing the work of the church has not been in the line of training theologians or producing biblical scholars; it has been rather in the line of general scholarship. And in this respect the success of the college has been remarkable. Its graduates have taken rank along with those of the best colleges and universities in the land, and are in constant demand among the higher institutions of learning. Wherever they have come in competition with the graduates of other institutions they have carried off more than their proportionate share of honors. Indeed it may safely be said that there is no other college in the State of whose graduates so large a per cent have achieved such signal success.

These successes are in no way to be disassociated, however, from religious instruction. On the other hand it is impossible to tell how much of them is due to it. The morning prayer service in the presence of the whole school, the silent moments of thankfulness at the beginning of each meal, the weekly Sunday-school and preaching service which all attend, and the prayer meetings and the services of the Missionary Society in which many participate, all these engender and perpetuate a religious atmosphere whose steadying and sustaining power in the lives of young people cannot be estimated. While the direct teaching of the college, therefore, goes out to a large extent in the line of general scholarship, there is closely blended and intertwined with this that religious precept and Christian example whose atmosphere envelops a young life and leads to rounded, symmetrical Christian character. And to the presence of this spirit in the college, which leads to high ideals in scholarship and character, and to pure and clean habits of living, is due in large measure the eminent success to which the graduates have attained.

To what results then has the training received at

the college, for the most part, led? Statistics will help us to decide. Taking first those who have completed courses of study and have received diplomas, we find that they have gone largely into three occupations: the Christian ministry, educational work and agricultural pursuits. Of the men graduates, (for women do not enter the ministry) twenty-two and one half per cent, or nearly one-fourth, are today active ministers of the Gospel. Thirty-three per cent of the whole number of graduates have taken up educational work, and the field of their activity is very broad. From the ungraded public schools they are found in all positions of the graded and high schools, as teachers or principals, to professorships in colleges and universities, and as presidents of colleges and higher institutions of learning in several parts of the United States. Nor are their activities entirely confined to the homeland, as the far-away Philippines claim several of them.

The men who have gone into agricultural pursuits represent twenty-seven per cent of all who have graduated, but as the ladies refuse to compete with the men in this field, a more significant estimate is based on the number of men graduates. On this basis the number is thirty-six per cent, so more than one third of the young men who have graduated from the college in all courses have returned to the farm.

Many of the lady graduates have taught for a few years and later abandoned the ferrule for the rolling pin, and are today among the happy home-makers of the land. Thirty-five per cent of the lady graduates have married since leaving school. This is the record for the last twenty years, from 1886 to 1906. Of those who have been out of school as much as five years sixty-eight per cent are married.

But these statistics tell only a partial truth. A large majority of those who have attended the college have not graduated at all. These have been in attendance from short periods of a term or more to three or four years. And among them are numerous instances of conspicuous success. In this group are many teachers in the public schools, some holding the principalships of high schools at handsome salaries. Others have gone directly into the study of one or another of the learned professions, medicine, law, dentistry and the like. Others have become bankers, merchants, clerks, government officials; while many more are amassing fortunes by tilling the soil, handling stock or growing fruit. And there is not wanting a large and important number who have laid their lives on the altar of sacrifice and are devoting their talents and their energies to the salvation of souls. Among these are about fifty ministers of the Gospel, scattered westward to the Pacific coast and northward to the Dakotas, and more than a dozen missionaries working in various States and cities of the Union for the redemption of mankind; all these in addition to those who have completed courses of study.

The comparative statistics of those who have graduated and those who have not are also interesting. Of the whole number of students who have been in regular attendance at the college about seventeen per cent have graduated in some course. Of the men who have not graduated about seven per cent have become ministers of the Gospel; of those who have graduated about twenty-two per cent are ministers. Of the young men of Brethren homes who never go away to school at all, it is doubtful whether two per cent ever attain to the ministry. Only a year or two in school, therefore, multiplies this proportion several times, and residence long enough to complete a course increases the ratio of ministers at least tenfold. It is very seldom that a young man is elected to the ministry in the Second District of Virginia, who has not attended or is not about to attend college. So it is only a matter of time when the ministry of the Brethren Church will consist almost exclusively of college-bred men.

In the Sunday-school work also similar conditions prevail. In almost every school of the district at least one and frequently quite a number of the leading spirits in the work are those who have caught the contagion from attendance at the college. As the years pass by the significance of all this becomes all the time more apparent. The church is being gradually officered, directed and taught by those who attend the college.

Whether we realize it or not, Bridgewater College is making the Brethren Church in Virginia what it is. According as the school is supported and developed will its influence for good be increased. When it is once placed on the financial footing it deserves, so that its direct power can shape the lives of our young people by the thousands instead of the hundreds, will it be in position to do the work possible for it. Its past is full of faithful service, true devotion to a noble cause, heroic sacrifice and splendid results. Its future is large with opportunity and possibility. The opportunity is ours, and it is for us to determine how many of the possibilities shall be attained.

In the six or seven years since the above was written, Bridgewater College has made rapid advancement in different ways.

In this time the material equipment has been very much improved. Two new buildings have been erected, one a dormitory, with accommodations for about seventy-five young men. The library has doubled in size, and today contains more than ten thousand well-selected volumes. These have been catalogued by the decimal system, which again doubles the working value of the collection. The laboratories have been provided with new equipment until they rank well with the laboratories of some of the best colleges of the State. The dormitories are provided with all the homelike conveniences, such as steam heat, electric light, baths and lavatories, and the furnishing throughout is modern and comfortable. A full supply of the best of lithia water has been provided in all the dormitories.

The endowment fund has also materially increased. Legacies, bequests and annuities to the college are coming to be the rule with many of the brethren and sisters who have money to dispose of. We are all learning that we can not devote a portion of our means to a more worthy cause.

The curriculum has been steadily developed and strengthened. The work in the various departments is standardized, so that the courses of study are such

Bridgewater College. Main Group of College Buildings.

as are given in the best special schools of the various kinds. The college course leading to the B. A. degree, for instance, is as thorough and provides as liberal a degree of culture as do similar courses in the leading universities and the best colleges. The commercial courses are of the same rank as those given by the best commercial colleges. Similar standards are maintained in all the departments of the institution.

Especially in the college work has Bridgewater made marked progress in recent years. In the last five years the number of college students has more than doubled, and the number of graduates in the college course in the last two years is nearly as great as in the ten years before.

The Bible School, too, has grown rapidly in favor. The Bible courses are attracting more young people every year, and the number of our young ministers who take advantage of this work is especially marked. Those enrolling in the fall of 1914 exceed twoscore in number.

In standing also the college has made marked advancement. Today Bridgewater College is one of the accredited institutions of Virginia. Its literary courses lead to State certificates without examination, and the graduates of the college department have been received into the graduate schools of the best universities without condition.

The alumni are a loyal body, ready to do anything in reason for their alma mater. They are found in many of the useful callings in life, and uniformly adorn the vocations they enter. Many of them are educators, and about one hundred and fifty are in the Christian ministry. At the last Annual Conference six of them served on the Standing Committee. They are found on the mission fields of India, China, and Denmark, and one is under appointment to go to South America. Their influence in the work and development of the church becomes year by year increasingly important.

Daleville College.

By C. S. Ikenberry.

Daleville College had its beginning in the year 1890 as a select school conducted for the families of two of its faithful patrons, B. F. Nininger and G. G. Layman. This school was conducted by Prof. I. N. H. Beahm, who so fittingly created an interest in the community that the idea of an academy was made manifest in the minds of a number of patrons. In the year 1901 a building was erected with private funds and dedicated in the month of October under the name of Botetourt Normal. Prof. Beahm called to his assistance in this initial educational work Prof. D. N. Eller, who has been closely associated with the school since that time, and C. E. Arnold, who later became president of McPherson College, Kansas.

The catalogue of the first year shows an attendance of sixty-eight students. The purpose of the promotors of this school was not the founding of a college, as it later developed, but the normal and academic idea was prevalent. During this school year a charter was secured from the Legislature of Virginia to confer degrees. The school progressed for a number of years, largely with a local attendance, and in the year 1895 the name was changed to Botetourt Normal College and the normal idea was held foremost in the work of the school. Hence the school early in its beginning put out a number of noble men and women who have served faithfully their day as successful teachers. Some continued their educational work teaching in other colleges and universities, others giving their service to the public schools.

In the year 1897 the educational spirit had grown in the community and there was a demand for college work. Consequently the Latin scientific course was added to the curriculum, which gave freshman and sophomore years of the collegiate course. At this time Prof. L. D. Ikenberry was called to take charge of the school as president. A new building was erected, known as Central Hall, and dedicated January 1, 1898, and the school assumed an attitude for more aggressive work along educational lines.

The departments of music and expression were added to the course of study, and among the teachers who gave a touch of art to these courses may be mentioned Flora May Nininger and Nellie McVey, both deceased. Their worth was probably not most felt in their day, but the growth of the sentiment for culture and higher Christian education may largely be attributed to these two efficient teachers.

Some years of the school became more eventful than others. One of these eventful years was the session of 1902-03. On January 9, 1903, the first building erected was burned to the ground. This was the real test for the success of the school that was destined to become felt in the community and church, for it was on the day following when the enterprising Board of Trustees met and freely gave their contributions and plans for the erection of a new building. This building was erected the same year and was dedicated and is known as Denton Hall.

We mention here, in connection with the presidents of this school, the name of James Z. Gilbert, who served as president for two years. Succeeding him Prof. D. N. Eller was again called to the responsible place, and served efficiently until the year 1910, when Prof. T. S. Moherman, the present president, became his successor.

In the year 1909 the benevolent spirit of our Board of Trustees, friends and patrons was manifested when the Ladies' Home, now known as the Nininger Memorial Hall, was erected. This was a donation largely from the relatives of Eld. Peter Nininger, and in connection with this Mr. B. F. Nininger donated to the college the old Peter Nininger Home, with the beautiful campus surrounding it.

It may be a difficult problem to answer the question, "What constitutes a college?" Evidently the grounds, buildings and endowment are a necessity, and we must attribute the existence of Daleville College through her years varied with prosperity and adversity to the liberal donations and bequeathments of two of her faithful trustees, B. F. Nininger and Eld. T. C. Denton. In fact, Daleville College will ever stand as a memorial to its first and most generous

President of the Board of Trustees. Bro. Denton's life has been associated with the college from its inception, and during his active years he not only gave needed funds, but exercised a faith that gave courage even through the most discouraging periods. He took a broad view of life in a hopeful prospect

Eld. T. C. Denton.

of the future church, realizing that the progress of the church depends upon the education of our young men and women. He made the success of the college evident by bequeathing to it largely from his estate. His death in February, 1914, left vacant the office of President of the Board of Trustees, and Eld. J. A. Dove was chosen as his successor.

The influence of Daleville College in the churches should be mentioned. We feel safe in saying that every congregation in the District has felt the touch of the educational spirit. Special Bible Terms have been held annually, conducted by some efficient Bible instructor, which have largely been attended by the

B. F. Nininger.

ministers of the District. While the school in its early years was not recognized or known as a Brethren school, at the same time its highest purpose was the Christian education of the young people of our church communities. But desiring a closer relationship with the churches of the District, the following query was presented for consideration at the District Meeting in 1908 and was adopted in 1909: " Inasmuch as it is the purpose and desire of the Board of Di-

Prof. D. N. Eller.

rectors of Botetourt Normal College, at Daleville, Virginia, to work more successfully and in harmony with the Brethren church in the preparation of young ministers, Sunday-school workers and missionaries, we, the Board of Directors, ask District Meeting to recognize the aforesaid institution as a Brethren

Denton Hall. Central Hall. Nininger Memorial Hall.

College Buildings, Daleville, Virginia.

school, and grant us the privilege of soliciting patronage from the several churches in the District."

A Bible department has been conducted in the school for the special benefit of our young ministers, missionaries and Sunday-school workers. A number of our young brethren and sisters have taken advantage of this course. The college at present offers a two and a three-year course, including a broad scope of biblical literature. The college has for four years maintained a full college course, and it is this department that the school purposes to make its most aggressive work.

Daleville College not only recognizes the moral and mental training as necessary, but holds for its motto, "A sound body for a sound mind." Well-directed physical culture is given, and the gymnasium erected by the Alumni Association in the year 1911 affords most excellent opportunities for its develompent. It was the sacrificing spirit of the students of that school year that made this building possible.

Thus, through the period of more than twenty years, the writer has seen chapter after chapter written in history which is not tabulated here. That the school, with her one hundred and fifty graduates and hundreds of old students, is a potent factor in the Church of the Brethren in the Districts that control the school is no more a question. The larger outlook is demanding the interest and thought of its teachers and Board of Trustees, that the dynamic influence of this institution may be directed to the greatest good to the church and state.

The Sunday-School Work.

Shoulder to shoulder with other lines of endeavor for the Lord, stands the Sunday-school worker with Bible in hand. His mission is to gather the young and old alike each Lord's Day to instruct them in the ways of Truth.

Among the churches in Virginia can be found many enthusiastic Sunday-school workers, and it is impossible to estimate the great amount of good they accomplish for the church and humanity. The organization is not unlike that of any other part of the Brotherhood. In the two Districts of Virginia it is almost identical.

The reader has already seen that in principle the Sunday-school instruction was used by some of the first Brethren who settled in Virginia. But, subsequent to this, for a time Sunday schools were not held in favor by the churches. However, time has wrought a great change and no church is considered fully equipped without a Sunday school. The growth in this line of Christian work has been very marked during the last several decades.

In the First District the work was organized by Eld. Jos. H. Murray, who did efficient work, creating a greater Sunday-school interest. At the District Meeting of 1905, C. S. Ikenberry was appointed as District Secretary. The number of schools since that date have more than doubled.

The territory of the District being large, the secretary had four assistants, each responsible for a division of the District. Brethren who have served in this capacity are Elders J. H. Garst, R. T. Akers, J. W. Barnhart and L. A. Bowman, and Brethren C. W. Kinzie, Homer Trout, E. E. Bowman, G. O. Reed, D. V. Shaver and C. E. Trout.

Annual Sunday-school Institutes have been held since 1909. At an institute held at the Brick church, Franklin County, in 1912, the following resolution was passed: "Resolved, That the Sunday schools of the First and Southern Districts of Virginia support a missionary in the foreign field." Sister Rebecca Skeggs Wampler was selected by the Districts and is now the representative of these schools in the China field.

After the division of the Old First District the Southern District elected E. E. Bowman as their secretary and C. S. Ikenberry was retained in the New First District. The fraternal spirit of these two Districts was made manifest when unanimously they agreed to coöperate in a Sunday-school Institute every two years.

Organized Sunday-school endeavor in the old Second District was inaugurated by the appointment of Bro. J. W. Wampler as District Secretary in 1899. He served the District in this work to the time of its division into three Districts, except the four years, 1904 to 1907, inclusive, when Bro. S. I. Flory was District Secretary. From the first the Sunday-school work showed improvement. The report for 1906 shows there were eighty-nine schools in the District, seventy-six of which reported five thousand and ten scholars with collections of $1,631.73.

At the organization of the Northern District, Bro. J. W. Wampler was again appointed District Sunday-school Secretary, with two assistants. The Sunday schools of the District show improvement in almost every line of work. A comparative report would be too lengthy for insertion here, but a summary for 1913 is given. There are in the new District fifty-seven schools with an enrollment of four thousand two hundred and forty-two and the offerings for the year of $1,682.27. In cradle roll there are three hundred and thirty-seven and the home department two hundred and thirty members. Teacher-training classes show a total of one hundred and eight. One hundred and eighty-nine conversions are reported from the ranks of the schools. The report further shows four front line, eight banner and six star schools. Division Institutes are held each year among the churches to raise the efficiency of the workers.

Bro. J. W. Wright, with two assistants, serves the Second District as Sunday-school Secretary. The report shows forty-one schools. Good work is being done in a number of the schools.

When the Eastern District was organized, Bro. Lewis B. Flohr was appointed Sunday-school Secretary. Bro. W. H. Sanger is Secretary at present: Brother J. J. Conner and Sister Martha Sanger are his assistants. Nineteen schools, with an enrollment of one thousand five hundred and thirty-nine, are shown in the report for 1913. Considerable endeavor is made in this District, also, to raise the standard of efficiency in this District.

THE CHARITABLE WORK OF THE CHURCH.

There is nothing relating to the Brethren that more fully commends itself to the thoughtful mind than their acts of charity. This has been remarkably true of the church in Virginia from its earliest history to the present. Neither have these benevolent acts been confined to the members of the church alone, but to the unfortunate regardless of church affiliation. Yet, to those within the church the obligation would seem the greater, for "Whoso hath this world's good, and seeth his brother have need, and shutteth up his bowels of compassion from him, how dwelleth the love of God in him?"

Wherefore, it has been the universal practice of the Virginia churches to care for its destitute members and not allow them to become dependent upon the almshouse. For years provisions have been furnished to their homes if circumstances permit. In other instances homes were provided for them in private families. But in recent years the Second District of Virginia established a home for the aged homeless or, as it is styled, an OLD FOLKS' HOME. This provides a comfortable dwelling for the declining years of those who have no homes. This was inaugurated by the appointment of Michael Zigler, Samuel F. Miller and Noah Beery in the spring of 1888 to take under advisement the feasibility of the district establishing such a home. The committee made a report to the District Meeting of 1890, favorable to the establishment of the home. The report was accepted and a Board of Directors consisting of five members was appointed with authority to raise money and construct a home. In this they were successful. Thirty-one acres of land were purchased near Timberville; suitable buildings erected; and on March 1, 1892, Bro.

Old Folks' Home, of the Second District of Virginia.

Daniel Wine and wife took charge of the home as superintendent and matron.

Since then it has been in constant use. In this time the inmates range in number from ten to twenty-five. While the home has had its trials, it has given comfort to many otherwise destitute lives, and is on a solid financial footing. In addition to bodily comforts it is the policy of the management to give such religious exercise as is best adapted to develop the spiritual life.

Prompted by the same spirit and for the present closely associated with the Old Folks' home is the

ORPHANS' HOME in the Second District of Virginia. This institution is little past the experimental period, but it has already demonstrated to an extent the possibility of such an institution in our midst.

In 1904 the following petition was presented to the District Meeting, which was passed with the appended answer:

The Beaver Creek congregation petitions District Meeting of the Second District of Virginia to appoint a committee of five to investigate the propriety of the founding of an Orphans' Home either in connection with the Old Folks' Home or separate, and report to District Meeting of 1905.

ANSWER.—Petition granted and D. H. Zigler, J. W. Wampler, P. S. Thomas, J. M. Kline and Minor Cline were appointed as the committee.

To the District Meeting of 1905 the committee reports that,

We, your committee, after securing information and getting reports from a majority of the churches in our District, would recommend the establishing of an Orphans' Home in the Second District of Virginia and would further recommend, for the consideration of the committee to be appointed, the proposition made by the Directors of the Old Folks' Home.

The report was accepted and the committee was authorized to carry its recommendations into effect.

A charter was at once procured and the proposition of the Directors of the Old Folks' Home made it possible to receive a limited number of orphans without delay. At present the institution is being run on the Home Finding plan, and a number of little lives are receiving blessings thereby.

Since the foregoing was written the orphanage work has moved onward, as told by the following, written by P. S. Thomas, Secretary:

" The Orphans' Home at Timberville, Virginia, was organized, and is supported by the Second, Northern

Orphanage.

and Eastern Districts of Virginia. It was chartered in 1905, and is managed by a Board of Trustees, of five members. Two of these trustees are from the Second District, two from the Northern and one from the Eastern.

" The work has been supported by freewill offerings, from individuals and from the congregations, but at the present time an effort is being made to maintain the work by apportioning to the churches the amounts needed, and in proportion to the wealth of the several congregations.

" Prior to the erection of the present building, the

children received were cared for at the Old Folks' Home. In 1909 a building was erected on a plat of ground purchased from the Old Folks' Home Trustees.

"The plan is to keep the children in the Home only long enough to find suitable homes for them. It is held that the family life is the ideal life, and the private home the one where best results can be attained and the greatest good done. Since the date of the organization, to March 1, 1914, fifty-one children have been admitted."

SISTERS' AID SOCIETIES.

No record of the church in Virginia is complete without mentioning the Sisters' Aid Society. So closely allied in church life is the work of our sisters that it is noticeable on every hand. In true loyalty to her principles, in attendance at services, in Sunday-school work, in missions and in charity they take a leading part. But it is through the coöperation in the Sisters' Aid Society they accomplish the greatest good.

These societies are found in nearly every well organized church throughout the State, and they have received the full endorsement of Conference. In each of the five State Districts there is a District organization which is a part of the general organization of the Sisters' Aid Societies of the church at large.

The amount of good accomplished by these societies can never be told. In their unselfish spirit they are helpers in every commendable work of the church. Like Dorcas of old, they choose the adornment of "good works" rather than worldly display.

Temperance.

Each State District has its Temperance Committee appointed by District Meeting. To these the church looks for leadership against the saloon, the arch enemy of mankind. It has been seen in a previous chapter how slavery was opposed to the last measure. No less uncompromising has been the attitude of the church against the rum traffic. At no time could a saloon-keeper or manufacturer of intoxicating liquors have been received into the church without abandoning his unrighteous vocation. The sale of grain or fruit to distillers by a member of the church is also incompatible with her councils. In the campaign against the saloon and the rum traffic in general there is no uncertainty about the attitude of the Brethren as a body being for its banishment. The use of tobacco is likewise discouraged as being useless expenditure of money and injurious to the health of the individual as well.

In doctrine the church in Virginia is in full accord with the Brotherhood at large. Like the founders of the church, it challenges all creeds and confessions of faith by turning triumphantly to the Word of God for its faith and the rule for its practice. Wherefore, the commands of the New Testament Scriptures are held by living obedience, as the author of " The Germans of the Shenandoah Valley," page 128, says of the Brethren:

" They observe as religious ordinances the kiss of charity, feet-washing, and the apostolic love-feast *(agape)* in connection with the communion in the eucharist; they practice the rite of anointing with oil, in cases of severe illness, though they do not at all neglect medical and hygienic aids; they avoid the taking of oaths (holding their simple word as binding all their powers), going to law, membership in secret societies, and fashionable dress; and are unalterably opposed to war and easy divorce of husband and wife. In consequence of their nonresistant principles, they, like the Mennonites, have been accused of a lack of patriotism, and have at times suffered much in consequence of this and their refusal to bear arms. But they are not lacking in patriotism. They only believe that war is always wrong and debasing. They believe, as a thoughtful writer of history has said, that 'there are few things, if any, more important to the steady growth of a free nation than the maintenance of domestic virtues and the sanctities of family life.' They believe in helping the State and the Nation, not by means of war and great standing armies, but by the useful and productive industries of peace; by earning an honest living, paying just debts and equitable taxes, by avoiding strife and contention as far as possible, by settling peaceably, man to man or by additional counselors, such disputes as inevitably arise; and thus making almshouses, jails, law courts, asylums, many policemen, and the expense of maintaining all these, largely unnecessary. They would apply this principle of peaceable adjustment of differences upon a large scale, and have nations, as well as individuals, observe the golden rule in business and diplomacy, and settle all disputed points by honest and just arbitration before, rather than after, the battle."

In almost every part of the State and surrounding territory where churches have been established they indicate a healthy growth. The combined membership of the five Districts number more than 13,000 communicants. In Rockingham, Augusta, and Shenandoah counties the membership is the largest. Rockingham alone has six strong local organizations with a considerable margin of two other churches jutting across its borders, the combined membership of which exceeds that of any other county in America. In the southwest the membership is large in Floyd, Franklin, Botetourt, and Roanoke counties. And with the blessings attendant on the simple life, with the present opportunities for spiritual and intellectual development, and with an unrestricted and practically unlimited mission territory on every hand, the Virginia churches have a responsibility they dare not ignore.

The organizers of the church, as well as the leaders during the different periods were men well qualified for the duties of their time. They displayed much wisdom in the guidance of the church in their day. We look back to them, not that they can guide us now, but that their clear insight into the needs of their time and their willingness to meet them may inspire us to nobler endeavor.

Greatly different are the requirements of the present, to meet which, the worker of today must be well equipped with a training coequal with the advancement of the age. We do not most honor the noble men of the past by adopting their methods, but by improving upon them. A greater work is upon the church today than ever before, but by devotion to duty and in the same true spirit of righteousness we can conquer for Christ. In this we can well be their imitators and in this way their greatest legacy comes to us.

THE END.

www.ingramcontent.com/pod-product-compliance
Lightning Source LLC
Chambersburg PA
CBHW060941230426
43665CB00015B/2017
* 9 7 8 0 7 8 8 4 3 7 8 2 3 *